# THE ART OF BILLY ROCHE: WEXFORD AS THE WORLD

# THE ART OF BILLY ROCHE: WEXFORD AS THE WORLD

## Edited by Kevin Kerrane

**Carysfort Press**

A Carysfort Press Book
*The Art of Billy Roche: Wexford As the World*
edited by Kevin Kerrane

First published in Ireland in 2012 as a paperback original by

Carysfort Press, 58 Woodfield, Scholarstown Road
Dublin 16, Ireland

ISBN 978-1-904505-60-0
©2012 Copyright remains with the authors

Typeset by Carysfort Press

Cover design by eprint limited
Printed and bound by eprint limited
Unit 35
Coolmine Industrial Estate
Dublin 15
Ireland

This book is published with the financial assistance of
The Arts Council (An Chomhairle Ealaíon) Dublin, Ireland.

For Patti Roche

with admiration and affection

# CONTENTS

## Close-Ups

# Acknowledgements

I wish to thank all the contributors to this collection, but would like to single out Christopher Murray and Patrick Lonergan for their encouragement and practical counsel. Dozens of other scholars, friends, and admirers of Billy Roche's work have helped along the way; unfortunately, space limitations permit only a listing of names: Steve Bernhardt, James Dean, Matt Kinservik, Sandy Robbins, and Jewel and Marge Walker at the University of Delaware; Tony Roche, and Declan Kiberd at University College Dublin; Mairead Delaney at the Abbey Theatre in Dublin; David Brooks at the Bush Theatre in London; Joanna Norledge at the Victoria and Albert Archives; Jessica Dromgoole at the BBC; the photographers John Hession, John Michael Murphy, Mick Harpur, and Charles Collins; James Silas Rogers, editor of *New Hibernia Review*; Tanya Dean at the Yale School of Drama; and good friends in Ireland: Patricia Burke Brogan, Michael and Maria Warren, Noel and Christine Fahey, and most especially Dermot and Mary O'Connell.

Acknowledgements are due to Methuen Drama, an imprint of Bloomsbury Publishing PLC, for permission to reprint the excerpt from Dominic Dromgoole's *The Full Room: An A to Z of Contemporary Playwriting* (London: Methuen, 2000); and to ArenaPAL for permission to reproduce three Bush Theatre posters, with photography by Mark Douet. An anthology of this sort requires extensive quotation of creative work, and I offer thanks to Faber and Faber for permission to quote from Brian Friel's *Dancing at Lughnasa*; to Nick Hern Books for permission to quote from all of Billy Roche's plays; to Pillar Press for permission to quote from *Tales from Rainwater Pond*; and to Tassel Publications for permission to quote from the revised edition of *Tumbling Down*.

I am grateful to Eamonn Jordan for inviting me to undertake this project, and for providing expert advice along the way; and to Dan Farrelly for his work, always smart and thorough, on the text and index.

Finally, I extend heartfelt thanks to Billy Roche for the generous help he has given to several of the contributors, and particularly to this book's editor.

As ever, my debt to my wife, Katharine, is too great to be expressed in words.

*Kevin Kerrane*

# Illustrations

# 1 | Introduction: Music and Myth

Kevin Kerrane

It would be impossible for any book about Billy Roche to do justice to his multiple accomplishments as actor, singer, composer, novelist, playwright, director, and screenwriter. The essays in this collection focus on his literary and dramatic work – but with a deep appreciation for the music that runs through all of Roche's stories like an electrical current.

Music appears in Roche's original compositions for the stage (the beautiful 'One Heart Broken' in *The Cavalcaders*) and in his allusions on the page (the traditional ballad 'The Wexford Girl' as an ominous motif in the short story 'Verdant'). But music is also audible in the rhythm of Roche's dialogue and even in the rhythm of his scenes. Alert to the lyrical potential of ordinary Irish speech – specifically the dialect of his native Wexford – Roche has imbued his characters with the poetry of the street. Colm Tóibín, in his seminal essay 'The Talk of the Town', shows how Roche transforms 'the tones and colours and cadences' of living language into moving dialogue, as in Steven's speech that ends *Poor Beast in the Rain*: 'It hits us like a line in a song that seems to have no obvious power. It appears, however, to have a hidden nervous system of its own, all the stronger because you do not know where the emotion is coming from.' Roche even finds ways to make silences articulate, dramatizing feelings that lie 'between the notes.' His own experience as a musician is obvious in his thinking through the 'movements' in a scene or story:

> I would be aware of the rhythm and the pace and I suppose a sort of key. I think it was the critic Michael Billington who once said that tragedies are invariably in a minor key. Well, I would

be looking out for that. And texture too of course. Is the speech played on an oboe or a French horn? Is it wistful or passionate? Does the scene call for a comical crash of the symbol or a roll of the drum? Soft or loud? Fast or slow? All of that![1]

Several essays in this collection stress Roche's affinities with Anton Chekhov, James Joyce, and Brian Friel. While acknowledging these influences, Roche has also been eloquent in his admiration for Tom Murphy, in whose plays Irish vernacular speech and realistic settings are infused with a sense of the mythic – as in *Conversations on a Homecoming*, which links an ordinary pub to the world of Camelot. Most of all, Roche says, Murphy reaffirms the power of 'the continuous past', analogous to the Irish verb tense *An Gnath Caite* – 'a place where technology is discarded, where only the fundamentals apply: emotions, feelings, colours, sounds, silences, and the like.'[2] The continuous past is a dramatic dimension without cellphones (perhaps even without landlines), in which the universal struggles of hate, love, sex, death, longing, and jealousy unfold as they always have and always will. Of course Roche means to apply this description to his own stories and plays. The difference, he notes, is that Murphy's plays channel much greater anger, often culminating in violence. 'Put my characters in a ring with Murphy's', Roche once said, 'and his will beat the shite out of mine.'[3]

It's not that Roche's work lacks ferocity. Act 1 of *Belfy* ends with the sacristan Artie using his belt to whip Dominic, the troubled boy who needs him most, in a frenzy of misguided blame. In the film *Trojan Eddie* the long-suffering protagonist, after hearing one taunt too many from his unfaithful wife, suddenly snaps: his violent attack on her is witnessed by the audience, and overheard by their two terrified daughters. In *The Cavalcaders* Terry never strikes Nuala, his young mistress, but he comes so close to doing so that the audience may flinch. After watching Liam Cunningham command the role of Terry at the Tricycle Theatre in London, the reviewer Benedict Nightingale wrote: 'Roche, a writer who combines finesse with large-mindedness and who can hop from the sunny to the dark

---

[1] Quoted by Kevin Kerrane, 'The Poetry of the Street: An Interview with Billy Roche', *Irish Studies Review*, 14/3 (August 2006): 377.

[2] Billy Roche, 'Tom Murphy and the Continuous Past', *Princeton University Library Chronicle*, LXVIII, 1 and 2 (Autumn 2006-Winter 2007): 627-628.

[3] Quoted by Eileen Battersby, 'The Boy from Wexford', *The Irish Times*, March 2, 1995.

in a twinkling, has not written a finer scene than the one in which [Terry] reduces a vulnerable girl who has been fishing for love-talk into emotional smithereens with a cruelty that makes you shudder.'[4]

One of the most intriguing features of Roche's writing is how scenes like these include so much *more* than cruelty. Performers like Gary Lydon and Ingrid Craigie, who have appeared in many of his productions, talk about the 'empathy' that Roche extends to all his characters, and his respect for the 'yearning' felt by even the less likeable among them. Roche's characters also seem to feel an instinctive moral imperative (whether or not they live up to it), usually without the scaffolding of religion. At the end of the scene that so impressed Benedict Nightingale, as Nuala leaves the stage in tears, Terry stares toward the empty doorway, sighs, and says simply: 'God forgive me.' Robin Lefevre, who has directed all three major productions of *The Cavalcaders*, observes that Terry feels unworthy of love, especially as offered by an unstable girl half his age. 'Terry comprehends the depth of his cruelty', Lefevre says. 'He knows exactly what he's doing.'[5]

Billy Roche was born in 1949 in Wexford, the town that has provided settings for almost all of his stories and plays. His grandfather, Jem Roche, the Irish heavyweight boxing champion in the early years of the twentieth century, is commemorated with a plaque in Wexford's town square, the Bull Ring. His father, Pierce Roche, ran a waterfront pub called The Shamrock. Billy worked in this pub as a teenager, and later fictionalized it as 'The Rock' in his apprenticeship novel *Tumbling Down*. After finishing his schooling with the Christian Brothers, Roche briefly attended the Abbey Acting School in Dublin. He would eventually build an acting career, appearing in Brian Friel's *Aristocrats* and in various films, as well as in several of his own plays, but at the age of eighteen he turned to a career in music. A self-taught guitarist, Roche performed solo as a singer-songwriter, and then as the leader of a new-wave pop group, The Roach Band – part of an eclectic era in Irish music fondly recollected here in an essay by another Wexford musician, Larry Kirwan. 'The Shamrock Shuffle', recorded by the Roach Band in the

---

[4] Benedict Nightingale, '*The Cavalcaders*', *The Times* (London), January 9, 2002.

[5] The quotes from Ingrid Craigie, Gary Lydon, and Robin Lefevre come from personal interviews conducted in June 2007. See my essay on *The Cavalcaders* in this collection.

late 1970s, was inspired by characters who frequented Pierce
Roche's pub. Billy also worked as a bartender, construction hand,
and automobile upholsterer before achieving success as a writer,
and his writing shows an easy familiarity with working-class
characters and settings.

In *Tumbling Down* (1986) several characters from 'The
Shamrock Shuffle' reappear – arguing, telling stories, betting the
horses, and especially singing – but the story is held together by its
young and very autobiographical protagonist, an aspiring musician
who works in his father's pub. Sketching a year of Wexford life, the
novel shuttles between the young man's coming-of-age narration
and omniscient chapters that look more deeply and sadly into other
lives. The rich comedy of the book includes an extended scene in a
barbershop, with one customer playing an elaborate joke on the
man cutting his hair, and the rhythm of that dialogue gives early
evidence of Roche's aptitude as a playwright. The turn toward
drama, Roche says, came halfway through the writing of the novel
when his protagonist, 17-year-old Davy Wolfe, 'stepped into a
dilapidated snooker hall and – eureka. I seized on the setting and set
to work on my first stage play, *A Handful of Stars*.'[6]

The main character in that drama, Jimmy Brady, is also 17 – but
he has none of Davy Wolfe's ambition or watchful patience.
Destructive and self-destructive, Jimmy ends the play as a petty
criminal waiting alone by a jukebox for the police to come and arrest
him. Yet this character transcends his depressed environment,
which is epitomized in the seediness of the play's single set. Jimmy
becomes compelling not just as a bold rebel but as a damaged soul
who sometimes tries, haltingly, to do or say the right thing. The
scene reprinted here, in which Jimmy and his girlfriend have
sneaked into the snooker hall at night, suggests why audiences have
been attracted to a dramatic character they would probably shun in
real life.

As Dominic Dromgoole recounts in the first 'Overview' essay,
Roche's script (originally entitled *The Boker Poker Club*)
immediately impressed the artistic staff at the Bush Theatre in
London – and, when it opened in 1988, the play found a most
appreciative audience. Roche received a John Whiting Award, was

---

[6] Billy Roche, untitled reminiscence in *'Close-Up Magic': 40 Years at
   the Bush Theatre*, ed. Neil Burkey (London: Millennium Press,
   2011): 77.

recognized by Plays and Players as 'Most Promising New Playwright', and became Writer-in-Residence at the Bush, which premiered his next two works, *Poor Beast in the Rain* (1989) and *Belfry* (1991). In 1993 the three plays were published together as *The Wexford Trilogy* and were revived under that title at the Bush and then at the Theatre Royal in Wexford as part of a 'Billy Roche Weekend', as recalled here by Dominic Dromgoole and Benedict Nightingale. In that same year the trilogy was adapted for presentation on BBC television, with major roles reprised by the original stage performers. Unfortunately, these adaptations, produced by Stuart Burge with intelligence and sensitivity, remain archived on videotape in London; their re-release would be a gift to all who care about fine writing and fine acting.

Although the trilogy plays have no recurring characters, they are linked by tones of rough compassion and gentle humour, and British critics have often used phrases like 'generosity of spirit' to describe their subtle appeal. Benedict Nightingale of *The Times*, Charles Spencer of the *Daily Telegraph*, and Aleks Sierz (a prolific freelancer) have remained the most enthusiastic of these commentators. Sierz characterizes Roche's plays as 'gritty, tough and hard,' but also emotionally rich: 'If his writing often smacks you in the gob,' Sierz once said, 'it can also lift you to the stars. To Friel's acoustic fiddle, Roche answers with an electric guitar.'[7] Spencer has been even more effusive: these Wexford dramas, he says, 'concern apparently inconsequential people and events. Yet like Vermeer, like Jane Austen, Roche transforms the everyday into profound, beautiful, strangely consoling art.'[8]

Many observers – including Karen Fricker, Kate Bassett, and Veronica Lee – have credited Roche's breakthrough in London as a breakthrough for Irish drama in general, paving the way for other productions at the Bush and the Royal Court of work by Conor McPherson, Sebastian Barry, and Mark O'Rowe. But Fintan O'Toole finds an 'oddity' in the initial success of the trilogy:

> Its well-made slice-of-life drama would be mainstream anywhere else ... But in Ireland, there are astonishingly few successful examples of such work in recent decades. An angular strangeness is, paradoxically, much more familiar in the work

[7] 'From Fiddles to Guitars', *New Statesman & Society*, January 14, 1994: 36.

[8] 'Little Shop of Despair and Hope', *The Daily Telegraph*, January 9, 2002.

of major Irish playwrights than well-worked naturalism. Thus the irony is that this most local and rooted of dramatists, whose universe is Wexford town, was ignored by the Irish theatre until he was feted in London.[9]

The real paradox here is not that Roche's realism is out of the mainstream of modern Irish drama, or even that yet another national artist had to be 'discovered' abroad. It is that Roche achieves dramatic universality while focusing relentlessly on one setting. How does it happen that, in Colm Tóibín's apt formulation, Billy Roche's Wexford stands for the world? There may seem to be precedents in fiction and drama – William's Faulkner's 'little postage stamp' of Yoknapatawpha County in Mississippi; John Steinbeck's lush Salinas Valley in California; and closer to home, Brian Friel's fictional village of Ballybeg ('small town') in Donegal. But Faulkner, Steinbeck, and Friel have been obsessed by history, and their characters' lives are seen as layered atop those of ancestors, and shaped by politics, migrations, and conquests. Roche seems indifferent to such concerns. Although Wexford is a central site of Irish history (invasions by Vikings and Normans, later massacres of both Catholics and Protestants, rebel uprisings in 1798 and 1916), Roche does not delve into his town's rich past. He once drafted a play set in Wexford during the Irish Civil War, based on real events surrounding the execution of three young men – but, uneasy about 'the vulgarity of political banner waving', he put the manuscript aside.[10] 'I'm fascinated by my characters', Roche has said, 'and my characters don't care about history. I'd be trying more to capture the lives of characters who think the world revolves around them.'[11] It seems indicative that this playwright gave the name of Artie O'Leary to the protagonist of *Belfry* without drawing a connection, even an ironic one, to the historical figure commemorated in the classic Irish poem 'Lament for Art O'Leary'.

If history provides no substructure for Roche's Wexford, what does underlie the universal quality of his writing? The answer, in a word, is 'myth' – understood in the widest sense. He draws upon

---

[9] Review of *Poor Beast in the Rain* at the Gate Theatre, *The Irish Times*, April 14, 2005.

[10] Roche discussed this play, *The Light in the Morning Sky*, in an interview with Claudia Woolgar when he was still considering going forward with it. See 'Tumbling Down to London', *Theatre Ireland*, 29 (Autumn 1992): 9.

[11] Kerrane, 'The Poetry of the Street': 371.

classical figures (Theo in *Lay Me Down Softly* as Theseus), tales of Camelot (a quartet of singers in *The Cavalcaders* as Arthurian knights), and Irish legends (the fugitive lovers in *Trojan Eddie* as Diarmuid and Grania). Roche rarely calls attention to such parallels – an exception is Danger Doyle's speech in *Poor Beast in the Rain* about Óisín's return to Ireland – and he seems not to care if audiences don't recognize them consciously in a story: 'on some level they know there's a *déjà vu* about it, or something that gives it a strength ... The trick is not to make it too obvious.'[12] One of his storytelling 'commandments' (adages for artists in his writing workshops) is 'Hide in the long grass.'

Roche has often referred to *The White Goddess: A Historical Grammar of Poetic Myth* as his bible, and it is clear that Robert Graves' compendium has helped him to think through patterns of characterization surrounding the 'eternal feminine.' Many of Roche's plays and stories dramatize a longing for an unattainable or ever-elusive woman, or for a wife who runs away. Usually remaining off-stage, but powerful nonetheless, is a mother who can betray as well as nurture. Occasional reviewers have detected a tinge of misogyny in Roche's work, but the great actress Ingrid Craigie has observed that, if anything, this writer idealizes women too much. In fact, as Belinda McKeon argues here, Roche typically focuses on men who are trapped by their superficial regard for the opinions of other men, and the narrowness of a male subculture is sometimes visualized in the narrowness of the stage – a small shop, for example, as a masculine enclave.

The world of competitive sport offers another window into the values of Roche's males, but it also constitutes an alternative dimension of myth. Perhaps because of his family history, boxing as a primal contest runs like a thread from *A Handful of Stars* though *The Cavalcaders* to Roche's most recent play, *Lay Me Down Softly*, in which a boxing ring is the centrepiece of the set. No bouts are seen on stage in any of Roche's plays – although his film *Trojan Eddie* includes a bare-knuckle fight at a muddy campsite, with bettors forming a ring. In the betting shop of *Poor Beast in the Rain* the risk and hard luck of horseracing reflect the characters' own lives, and most of their conversations (and eventual celebrations) circle around the county team's fortunes in the All-Ireland Hurling

---

[12] Quoted by Jimmy Lacey, 'Stories in the Key of Life', *The Irish Book Review*, II, 3 (Spring 2007): 31.

Final. Roche has an abiding love for hurling: a game embedded in Irish myth, and a brilliant spectacle in its own right. In 'Some Silent Place' – the long story that concludes *Tales from Rainwater Pond* – the athletic scenes gain credibility and almost cinematic detail from Roche's allusions to real events, sometimes in an omniscient narrative voice, and sometimes in the florid prose of 'The Scribe' who writes of hurling matches as Homeric contests.[13]

'Myth' for Roche shines through popular culture as well. Pop music amplifies feelings that characters on their own can barely express, as illustrated beautifully in the tale 'A Lucky Escape,' in which pop songs from the author's own youth (like "Cupid' by Sam Cooke) provide an imaginary soundtrack. The protagonist of that story, the singer Tommy Day, is a recurrent character in Roche's writing and, as a soulful figure and an inveterate gambler, he comes to represent something essential in the town's collective identity.[14] The mythic power of music is even greater on stage. *The*

---

[13] Roche recasts real events, most notably when he narrates the heroics of one Wexford player with just seconds to go in the Leinster semi-final, his team trailing by two points. An Offaly full-back, near his own goal, tries to clear the ball by whipping it out to the wings. But Tommy Hawkins 'blocked the shot, scooped it up into his hand with a slice of his hurl, half turned and with one last beautiful strike he slammed it into the roof of the net. Bang! Poetry!' This sequence is a direct replay of a dramatic shot by Wexford's Michael Jacob in the 2004 Leinster semi-final against Kilkenny at Croke Park. In the last seconds, with Wexford trailing 1-16 to 1-15, Jacob blocked a clearance from Kilkenny's Peter Barry, and (just as described) miraculously caught it, turned, and fired home the match-winning goal.

[14] Prior to Tommy Day's appearances in the *Rainwater Pond* stories, Roche had used him as an important off-stage character in *On Such As We* (London: Nick Hern Books, 2001). The play's protagonist, Oweney, is infuriated that Tommy has been beaten and hospitalized because of gambling debts. When the thuggish Eddie says that this 'nothing' character is not worth caring about, Owney angrily replies: 'Tommy Day is Tommy Day! ... He's Tommy fuckin' Day! ... and if a fella like that can't walk around owin' someone a couple of quid then what's it all about? I mean he did his bit. He paid his dues' (48). In 2008, when Roche published the revised version of his novel *Tumbling Down*, he slyly inserted a new reference near the end when his teenage narrator goes to a dancehall: 'We took in the relief band – Tommy Day and the Bandits, belting out *Boys* ...' (Wexford: Tassel Publications: 150).

*Cavalcaders*, for example, highlights rehearsal performances by a quartet of supposed friends, and Fintan O'Toole has pointed out that their lyrics ironically convey their sense of helplessness amid a swirl of infatuation, lust, and treachery:

> All, in other words, are living lives in which love functions as it does in the pop songs: an inexplicable, irresistible and irrational force that sweeps away everything in its path. The great poignancy of the play is that the singers are victims of the things they celebrate in their songs. Like devotees of some ancient cult, they worship the cruel goddess that toys with their lives.[15]

Cinema has provided Roche with another set of archetypes. The sawdust-and-canvas world of *Lay Me Down Softly*, for example, is not a nostalgic recreation of Ireland in the 1960s; it is an evocation of the timeless melancholy world of Federico Fellini's *La Strada*. Roche has written wittily about growing up in a town culture dominated by film: 'I didn't see much theatre when I was growing up, so I learnt a lot from the pictures. Sharp, snappy dialogue – I loved wise-guy quips. One of my favourites was *Cool Hand Luke* – and my own film *Trojan Eddie* is a little nod to it. I love misfits and those who challenge authority.'[16] *A Handful of Stars* was dedicated, Roche says, to the era of rebel heroes like James Dean, and other plays have been influenced by western movies: 'I grew up on the mythology of westerns. John Ford was our Homer really.'[17] Patrick Lonergan's essay shows how *On Such as We* recasts several conventions of the western, culminating in an off-stage showdown on the main street. And when *Poor Beast in the Rain* was revived at Dublin's Gate Theatre in 2005 (directed by Conor McPherson), one of the advertisements announced: 'Danger Doyle Is Back in Town.'

This anthology concludes with an essay suggesting that Roche's Wexford is itself a mythic construction. Hilary Sophrin shows how this storyteller, unlike Joyce, freely remaps his town. Roche changes

---

[15] '*The Cavalcaders*: Lyric Theatre, Belfast', *The Irish Times*, October 31, 2002.

[16] 'Billy Roche in conversation about memories of Wexford cinemas', in *Here's Looking at You, Kid! Ireland Goes to the Pictures*, ed. Stephanie McBride and Roddy Flynn (Dublin: Wolfhound Press, 1996): 116.

[17] Jimmy Lacey, 'Stories in the Key of Life': 31. See also Roche's Afterword to *The Wexford Trilogy* (London: Nick Hern Books, 1992): 187.

the location of buildings, enlarges an off-shore ballast bank into a mysterious island, and combines two tidal pools into a single entity, unfathomable and ever-changing, that mirrors the lives of people in the town – and perhaps of people anywhere in the world.

Despite the range of Roche's mythic imagination, his work does not have some of the obvious 'hooks' that attract academic analysts. (Conor McPherson once observed that Roche writes about love without irony.) And the plays, in particular, have a deceptive transparency that can baffle critics – as when John Peter of *The Sunday Times* reviewed a revival of *The Cavalcaders*: 'The writing has virtually no style, only a casual simplicity, as if the actors were speaking their own thoughts. Roche is using the innate theatricality of Irish speech, and has created a play that unfolds like life.'[18] Nor are these dramas issue-driven. Instead of creating what Fintan O'Toole calls 'power plays' – works that tackle big social issues – Roche writes in the spirit of James Joyce, or at least the side of Joyce summarized by Patrick Kavanagh:

> The exciting quality about Joyce is that when you read him you are not told of the large public issues that were agitating the minds of politicians and journalists in those days. Joyce takes the unimportant lives of people and shows that in the end these private lives are the only lives that matter; the only thing that matters is people – thinking, dreaming, hoping, loving.[19]

Roche seems most Joycean, and perhaps most Irish, in blending tragedy and comedy, often shifting the mood of a scene in a heartbeat. O'Toole himself has credited this playwright with an unsentimental compassion, 'a vision that combines astringency with absolution.' Among the most remarkable features of Roche's work, O'Toole says, are 'the vivid appropriation of Wexford dialect, the deep affection for unheroic people, the deadpan wit, the patient attention to the quiet notes of sorrow beneath the babble of everyday conversation.'[20] To that impressive list one might add the creation of countless characters who never appear on stage, but who seem to be hovering just out of sight in the wings. As a result,

---

[18] John Peter, '*The Cavalcaders*: Tricycle', *Sunday Times* (London), January 6, 2002.

[19] *Kavanagh's Weekly*, No. 7 (May 24, 1952): 2.

[20] Fintan O'Toole, '*On Such As We*: The Peacock', *The Irish Times*, November 20, 2004. See also the 1990 review of *Poor Beast in the Rain*, reprinted in *Critical Moments: Fintan O'Toole on Modern Irish Theatre* (Dublin: Carysfort Press, 2003): 101-102.

Roche's audiences are invited to consider the shared life of a community, both in the play and in their own lives.

Roche's gift for finding the universal in the local, the world within Wexford, illustrates Kavanagh's famous contrast between two artistic mentalities, the *parochial* (literally 'of the parish') and the *provincial*. One is authentic, grounded in the fundamentals of life; the other is merely ambitious, looking for approval from outside: 'The provincial has no mind of his own; he does not trust what his eyes see until he has read what the metropolis - towards which his eyes are turned – has to say on the subject ... The parochial mentality on the other hand never is in any doubt about the social and artistic validity of his parish.' Thinking of life in his native Monaghan, Kavanagh once said that his idea of a cultural parochial entity was 'the distance a man would walk in a day in any direction.' That sounds like an amusing definition of the Wexford walking tours that Roche is so fond of providing.

But Kavanagh's insight cuts much deeper when he characterizes the parochial writer as someone with 'the right kind of sensitive courage and the right kind of sensitive humility' - a beautifully apt description of the artist Billy Roche.[21]

---

[21] Patrick Kavanagh, 'The Parish and the Universe' in *Collected Pruse* (London: MacGibbon and Kee, 1967): 282-283. See also 'Studies in the Technique of Poetry: Extracts from Ten Lectures', reprinted in *Patrick Kavanagh: Man and Poet*, ed. Peter Kavanagh (Orono, Maine: National Poetry Foundation, 1986): 243.

# 2 | From *A Handful of Stars*

Billy Roche

## Scene Three

> *The Club a few nights later in darkness. There is some commotion off stage and soon Jimmy comes into view, coming out of the toilet door. He goes across to the front door and opens it up. Linda steps in, Jimmy closing the door gently behind her and switching on the light. Linda stands just inside the door, looking around at the place, seemingly unimpressed. Jimmy goes across to the pot-bellied stove and starts banking it up with coal.*

**LINDA.** I thought you said you had your own key.

**JIMMY.** No I said meself and Tony had our own private entrance.

**LINDA.** (*Moving a little deeper into the club*). Oh! ... How did you get in as a matter of interest?

**JIMMY.** What? There's a window broken in the jacks. It's been like that this ages. Meself and Tony let ourselves in and out of here whenever we've no place else to go. It's queer handy.

**LINDA.** Won't someone see the light shinin' from the street?

**JIMMY.** No. We checked that out. I had Tony stand down there one night and look up. Once those shutters are drawn you can't tell a thing.

**LINDA.** You have it well planned. All the same I think I'd prefer to be somewhere else.

**JIMMY.** Look stop fussin'. I told yeh it was alright. (*Jimmy rubs his hands together and stands up.*) A bit of heat now and we'll be elected. Poor Paddy will be hoverin' over this yoke tomorrow night, tryin' to figure out where all the coal is gone. I'm not coddin' yeh, meself and Tony were often here breakin' our hearts laughin' and Paddy looking at the half empty bucket and scratchin' himself. We'd be after usin' all the coal up on him.

**LINDA.** Oh now you're a right pair of chancers. (*Jimmy sits on the bench. He watches her ramble around the club, touching the cues, caressing the table and finally coming to a standstill in front of the glass panel. She tries to see in but it is too dark.*)

**JIMMY.** What do yeh think of it?

**LINDA.** What's in there? The auld fella's office or somethin'?

**JIMMY.** What? No that's where the whatdoyoucallit go ... the elite.

**LINDA.** The elite?

**JIMMY.** Yeah. Conway and all. (*She cups her hands and peers in. Jimmy rambles over closer to her, standing behind her.*) That's Tony's main ambition yeh know?

**LINDA.** What is?

**JIMMY.** To get inside there.

**LINDA.** (*Ponders on the remark.*) Why don't he just break in some night when the pair of yeh have the run of the place?

**JIMMY.** That's what I said. But no, that wouldn't do him at all.

**LINDA.** Why not?

**JIMMY.** Tony's waitin' to be invited in.

**LINDA.** Invited? Who's goin' to invite him?

**JIMMY.** (*Putting on a deep voice.*) The men. (*He steps up to the slot machine and puts some money in, banging away at it.*) It's not just getting' in there that matters to him yeh know? It's ah ... I don't know.

**LINDA.** He wants to be accepted I suppose?

**JIMMY.** Yeah.

**LINDA.** (*Sarcastically.*) By the men?

**JIMMY.** I suppose so. (*Linda smirks at the very idea.*)

**LINDA.** (*Taking down a cue, awkwardly taps around with a few loose balls that have been left on the table.*) And what about you?

**JIMMY.** Me? What about me?

**LINDA.** You mean to tell me you don't dream about gettin' in there too?

**JIMMY.** (*Smiles at this remark.*) Naw ... I don't belong in there.

**LINDA.** Where do you belong then?

**JIMMY.** What? Where? I don't know. Not in there anyway that's for sure. (*Jimmy is standing close to her now and the intimacy seems to make Linda uneasy. She breaks away, placing the cue across the table.*)

**LINDA.** What's in there?

**JIMMY.** The jacks. (*Linda backs out of the doorway, cringing at the stink of the place. She spots a cutting from a newspaper pinned up on the door that leads to the back room. She goes across to read it. Jimmy picks up the cue and starts to show off, taking up an exaggerated stance, sprawling himself across the table.*)

**LINDA.** 'Chase over rooftops.' (*She glances towards him.*)

**JIMMY.** (*Takes his shot*). 'A dramatic chase took place last Sunday night over rooftops on the South Main Street when a young man who was suspected of breaking and entering was pursued by Detective Garda Swan. The drama occurred when Detective Swan slipped and went tumbling down the slanted roof. Eyewitnesses said that he was dangling from a considerable height, holding on to the gutter by the tips of his fingers. Ah ...'

**LINDA.** 'His cries for help ... '

**JIMMY.** Oh yeah ... 'His cries for help were answered when the young man that he was chasing came back to assist him, a factor that later contributed to the leniency of the sentence.' That's a deadly word ain't it? Leniency.

**LINDA.** 'The judge said summing up that the defendant James Brady was a nuisance and a danger to the public. He resisted arrest and was constantly in trouble with the police. "The sooner he grows up the better for all of us."'

**JIMMY.** Hey don't forget. 'The probation act was applied.'

**LINDA.** What did you do Jimmy, learn it off by heart or somethin'?

**JIMMY.** The whole town has it off by heart. I'm famous sure. They don't know whether I should be crucified or ascended into heaven. I have about twelve of those cuttings at home. Every time Paddy rips one down I stick another up. Conway is ragin' ... I don't know what you're lookin' at me like that for. I did it for you.

**LINDA.** (*Baffled.*) For me?

**JIMMY.** Yeah. I was skint. If I was goin' to take you somewhere I needed some money fast didn't I? I mean I couldn't turn up with no money again could I?

**LINDA.** And that's why you broke into the shop?

**JIMMY.** Ah I've been knockin' off that place for ages. It was a cinch. In through the window and the money was always left in the same drawer. The only thing was they had set a trap for me. There was all this dye or ink or somethin' all over the money and it stained all me hands and clothes. So when he picked me up he knew straight away that I was the one.

**LINDA.** And that's when you took off up onto the roof? (*Jimmy nods.*) I mean you must have known that you couldn't get away. It was stupid.

**JIMMY.** Yeah I suppose it was.

**LINDA.** Why did you do it then?

**JIMMY.** I don't know. I just felt like it at the time. (*He goes across to the cue stand.*)

**LINDA.** You just felt like it?

**JIMMY.** Yeah. It seemed like a good idea ... (*He puts up the cue.*) at the time. (*Linda shakes her head and smiles in disbelief. He smiles across at her.*) Look, I've always enjoyed knockin' off stuff. Ever since I was a young lad and I'd rob me da's pockets while he was asleep in the chair. He'd have come in stocious drunk and gave me poor ma a couple of belts and maybe broke the place up too into the bargain. Then he'd flop down into the armchair and demand his dinner. When he was asleep, snorin' his big head off, I'd rifle his coat pockets. He'd wake up dyin' and not a penny to his name.

**LINDA.** You'd rob your own da?

**JIMMY.** Yeah. Why not? If somebody has somethin' I want I'll take it.

**LINDA.** What, anybody?

**JIMMY.** No, not anybody. Yeah, though, anybody. Why not?

**LINDA.** Aw I can't believe that. What, even Tony yeh mean.

**JIMMY.** Yeah, if he had somethin' I wanted.

**LINDA.** (*Shakes her head.*) I can't ... I mean I know your brother Dick real well and he's terrible nice.

**JIMMY.** Yeah well Richard follows me ma.

**LINDA.** And who do you follow?

**JIMMY.** (*Shrugs.*) Naw I wouldn't rob Tony though. The fucker never has anythin' worth talkin' about anyway.

**LINDA.** But yeh would rob your da?

**JIMMY.** (*Nods that he would.*) If your da was like mine you'd rob him too.

**LINDA.** (*Shakes her head in disbelief.*) Your poor ma must be addled between the two of you. (*Jimmy falls silent. He is sitting up on the pool table now, his legs dangling over the edge.*)

**JIMMY.** I once caught them kissin' yeh know. Me ma and da I mean. I was only a little lad at the time. I ran out to tell Richard and when we got back me da was singin' at the top of his voice and the two of them were waltzin' around the little kitchen. Me and Richard just stood starin' up at them. 'There they are now', says me da. 'James the Less and his brother Jude.' He had his good suit on him and a gleamin' white shirt and the smell of Brylcreem off him would nearly knock you down. Me ma was breakin' her heart laughin' at the face of us, her own face lit up like a Christmas tree. I'm not coddin' you she looked absolutely ... radiant. (*Pause.*) Richard says he doesn't remember that happenin' at all. Me ma don't either. Maybe it was just a whatdoyoucallit. ... a mirage. (*Linda has come closer to him now. She picks softly at his shirt, pulling at the loose threads.*) Richard kicked me da out of the house yeh know when I was away with the F.C.A. that time.

**LINDA.** I never knew you were in the F.C.A.

**JIMMY.** Yeah I used to be. They threw me out of it. I got fed up of your man shoutin' at me. Whatshisname ... yeh know your man lives up by you there ... Brown! I told him to go and cop on himself. Anyway when I got home I found me da stayin' down in that auld hostel. I felt terrible. He was just lyin' there, reading a war book or somethin', a couple of those army blankets tossed across his feet. I wanted to burn the place down. I told him to get his things and come on home but he wouldn't. Well let's face it fellas like meself and me da don't have a ghost of a chance do we? Like when I went looking for a job at your place. What did your man O'Brien ask me? What Brady are you then? Well that was me finished before I even started wasn't it?

**LINDA.** Aw he was probably only ...

**JIMMY.** Yes he was yeah. He wrote me off straight away. Even if I had never been in trouble I was out. I wouldn't mind but he was knockin' off stuff all over the place himself. They found the generator in his car didn't they?

**LINDA.** Yeah.

**JIMMY.** And I heard they found a load of more stuff up in his garage – stuff belongin' to the firm. And he didn't even get the sack out of it did he?

**LINDA.** He's still down there anyway. (*Jimmy shakes his head and smirks at the idea.*)

**JIMMY.** It's just as well I didn't get a job down there anyway. I'd never have been able to stick that Conway. I can't stomach that fella I'm not coddin' yeh. Did you know he's after talkin' Tony into getting' married?

**LINDA.** To who? Not to that young one surely?

**JIMMY.** Yeah. She's up the pole sure. And now Conway is preachin' to him that the decent thing to do is to marry her.

**LINDA.** Well if it's his child ...

**JIMMY.** Look Conway never stopped at him when Tony started goin' out with her first. Did you do this yet and did you do that yet? Badgerin' and jeerin' the chap and makin' a holy show of him in front of everyone. And now all of a sudden he's preachin' about what's right and what's wrong. All of a sudden she's a grand little girl ... Tony don't want to marry her anyway.

**LINDA.** Poor Tony. He's real nice. (*She studies Jimmy's face.*) What would you do if you were in his shoes?

**JIMMY.** I'd run for the hills.

**LINDA.** Aw you wouldn't.

**JIMMY.** No not half wouldn't I. (*Linda watches him carefully, trying to see if he is only joking. Earnestly*) I would.

**LINDA.** (*Disappointed. Turns away.*) Let's get out of here Jimmy. This place is stinkin'.

**JIMMY.** We only just got here.

**LINDA.** I know but ...

**JIMMY.** (*Going to her, putting his arms around her, kissing her gently.*) What's wrong with yeh?

**LINDA.** Nothin'. I'd just prefer to be somewhere else that's all.

**JIMMY.** Yeah well we're not somewhere else are we? We're here.

**LINDA.** I know. But I'd prefer to go someplace else.

**JIMMY.** Where?

**LINDA.** I don't know.

**JIMMY.** Do you want to go to the dance?

**LINDA.** How can we go to the dance when you're barred from the club?

**JIMMY.** Yeah well you can go in on your own can't yeh. I don't mind.

**LINDA.** Look Jimmy if I'm goin' with a fella I'm goin' with him.

**JIMMY.** I know that. I just thought you liked dancin' that's all.

**LINDA.** I do like dancin'.

**JIMMY.** Well then?

**LINDA.** I'll just have to live without it won't I? (*Jimmy sighs and winces.*) What's wrong?

**JIMMY.** You'll have to live without goin' to the pictures too.

**LINDA.** Why? What did you do up there?

**JIMMY.** I asked the auld fella do be on the door how much would he charge to haunt a house? Did you ever see the face on him? He's like a ghost ain't he? (*Jimmy is laughing and so is Linda in spite of herself. Jimmy kisses her, hugs her, wraps his arms around her. Linda responds. Jimmy gradually caresses her all over, her hair, her neck. Eventually he tries to slip his hand up her jumper. She stops him. He whispers:*) What's wrong.

**LINDA.** I don't want you runnin' for the hills do I?

**JIMMY.** I said if I was in Tony's shoes I'd run for the hills. I'm not.

**LINDA.** You're in Jimmy Brady's shoes are yeh?

**JIMMY.** Yeah. (*Linda considers this answer.*) Well they're me brother Richard's shoes actually but ... (*Linda smiles. She then takes the initiative and kisses him, running her fingers through his hair. Lights down.*)

*End of Act One.*

# 3 | A Lucky Escape

Billy Roche

Tommy Day? Yeah, I know Tommy Day. Tommy Day the singer, you mean? Yeah! He used to sing with a dance band called The Toreadors once upon a time. Well, he sang with other bands too, but that's what most people remember about him. A nifty sort of fellow. You'd often see him coming out of a side street or nipping up a back street or slipping in and out of betting shops and all the rest of it. That's more or less how he lived his life really. Plenty of talent. No ambition. No plan. Some people are like that. Until they wake up one morning and realize it's all over.

He'd be over fifty now, Tommy! He was never much to look at, but there was always something about him, especially when he sang - deadly hand movements and that kind of thing. I mean he had something, you know, heart or soul or something. I don't know... It's hard to explain. I mean you knew that he meant what he said when he sang, let's put it that way. And I'll tell you something else for nothing but no one could ever sing a love song like Tommy Day. And I know most people say they were just words to him, that there was never really anything to him, but ... no. He knew about love all right. He'd been to the garden.

He never married, lived with his mother all his life. His father died young so I suppose Tommy was a source of comfort for her, singing to her and that. Not financially of course. No, Tommy was no breadwinner. Although to be fair to him she always knew exactly where to find him if ever she was looking for him: hanging over a jukebox or down in the snooker hall or up to his ears in a back room card game. He'd bet on two flies going up the wall, the same fellow.

Tommy joined The Toreadors when he was seventeen, singing at the Saturday night dances in the local Desert Hall. So by the time his eighteenth birthday rolled around he was a fairly seasoned singer. Johnny, the old bandleader, came through the double doors at the back of the room with a cake and he carried it across the powdered dance floor towards the bandstand. Tommy was mortified. He was on stage, surrounded by an eight piece band, trumpets and trombones and saxophones and what-not, and big Leo What's-his-name - I can't think of his surname now ... he was a baker ... on the drums. The musicians were wearing these red sparkly coats and white frilly shirts. Next week the coats would be turned inside out and they'd be blue. Ingenious? Yeah, well, maybe. It wouldn't do to look too close though. All that glittered wasn't gold back then.

The band played 'Happy Birthday' and the dancers sang along and then Tommy blew out the candles with three half-hearted puffs. 'Take your pick', Johnny said to him, picking up his old battered saxophone and Tommy looked at him with wide eyes and wonder.

'What do you want to sing?' Johnny explained and a stillness fell over the hall.

Now this was 1967, don't forget (*Flowers In The Rain,* and *Strawberry Fields Forever,* and all). But Tommy was basically an old fashioned singer at heart and everybody knew that he wouldn't pick something straightforward from the charts. In fact the band had made bets on it and everything. It was bound to be Sam Cooke, Bobby Darin or Conway Twitty – Tommy's idols. For that very reason he was rarely allowed to pick a number.

'Somethin' from this century, Tommy', Leo called from the back of the band.

'Yeah and preferably before the century is over', Johnny chirped and the band launched into an old Laurel and Hardy riff to highlight the joke.

'Cupid?' Tommy eventually suggested and Leo What's-his-name gave a triumphant roll on his snare drum.

'Fair enough', Johnny said and counted them in. 'A one, two, a one two three and ...'

Cullen ... Leo Cullen! That's it.

'Cupid,' Tommy crooned, stepping into the spotlight. 'Draw Back Your Bow/ And Let Your Arrow Go/ Straight To My Lover's Heart For Me / Nobody But Me ... '

She was standing down at the back of the hall, flicking her hair behind her ears all the time as young girls do and singing along to

the song and smiling at Tommy's hand movements and lovely –
what only could be termed – Frank Sinatra gestures: the wry smile,
the slight tilt of the head, the expressive shrug of the shoulders and
so on. She blushed when someone asked her to dance, but she got
up anyway and before the song was over she was dancing close to
the bandstand, laughing at the winking musicians and thrilled by
Tommy's beautiful stage antics.

Tommy couldn't take his eyes off of her. He watched her all night
long as she moved about the dance floor – sitting down and
standing up and dancing and trying to hold the hard cases at bay.
Her name was Clare Kearney and from the moment he saw her and
heard her name spoken out loud I'm afraid it was all over for him.
And I'm sorry to have to report that from that day on Tommy's life
was just another sad, sad song that he'd never get to sing.

That night Tommy didn't sleep a wink. He tossed and turned and
thought about her all the time. He wanted to hold her hand. He
wanted to say her name out loud. He wanted to marry her. *When
My Little Girl Is Smiling* kept cropping into his head. The next few
days he spent in a trance, mooning and moping about. His mother
was worried about him because he wasn't eating his dinner. 'You
don't owe anybody any money or anything, Tommy, do you?' she
asked him one time after tea. She knew well enough, like his father
before him, that he was a bit of a gambler.

The following Saturday night Clare was back at the dance again
and every other Saturday night after that. It was about the third or
fourth Saturday though before Tommy got a chance to talk to her.
She came up to the bandstand to put in a request for her friend's
birthday.

'What would you like me to sing?' Tommy asked her, going down
on one knee.

'Far away', Leo cried from behind his drums.

'Bus Stop', she said. 'She loves Bus Stop.'

'Alright', Tommy promised. 'Bus Stop it is', and he took the slip
of paper from her and stuffed it into his top pocket and watched as
she kind of tiptoed her way back to her place by the wall.

'A bit recent for you, Thomas, ain't it?' Johnny said to him when
Tommy whispered the request in his ear. 'What's her name again?'

'Breda Lacy,' Tommy told him.

'Alright,' Johnny said. 'Fair enough ... Ladies and Gentlemen, a
special request for Freda Lacy who's seventeen today. And it's the
one and only Tommy Day to sing *Bus Stop*.'

'I wish the bus would stop', Leo said, 'Til we all get off.'

That same night (or perhaps it was some other night, I don't know) after he had helped to put all the gear into the back of Johnny's old battered van, Tommy fastened up his coat and rambled home alone. She was standing at the foot of John's Gate Street hill, looking a little apprehensive to say the least. A drunken man was out in the middle of the street singing, *Don't Laugh At Me Cause I'm A Fool*, at the top of his voice and she was afraid to pass him by. Tommy went over to her and told her not to worry and volunteered to walk her home.

*I'm Not Good Lookin'*, the old man sang as they passed.

'That's for sure', Tommy said under his breath and Clare laughed with relief: a fairly husky sort of sound.

And so the young couple walked through the deserted streets of the sleeping town – Tommy on air. They must have passed other people along the way, someone putting out a bin or a man and his dog or some courting couple arguing or something, but if they did Tommy never noticed, he never noticed a thing. And I know it wasn't a date or anything. I mean he wouldn't get to hold her hand or kiss her goodnight at the door, but it was still lovely nevertheless. It was still something worth remembering. 'Cause there were stars in the sky and everything.

She told him she was working in Rafferty's Department Store now, which he already knew: in the office. Mister Rafferty she said was all right to work for, a bit cross at times, but generally speaking he was all right. Mrs Rafferty on the other hand was a right bitch. You wouldn't want to put your hand in her mouth. Clare told Tommy then, confidentially, that she'd much sooner be working down in the shop with Thelma Mahoney and all the other girls; but Clare had Commercial Commerce you see and so her mother had insisted that they put her in the office, which could be a dull old place at the best of times if the truth be told. When she spoke Clare had a slight catch in her voice, and although she talked all the time you always got the feeling that there was something about herself that she would never tell you, that there was something about her you'd never know, something she'd never reveal. Tommy wasn't so sure he liked that about her.

Her friend, Breda Lacy, was going out with Apache Byrne now and that's why she was walking home alone. She asked Tommy about Apache Bryne, what kind of a person he was and all that, and Tommy told her that he was all right, that he wasn't half as wild as he pretended to be. On the other hand, he said, he wasn't called Apache for nothing.

Her mother was waiting for her at the door when they got there, wondering what kept her. So she told her mother about the drunken man singing, *Don't Laugh At Me 'Cause I'm A* Fool at the top of his voice and about Tommy coming to her rescue.

'Who was it, Tommy?' her mother wanted to know and when Tommy told her she just folded her arms and threw her eyes to heaven.

'She had to go home early 'cause she felt sick', Clare replied.

'What was wrong with her?'

'I don't know', Clare said. 'She was sick, that's all. '

'Mmn. ... How's your Mammy, Tommy?'

'Grand.'

'She misses your Daddy terrible though I think, don't she?'

'Ah yeah,' Tommy agreed.

'She looks lost sometimes – without him ... God help her ... Yeah. Sick, hah! You must think I came down in the last shower or somethin', Miss, do you? Huh? Go ahead in there. Night Tommy.'

'Night Mrs Kearney.'

'Thanks Tommy', Clare called softly from the hallway.

'Yeah, right, Clare. See yeh, eh?' Tommy said and the door was gently shut in his face.

The drunken man was singing his way up the street towards him as Tommy turned for home. A milk float came silently round the bend. *On The Street Where You Live* sprang to mind. Vic Damone, eh!

\*

The following week Marty Maher came home from England with two French letters in his wallet and all hell broke loose. Tommy took a break from the bandstand and went into the Gents to find big Shamey Shiggins with a bursted lip and spouting blood all over the shop. There was blood everywhere: in the sink, on the floor and caked on the wooden frame of the cubicle. Marty Maher had dropped him with a head butt. Everyone just stood around in awe. No one had ever dropped big Shamey before. Shamey looked dazed. Or pale and wan as they say.

To make matters worse when Tommy went back outside Marty Maher was dancing with Clare. Luckily enough it was a fast set. The next set was a slow one though and he danced that one with her too. It nearly killed Tommy to watch her snuggling into him. *The Twelfth Of Never, Unchained Melody*, and ... I can't remember what the third number was now.

She danced with him all night after that. At one stage she was sort of sitting on his lap. Tommy was dying up there. He was hoping that she'd shake him off as the evening wore on, but she never did. At the end of the night, as the band played, *'The National Anthem,'* Tommy watched them like a hawk. He could read their lips from afar as Marty asked her if he could walk her home. 'O.K.', Clare replied. 'Hang on 'til I get my coat', and as she tripped gaily out to the cloakroom Tommy's heart sank like a roller coaster and to his own astonishment he heard himself gasping her name under his breath. 'Clare', he said, and he was suddenly consumed with a terrible, old aching disappointment.

*

Sunday afternoon at Rainwater Pond. Blackberry pickers moved from bush to bush as Shamey Shiggins nursed his swollen lip and Apache Bryne boasted about his exploits with Breda Lacy (or Freda Lacy as she became to be known from then on). Tommy Day lay on his belly, plucking moss from the big rock and dropping it down into the dark water below. An abandoned boat lay stranded in the long grass and beyond the waving meadow the sea shimmered like a fragmented mirror in the sun. A train trundled by and a passenger looked out upon the gang of wayward boys who basked beside this strange looking lagoon. The stranger seemed to wonder too about Tommy's lonely frown and he appeared to understand. Perhaps that's the answer, Tommy thought as the man's face evaporated. Get on a train and go away.

A bunch of spancelled old timers arrived then with walking sticks and blackthorn sticks and dogs, talking all the time about everything under the sun – this, that and the other. The dogs dived in and swam about and came out glistening with brine. One old man, Jakey Brown, called out to the lads, 'Morrow boys.' Jakey was an expert on birds. He could imitate the plaintive cry of the curlew and the back to front wolf whistle of the grey plover. The sparrow has twenty different melodies he'd tell you too and if you gave him half a chance he'd whistle them all for you. 'Never trust a peacock', was another one, 'because it was the one that showed the Devil the way to Paradise.' And then he'd throw back his head and cry like one.

'I wouldn't have a blackthorn stick next or near me', Jakey was telling one of the other old men. 'The blackthorn is a terrible unlucky tree, you know.' Tommy had heard that before somewhere: The Crown of Thorns or something. Is this what's in store for them? Tommy wondered as the old timers yapped their way out of sight – himself and big Shamey and Apache Byrne rambling the roads in forty years time with blackthorn sticks and dogs, whistling like curlews and crying like peacocks. Men without women!

And then Marty Maher and Clare showed up, hand in hand or arm in arm – I don't recall. Of all the places to come! Or was that that day at all? Maybe not. So long ago now!

'He must be runnin' out of French letters by now, lads', Apache Bryne declared as the two lovers climbed over a gate and disappeared across the meadow. 'Unless of course he's havin' them dry cleaned or something', and big Shamey, in spite of everything, spluttered out a painful laugh.

Tommy watched her going towards the ocean to vanish into the waving corn and he told himself that he must learn to despise her otherwise the pain will be too hard to endure. He must relinquish all hope. The nape of her neck though!

*

A month later Clare announced to her mother that she was pregnant and Marty Maher bailed out for London and left her in the lurch. Needless to say she was the talk of the town. She lost her job in Rafferty's and everything over it, for fear she'd lower the tone of the place. And she was the butt of everyone's jokes for the next few months – on the street corners, in the bars, at the Saturday night dances, her name bandied about like Salome. And I wish I could say that Tommy Day became her Lancelot, but no, he didn't. He scoffed with the rest of them or pretended to at least and in his heart he told himself that he didn't care, that it didn't matter. She was never anything to shout about anyway.

The Toreadors got the sack from The Desert Hall around that time. Father Howlin took Johnny to one side and told him that he wanted to try something different. He said from now on he was going to hire a small group known as *The Bandits.*

The following Saturday night Johnny turned up with his gear as usual and Father Howlin came to him, red faced and fuming.

'Johnny,' he said, 'I told you last week that I was hiring a group called *The Bandits* from now on.'

'Yeah I know you did, Father, 'Johnny said. 'We are The Bandits.'

Tommy Day was the lead singer with The Bandits and people swear there was a hurt in his voice that hadn't been there before and maybe there was. He seemed a bit rougher certainly. A little angrier maybe as he belted his way through Johnny Kidd and The Pirates' *I'll Never Get Over You.*

*

Ash Wednesday, the beginning of Lent, and Tommy was out of work again. No more dances for the next seven weeks, no more weddings or reunions either. Tommy rambled around the place, skint. Now and then his mother would take pity on him and throw him a couple of quid, but Tommy would only squander it on a horse or try his luck in a poker game and before he knew it he'd end up back where he started.

He got a job as a night porter in The Menapia Hotel for a few weeks, which turned out to be a fairly handy number until the manager paid a surprise visit in the middle of the night one night only to discover big Shamey Shiggins and Apache Byrne and all the boys drinking on the house in the resident's lounge at four o'clock in the morning. Everybody out!

One night as he was going home with a bag of chips Tommy happened on Clare who was sitting on the wooden seat at the end of Saint John's Road. She called out to him and he said goodnight to her, matter-of-factly. He had intended to just go on by about his business, but he didn't in the end. He crossed the street and sat down beside her and before he knew it she was dipping into his bag of chips and telling him all her news. He was surprised how chirpy she was, considering, like! She only had about six weeks to go now, she told him, all being well. She was hoping for a girl, but it didn't really matter, she said, as long as everything turned out all right. That was the main thing. She got a letter from Marty a while back, she said. He didn't really want anything or anything, just wondering how she was getting on and that.

'That was nice of him', Tommy mumbled, sarcastically, and her eyes sort of darted in his direction as if she didn't quite get the drift.

She had really tiny ears and a perfect mouth and her eyes were of the faintest blue, kind of drained of colour, almost soul-less in fact. Another reason not to love her?

Tommy walked her home that night and shortly afterwards when the child was born, about three weeks prematurely, he went up to the hospital to see her with a squashed bunch of flowers under his coat. It was a baby girl – Deirdre – and the first time she wheeled the pram down the town Tommy went with her. He took her into Nolan's Cafe for a sundae and a coke and they listened to the jukebox. He knew that people were talking about him, laughing at him more than likely. He wished that people thought the baby was his, but he knew well enough that they didn't, that everybody knew the whole story. His mother was looking at him sorrowfully. Mrs Kearney on the other hand was all over him. Cups of tea and plates of biscuits to beat the band, his feet under the table as they say. *Alright!*

And when it came time to christen the child Tommy was invited to the party. The party (well it wasn't exactly a party, just a few cakes and sandwiches and tea and soft drinks) was held in the spacious living room. Apache Byrne was there with Breda Lacy. And later on Tommy nipped out and got Sean Corcoran who played the guitar with The Toreadors and Eddie Shaw who played the trumpet and they had a right session. Eddie Shaw had to put the mute on his trumpet to dampen the sound. Mrs Kearney came into the room at one stage as Eddie was playing, *Oh My Papa*.

'I can't believe that child is sleeping through that racket', she said. 'Rip Van Winkle has nothing on her!' and everybody laughed.

At the end of the evening Clare gave Tommy a huge hug in the hall on his way out. He was tempted to kiss her there and then but something stopped him and he didn't in the end. He knew in his heart and soul that he would regret not kissing her later, but, apart from everything else, Eddie and Sean and Apache Byrne were waiting for him outside the front door. (Breda had gone ahead home in a bit of a sulk because the boys kept calling her Freda all the time.) And then, as if to stem the tide, Clare gave Tommy a harmless peck on the cheek and she raced to the door to say thanks and goodnight to the others.

The next morning Tommy woke up in a state of confusion. Things were going all right, he assured himself. Clare had invited him to the party. She had sat beside him most of the time and she had given him that big hug in the hall on his way out. Her face glowed when he sang to her and she laughed at the funny things he said sometimes. And the other day they had gone out to Rainwater Pond together, sat in the sun and returned home along the railway tracks, the two of them talking and laughing and singing and the first two buttons of her blue blouse open and she kept asking him questions all the time.

'What do you feel when you sing a sad song now?' she wondered. 'I mean do you feel anything? Or do you just sing it, like?'

'Oh no', Tommy told her. 'I feel it. I feel everything.'

'Yeah?' Clare said and she made a bit of a face as if she didn't quite approve or understand what he was getting at.

'I can't imagine it', she said. 'I mean how you do it, like!'

And that's the way it went all the way home. It was as if she was trying to fathom it all. And just before they reached the edge of town she said something strange to him.

'Did you ever think of livin' somewhere else, Tommy?' she began.

'Yeah', Tommy lied, 'sometimes.'

'Yeah, me too,' she confessed. 'I often think about going away and living somewhere else, somewhere foreign maybe. Then I could really be myself for a change instead of going around pretending all the time.'

Tommy was disappointed to hear her say this and he looked towards her to witness her gazing moodily out to sea as if the place she dreamt of going to was just somewhere over the horizon. A dark shadow shaded her face and her eyes were vague and distant and Tommy felt a meanness welling up inside of him. Did she intend to go to this other place without him or what? And if she was not who she pretended to be all the time then who was she? I mean who was this girl that he thought he had got to know lately? Or had she only gulled him again? On the other hand he was well aware that she had just confided in him, let him in on a secret that, in all likelihood, nobody else had ever heard before and he was glad about that. No, at the end of the day and taking everything into consideration, he was convinced she felt something for him all right! He was sure of it in fact. Absolutely! He'd put money on it!

So why did he feel so inconsequential then? Huh? The friendly kiss on the cheek? The distance between them when they walked? Those vacant, soul-less blue eyes looking through him all the time? What?... Who knows? He just did.

*

As it turned out he was right to feel that way. Tommy went down to Kearney's one night before tea only to find Clare doing herself up for a date with Marty Maher who had just come back for the summer. He was taking her to the pictures. Wasn't it great? Yeah. Great.

Tommy got into a row down in the snooker hall that night and had to be put out of the club. Over tea earlier on he had snapped at his poor mother and made her cry. And in the pub when someone asked him to sing a song he sang something so vulgar that everyone wondered what was up with him. Around midnight he went up and hung around outside Clare's house and waited for them to come home. He intended to tell them exactly what he thought of the pair of them and maybe fight Marty Maher too if that's what he wanted. But it turned fairly cold and started to rain and in the end he just skulked on home via the back streets with tears in his eyes.

Tommy bumped into the two of them on and off over the next few weeks and whenever he did he averted his eyes or crossed the street or pretended he never saw them in the first place. Clare seemed to be going out of her way to let everybody see that she was going out with Marty now, holding his hand in public and linking him and sitting on his lap at the back of the dance hall and all that carry-on. She never once came to Tommy to explain it all to him. In fact it was Marty Maher who eventually came and put him out of his misery.

Tommy was sitting at the counter in the Banjo Bar and Marty sidled up and sat beside him.

'Listen Tommy', Marty said. 'I know you were fairly fond of Clare and all the rest of it and you're probably wondering what's going on and all that but ... Well, the truth of the matter is Clare is going out with me now.'

'So I see', Tommy said and he looked directly into Marty Maher's lousy eyes.

'Yeah well ...' Marty said and grimaced as if he understood what Tommy was going through. 'Clare and I have to do the best for the child's sake, Tommy, like you know. I mean ... whatever, you know.'

'I know', Tommy said. And he meant it when he said it.

'I'll be straight about it', Marty told him then. 'She's always talking about you. Gets on my nerves sometimes to tell you the truth, but sure what can I do? ... Anyway, I just thought you should know all of that and not be avoiding us all the time. Alright?

'Yeah.'

'Wish us luck?'

'Of course.'

Shake on it.'

Yeah', Tommy said and held out his hand. 'Good luck.'

Clare married Marty Maher before the year was out. She had two more children for him - a boy and another girl- and Marty sort of settled down after that. Of course there was the odd scrape, the odd fight in a bar, the odd day in court, the odd affair with another woman. But generally speaking he settled down all right, generally speaking he did all right by her. Generally speaking!

Clare turned more matronly with each passing year. She put on a fair bit of weight and her legs grew sort of dumpy and her clothes looked on the staid side and her conversation was inclined to be old-womanish. In fact if you saw her now you'd probably wonder what Tommy ever saw in her in the first place, but there you go.

Tommy moved from one band to another after that. After The Bandits he sang with The Ray Flynn Quartet and one or two other groups he'd rather not mention. He entered a few national talent competitions, which were sponsored by *The Golden Brown Boot Company*, and although he sang on the radio a couple of times he came nowhere and eventually he lost heart and just gave up the ghost and stopped trying altogether.

He sings in the Banjo Bar every weekend now with the hunch backed Ray Flynn on the piano. Real moody sort of stuff: Frank Sinatra and Paul Anka and that – *Blame It On My Youth* and *Diana* and *The September Song*. And an upbeat version of *Mona Lisa* – Conway Twitty's version.

Did he ever fall in love again? No, I don't think so. Although he did take up with this girl called Eithne Reilly somewhere along the line and she was absolutely mad about him and would do anything for him until she got fed up of him turning up late and turning up drunk and turning up broke and sometimes not turning up at all. She eventually opted for a more sensible chap who she married. She continues to see Tommy on the sly though when her husband is working the night shift.

'Tell me you love me, Tommy', she says.

'I love you', he tells her as he buttons up his pants.

Most weekdays he'll ramble the roads now with Shamey Shiggins and Apache Bryne: walking sticks, dogs, the lot, talking about everything under the sun – this, that and the other. They marvel at all the people dying all around them. Marty Maher for instance who died of heart failure at forty-eight years of age. Apache Bryne said it served him right when he heard the news and laughed and glanced in Shamey's direction and big Shamey flashed a forgiving smile and muttered 'Poor Marty' under his breath.

Every Friday night Tommy slips the two boys into the Banjo Bar for free. They sit down in their favourite corner to watch the show. Once in a while a drink on the house arrives for them.

'Fair play to you, Tommy boy!' Apache Bryne says as he takes another gulp and he sits back to enjoy Tommy singing, *It's All Only Make Believe.* 'I like this one', he says to Shamey over the introduction.

'So do I', Shamey agrees. 'So do I.'

*It's All Only Make Believe.*

Tommy saw Clare the other day, clattering down the street with a couple of – what must have been – Deirdre's children hanging out of her (a grandmother now if you don't mind). She called out to him from the other side of the road. She seemed genuinely pleased to see him too. He was tempted to go on over and talk to her, but he didn't in the end, he just walked on by. Better not start all of that up again, eh? A lucky escape really when you think of it.

*Yes It's All Only Make Believe.*

# 4 | Billy Roche in Conversation with Conor McPherson (excerpts)

[This interview took place in 2001.]

**Conor McPherson**: I think that if there is a recurring theme in your work, it is this idea of being lost. Have mercy on such as we, it is kind of looking for some kind of help or looking for some kind of comfort. It seems to be a very universal theme and I think it is probably what people relate to in your work. I think that people take your plays quite personally and remember them.

**Billy Roche**: I think redemption, forgiveness and understanding are prominent. I do get surprised at how judgmental people can be about little things, about other people's misdemeanors and sexual adventures, and they take it all so personally, 'but what has it got to do with you?' People live their own lives, and the person that doesn't go astray is a person that I don't particularly want to meet. When I wrote *Tumbling Down* I wouldn't have had any notion of metaphors or allegories or themes, I was just literally writing a novel. As I went to do this one-man-show, everything pointed back to that novel. Actually I was on stage when I realized it.

**CMcP**: I think that, when you look at a writer, there does tend to be the same refrain going through the work; if you are inspired to write, it is probably going to be the powerful thing that is going to drive you.

**BR**: That's interesting because I have been reading John Banville a lot, an amazing writer, and if you trace back through his books, you find a linking story that he always knew right from the word go. At a reading recently in Enniscorthy, somebody said to him 'why do you keep writing the same book all of the time?' And it is beautiful that the story is one he just keeps telling all the time, just from a different perspective. And always at the heart of it there is always an extremely articulate lost soul, who is desperately trying to be stoic against the world. I have to say that I admire him and envy the fact that he has discovered this personal myth. I know that Ted Hughes reckoned that Shakespeare also had an equation that he was trying to work out and that it ran through all of his plays, even the comedies, with the male trying to come to terms with the feminine aspect of life. He wouldn't have written so many plays had he not got some kind of – formula is the wrong word – equation into the work.

**CMcP**: It's a kind of an engine, that's always kind of motoring away. You're never quite right, so you try again and again. So how do you think that such a theme manifests itself in *On Such As We*? What's the story?

**BR**: Well, it's set in a Wexford barber shop and Oweney, who at forty is separated from his wife and family, has been around the block a few times and as one character says 'Why did you leave your wife?' and he says 'Well I didn't leave her, she put me out', and he asks 'Well what did you do?' He replies 'Well rambling and gambling and staying out late at night.' Living above the shop is a young artist and there is a hotel porter that comes straight from the orphanage into the hotel and the hotel has closed down, he now goes out into the world and he is alone. So really the shop is buzzing with orphans of every description, not necessarily literally, but they are all lost and alone and Oweney is kind of a lonely angel who guides them all into a safe harbour. That is the theme really of the piece.

**CMcP**: I relate very much to your work and I think that it is what my plays are about as well, it's about that search for comfort, and I wonder if it is because you feel out of step with everything? Have you always felt that you need to somehow explore your place in the world?

**BR**: Well absolutely, I was reared in a small town. Lucky enough, it was a town that looked out rather than in, we were not a céilí town, we looked out to pop music and Hollywood and everyone went to the cinema and everyone listened to pop music as opposed to listening to Radio Eireann. I always said that the quintessential Wexford man has no idea that he belongs to a small town. He thinks that he comes from a big cosmopolitan place with the Opera Festival and things like that. We were born into this world daring to dream. Nevertheless it was a rather small town and you can imagine having these dreams in your head. Very often small-town people think that having gone into theatre you might have joined an amateur dramatic group. But that was never for me because I was thinking more of Broadway and the West-End. When I first began writing my first play, *A Handful of Stars*, it had loads of locations in it: it was the snooker hall, the factory and the street. I remember Patrick Mason desperately trying to guide me into the one spot and at the time I was thinking, no the set is going to be coming down out of the ceiling and up out of the ground. And I knew nothing about the mechanics of theatre. I learned that lesson, as it was, it wasn't going to be feasible to put this play on, so I re-worked it. But I think that that's right for a new writer to dream like that.

**CMcP**: This theme that you come back to of someone staring at a handful of stars and people who are out of step, the dynamic that really seems to drive your work is the difference of those who know it and those who don't, essentially. Everybody seems to be out of step but there are then ones who are sort of cowboys who cover that insecurity with a lot of talk and a lot of boasting and putting people down and setting themselves up as some sort of judge and jury and then there are the characters who are watching really from the sidelines. And it is those kinds of characters who always emerge quietly as the heroes of your plays. I am just wondering personally what your own sense of morality would be? There seems to be a lot of sympathy for characters who are dysfunctional or unhappy in your work. In *A Handful of Stars*, the character Jimmy is a lawbreaker, but the play does essentially seem to be on his side in the sense that we hear his story and in the sense that somebody has to fulfill that role in the community. Do you have that sort of ambiguous sense that you wouldn't judge somebody?

**BR**: Certainly for Jimmy Brady his destiny lies in what happened. That is his destiny. His destiny is also to give other people wings in some way. Without somebody like that, nothing would have happened. We would be stuck in a doldrum. Really you shouldn't like him; the audience shouldn't have sympathy for Jimmy Brady because he is a pain in the neck. So I do like to challenge the actor and myself as a writer. For instance I am writing a screenplay at the moment about a hurling hero – an Irish version of *This Sporting Life* or a *Raging Bull*, if you like. This guy is just impossible, but somehow as a writer I have to learn to love him and I have to hope that you love him too, in spite of all of the things that he does.

**CMcP**: Do you think that a production which works on that level and has managed to bring those seemingly conflicting things together, do you think that it serves a kind of function in the community?

**BR**: Yes I do. I don't write it from a social point of view. But it was interesting at *A Handful of Stars*, so many older women would come and say 'that poor chap' and in real life I am sure they'd say 'it serves him right.' Stephen in *Poor Beast in the Rain* is a very morose and sad creature. People say it is because his wife left him. No, I say, Stephen is like that anyway. If she had stayed, he probably would have been like that anyway. He'd probably feel more control but that is the way he always was. That's why he lost her.

**CMcP**: The response to your plays is always very warm: it is very emotional, human. I would say a very open and lovely response to your work which is heartfelt and I think it is because people identify with the fundamentals because I think that you are writing about very primal instincts that people have, which probably aren't even very articulatable – for instance, love in *Poor Beast in the Rain*. Georgie is completely besotted with Eileen and you know just the way the play is structured that it is never to be. He really drinks her in every time that he looks at her. I think that because you are unashamed to write about that stuff in a very direct and honest way it allows people to identify and I think probably take away something from your plays which you really are not even aware of.

**BR**: On the good days at the office you do see it, that thing, and then it disappears and you just get on with making the work and it is always a lovely surprise when you can feel that certain something in the audience and you know you have everyone connected. Because it is a risky thing that we do. Nothing might happen, if an audience is not tuned in. I have been very lucky with actors. The acting has to be impeccable. There is just no way that you can fake this stuff at all. So if you get all of the elements right and everybody is tuned in, then it can be a beautiful feeling. Plays have to work on the off-nights too and maybe they don't work so well if everybody is not tuned in or if you happen to have a cynical audience for example.

**CMcP**: I think that your plays are different from what might be deemed fashionable work, which comes with some stamp of academic approval. In Ireland, the plays that are regarded as very good plays always seem to be intellectually challenging in the sense that I think that people like Frank McGuinness, who is an academic, writes about major themes, historical themes. Tom Murphy, for example, with his best play, *The Gigli Concert*, is really exploring a whole notion, but on a very rational level. I think that your work is really much more than that. If you have got a big play, which is a play of ideas, the actors on an off-night still convey that, whereas I think that your plays always need a 110% commitment from the actors because it is about much more than what you can talk about.

**BR**: One of my favourite books is *The White Goddess*. One little secret in there is that you hide in the long grass. It is difficult to do. As a writer I usually sit down to write a scene and decide what I have to say in that scene and then I have to proceed not to say it. How does an audience figure out what it is, without me saying it? The first draft is always quite vulgar, if you can be brave enough to take it out, you are playing to the best minds, you imagine a very imaginative audience.

**CMcP**: The thing about your work as well is that it needs that essential credibility, it needs that someone isn't suddenly saying 'listen to me.' Your plays tend to have a strong realistic basis. I know that you never would do something that was banal and just capturing life, for capturing something very accurately could be very boring. You have a great craft in that you make it seem as though these people are saying these things for the first time because they are inarticulate: and that is the trick. Most people, if they have a problem, don't really express it and it is how you convey that ...

**BR**: They say everything except that. I just want to say something about the things I learned growing up in my father's waterfront bar in Wexford. People say to me you must have listened to a lot of talk. Yeah I did. But nobody ever said anything. No man ever divulged a single secret out loud. They never spoke about sex, never spoke about marriage, about love. So I wonder what really happened in the five or six years that I was behind the counter. I think I learned what we don't say to one another basically, what's lying in the middle of it all really. But it is a theatrical trick really isn't it? If you look back through many plays you will find an exceptionally articulate character who is, by accident, able to use every word in the English dictionary if he has to. He is a professor or something. Therefore the world is your oyster. It is a beautiful theatrical trick that you could use if you wanted to.

*

**CMcP**: Robin Lefevre has been a longtime collaborator and now it seems that you have a relationship with Wilson Milam. What do you look for in a director of your work?

**BR**: Music.

**CMcP**: Music?

**BR**: Because if he picks the wrong track he's gone.

**CMcP**: That's it?

**BR**: Yeah, absolutely. If I have a drink with someone and I can see that they are musical, and on the right wave-length. When we did *A Handful of Stars*, my first play, I was unaware of Robin's previous work. And during rehearsals, when we came to the end of the play I suggested Johnny Rotten from the band Pill, doing 'I should be right, I should be wrong.' So I gave him the tape and asked him to have a listen overnight to it. Next morning he came in and said, 'yeah, you are right about that.' So he heard it, knew it. On one of the nights during the previews I was sitting beside this young couple, and when that song came on at the end, the guy lit up. It was one of those things you never forget that you see in small theatres, when they don't know who you are. A less musical director would not have seen that effect.

**CMcP**: Robin makes decisions very quickly and he sticks to them.

**BR**: Absolutely.

**CMcP**: Once they are made, I think that he is someone who would suit your work very well because he trusts his instinct implicitly and I have worked with directors who talk around an issue for a very long time, until reaching some sort of agreement with the actor which may last and may not last. Robin is always very strong ...

**BR**: Very strong, he has a brilliant directorial mind. He makes that decision and lives with it. When we did *Belfry* for the first time, there was one line that neither of us was sure about. Artie, at the end of the play, says that he has been seeing another woman, a young widow called Rita. He claims that he met her at the bacon factory re-union. Robin was unsure and he kept pushing me. 'Maybe it is vulgar.' The fact is that Artie found love in the strangest of places. It was decided just to leave it in for a preview and see what happens. On the line, that first night, there was a great response from the audience. He was sitting behind me and just tapped me on the shoulder. We never spoke about it ever again. That line is there for life now and I would have taken it out had he pushed me, as I was unsure too. The audience got the exact message that someone could find love at a bacon factory reunion. Unbelievable really, even to go to a bacon factory reunion. Robin has those wonderful decisive powers really.

**CMcP**: There are always those small things in your plays, like where you say 'the bacon factory' and suddenly the whole thing resonates, because everybody has this idea of a place, and it probably slightly jars and you have to start thinking about it for a second and that makes it all the more real. There is the priest in *Belfry*, who is terribly lonely and there is a whole play in him and at the beginning of Act Two, we get his story and it is really left as a whole sort of open book to be explored and it is very sad really. Robin is a good collaborator in a sense that he will allow it to breathe and just to leave it, where another director would probably try to drive you to resolve it.

**BR**: And do a little more. When I started to write Father Pat in *Belfry*, I was as riddled with prejudice as any young man would be in this country. He was going to be a typical priest and he just refused to be. I learned so much from that. I know a young man who had become a priest and had left the priesthood. After he saw that play many times, he went back in again and I am not saying because of the play. He was going through a really hard time. He must have thought that you can be a priest and be human at the same time.

**CMcP**: The play helped him to crystallize what he was thinking about.

**BR**: I hope so. It is a very hard life.

**CMcP**: Father Pat, he is a young man and it is a dying breed. You don't get the young bucks going into the priesthood. So he really is a very isolated character.

**BR**: He clearly believes. For Father Pat, the Mass is not just symbolism. God is coming down onto that altar. It is an amazing mystery, when you take it apart. I was in New York for St Patrick's Day and we went into Mass, and to hear a priest with a New York accent celebrate 'the mystery of the mass.' It put a whole new spin on it. The mystery of the Mass, I had forgotten about those words. Taking it from that ritualistic, almost pagan origin, it is almost incredible.

**CMcP**: Particularly when Father Pat describes himself seeing a woman on the other side of the road with a small family, the details of when he was studying in Rome and his description of the swish of the girl's skirt that he befriended. It is in those tiny details that the devastating recognition comes to your work. I think that you have almost a painter's eye for what will register with people. Do you think that you have a good visual sense?

**BR**: Always for me it starts with the visual. It will never be a kitchen sink. I think that there is an aesthetic that we owe to our audience that when they come in and the lights go out, it is a painting in itself. The new play at the Abbey has a painter who lives upstairs, every scene is one of his paintings. The director has that clear vision of a visual aesthetic. That is essential.

**CMcP**: In a way it stems from the fact that all of your life you have worked as a showman in one way and you know how important it is not to let your audience down.

**BR**: Absolutely. My job as a singer – and I couldn't do it now, you lose the power – I played all over Ireland and I played in some of the roughest bars. My job as a front man of that band was to make them look at me. And they did. They might not necessarily like me, but they were going to look at me.

**CMcP**: And your job was to make them forget about everything else.

**BR**: There for an hour and a half, whatever it takes. There was quite a theatrical quality to The Roach Band. There was a kind of a Chaplinesque quality to the character I played. I would put that suit on me and forget that two hours previously I had just come out of a factory somewhere.

**CMcP**: Where do you think that confidence came from with you? Is it a feeling or restlessness that you want to shake things up a bit or do you think that it is more an ego thing?

**BR**: Ego certainly drives you out there. But I always was attracted to performance. I think in a strange way that the character I played in the band is not unlike many of the characters in the plays: Oweney, in my new play, and Artie and Joe from *Poor Beast in the Rain*. Everyman. There was a hidden depth to Artie that he didn't know about. In fact *Belfry* was supposed to be about the barber. I set out to write this play, I didn't know what this story was going to be, maybe they met every Thursday in the barber shop and played poker. Men that came over were going to tell me about Oweney.

There was a women involved who ran a boutique across the street, she was going to be the beautiful aspect to the play. The first one I elected to talk was a lonely mammy's boy, middle-aged sacristan. When he started to talk he said, 'I know what they think of me, I know what they say about me behind me back. "There he goes, Artie O'Leary."' And this was complete news to me. I went with *Belfry* and saw where it took me.

\*

**CMcP**: I remember reading in Nick Hern's book catalogue that you had a forthcoming play to be published called *Haberdashery* but it never seemed to appear anywhere?

**BR**: No. I have been struggling with it for a long time. People have been showing interest in the play, maybe it is slightly flawed or something. I turned it into a short story, which I do on stage now and that lasts about twenty minutes. I condensed all of it down. I am really in love with the story and I am delighted to have found it. I don't know if the play will ever see the light of day. I don't know if it should actually. My mother was dying, and I began working on this short story *Haberdashery*. It was like all hell was breaking loose around me, and I was obsessed with this short story. It was like as if the gods were giving me something to take my mind off it. So I created it and tried it out on stage a few times actually. I was toying with the idea of going on the road and doing an evening's performance, a kind of modern ... *seanachaí* is the wrong word. I don't want it to be a theatrical piece. I don't want it to be a reading, because I do actually perform them. I don't need it to be regarded as a play. I have been trying to write this series of short stories, or tales might be a better word, that are centred around this place called Rainwater Pond. All of them have this mystical place at the centre.

\*

**CMcP**: What would your relationship be with the theatre administrations in this country, in terms of the people who have the power to produce your play or not?

**BR**: I think it is pretty good. I deliberately stay out of the centre of things. I am glad to be living where I live. I don't attend many opening nights. I like to slip in and see a play in my own time, later on, when the fuss has died down. I am not on committees and I don't join boards. Maybe people like us should? Maybe it is a cop-out. I am just not interested in politics of any description. I'd like to go a gentle Sam Shepard route, just plough my own furrow. It will happen. If it doesn't happen, as it didn't with *Amphibians*, I will get up and make it happen.

* A longer version of this interview appeared in *Theatre Talk: Voices of Irish Theatre Practitioners*, ed. Lilian Chambers, Ger FitzGibbon and Eamonn Jordan (Dublin: Carysfort Press, 2001): 409-423.

# 5 | Billy Roche*

Dominic Dromgoole

One early January night, 1993, I stood alone in a thin scutty Wexford street, a terrace of grey stone houses. A low hanging mist had settled over the town, a fog so thick it seemed there was no one else in the world. The entrance to the opera house, disguised behind modest front doors, was in front of me. Our production of *The Wexford Trilogy* by Billy Roche was coming to play in the author's hometown. All was quiet, but nervous with anticipation.

I had hung around in the dressing rooms, until my uselessness had started to irritate even me. Someone politely recommended that I go outside and watch the people arriving. Better that than nothing, I thought, so I stepped out and waited.

At about twenty to eight, a few desultory figures started to solidify out of the mist. A family here, a gang of kids there, a group of friends there, just a few at a time. The noise started to grow, and with it an excitement. The occasional brightening shadows turned into thick clusters of bodies. Then as curtain up approached, it became a solid wall. A wall of people marching with joy to the theatre. They filled the street. A couple of thousand had turned up, eight hundred to see the show and the other thousand-odd to savour it. The chat was high, the heads were up, the glint was in the eyes. They were excited and they were proud. My eyes were wet with tears. Wexford had come out to claim its own.

Almost six years earlier, in 1987, I sat in a toilet in the *Daily Telegraph* tower on the Isle of Dogs, frantically reading a script. I was very angry with it. It was good. If you're reading scripts in a hurry, you want them to be bad, so you can dismiss them. If they're good you have to be careful. This was very good. I was trying to combine a temporary job at the *Telegraph* with my script-reading duties for the Bush. That's why I was hiding in the toilet. The quality of the script, *The Boker Poker Club* (later entitled *A Handful of Stars*), meant that I had to spend a couple of hours closeted away.

I duly handed the script in to the then Bush management with a recommendation that they should produce it. They duly did. Two years later they produced Billy's second play, *Poor Beast in the Rain*. Two years later, by which time I had become artistic director of the Bush, we produced his third, *Belfry*. A year later we reprised all three as *The Wexford Trilogy*, performed them in repertoire at the Bush, took them to Wexford for one performance each, played them for a couple of months in Dublin, and then had all three televised by the BBC. Wherever it went it triumphed.

That is the bare bones of a much more colourful and interesting story, which would include, if anyone wanted to tell it, tales of some great parties, of some great fights and some enormous goodwill. The plays were peerlessly directed by Robin Lefevre. He assembled one of the three great post-war acting companies to perform them. The Billy Roche company was in the same rare class as Joan Littlewood's company at Stratford East and Bill Bryden's at the National. And each play was designed to perfection by Andrew Wood, who died shortly after the last, happy and proud in the knowledge that he had been involved with such high work.

As Jimmy Ellis, a highly respected Belfast actor, said to the company after the last performance at the Bush: 'There. You've done them. Now you can watch everybody else fuck them up.'

The plays afforded me probably my best two nights in the theatre – the first and second press nights of *Belfry*. The rarest pleasure that theatre can offer is when it provokes an action of the soul. Awareness is heightened, each individual and the group together feel their hearts and spirits growing. A bliss that is stretched to an airy thinness over despair spreads throughout the room. All that is played before the united congregation seems to live on the paper-thin, feather-light line between life and death. Each moment is beautiful because it is alive, each moment is beautiful because it must die and give way to another.

In a Shakespeare play, at a good production, on a good night, if you're lucky, you'll get about five minutes of this. At a Chekov, if it's motoring, you might get about three. To enjoy just thirty seconds of it on a night out makes any ticket worthy of its price. On those two nights of *Belfry*, like rolling thunder, that feeling just went on and on. The audience sat stock still, their mouths open, their hearts squeezed up into their throats, praying that it would not stop. They could not credit that it could be so precise and so strong, so light and so deep, so trivial and so profound.

This is all a tremendous amount of wind around the plays themselves. All the wind serves as an excuse for me to say I do not really know why they are as great as they are. Small-town Chekhovian drama is one way of looking at it, but does no justice to its huge effect. *A Handful of Stars* follows the rage and explosions of a young rebel as the society around him tries to destroy his originality. A perfect concise parable of how greyness loathes colour, and how good is turned to bad by fear of its own simplicity. *Poor Beast in the Rain* is the perfect well-made play. Set in a betting shop on the weekend of the All Ireland Hurling Finals, it chronicles the return of a mythic outsider and how he disturbs some delicate equilibriums. *Belfry* is a time play dancing backwards and forwards around some incidents backstage in a church – an affair, a drink problem, a death. It is the most meditative and the most deceptive.

These plays defy analysis or description. They celebrate the mystery of life, as completely as they celebrate life. This has meant trouble for Billy with certain theatre managements and critics, who like to proscribe and categorize their work. If they can't find a box, they don't know how to cope with something.

It is enough to say that their creator Billy Roche is a man touched with genius, and that the plays are the best.

* This essay originally appeared in Dominic Dromgoole's book *The Full Room* (London: Methuen, 2002), and is reprinted here with the kind permission of Methuen Publishing Limited.

**Figure 1:** Poster for the 'Billy Roche Weekend' (1993). In the bottom photograph, behind Billy Roche, Gary Lydon performs as Jimmy Brady in the Bush Theatre revival of *A Handful of Stars* (1993). (Photographs by Mark Douet)

# 6 | A Weekend in Wexford

Benedict Nightingale

It's not so surprising, since I regard Billy Roche as maybe the finest talent to emerge on either side of the Irish Sea during my 21-year stint as *Times* theatre critic. It's probably even less surprising, since I've even been heard to claim, quite untruthfully, that I discovered a dramatist who had actually won several awards by the time I encountered his work in London's Bush Theatre. But I don't think I've enjoyed any theatrical celebration more than the one that took me and my wife to his native Wexford back in 1993.

It was the Billy Roche Weekend, and came complete with a Roche symposium, featuring such notables as Fintan O'Toole and Colm Tóibín, a walk around Roche landmarks conducted by Roche himself, and, of course, a performance of Roche's *Wexford Trilogy* in the town's magnificent Theatre Royal. The actors who were reprising their original roles were nervous, as indeed was Billy himself. The photos of him plastered around town, his face sunk into a hand, were meant to make him look seriously creative but actually suggested he was biting his fingernails. How would a trilogy successfully performed in a small fringe theatre fare when it was transported to the gorgeous green acres of the home of the Wexford Opera Festival? Even more to the point, how would the Wexford citizenry react to portraits of themselves and their town which, though always caring and often affectionate, were very far from glamorizing either?

Well, we needn't have worried. Halfway through *A Handful of Stars*, which is the *Trilogy*'s opener and seems at least as sympathetic to the tearaway at its centre as to the repressed chum who craves acceptance by the men of the town, you could sense Wexford making its decision. It found the play funny and moving, as it did *Poor Beast in the Rain* and, especially, *Belfry*. At the end of a long day the house stood, cheered and, hearing that the dramatist was to turn 44 the very next morning, chorused 'Happy Birthday to You.' Roche might have had some sharp things to say about his home town, but, unlike Synge and O'Casey in riot-torn Dublin, he was clearly a prophet with honour on his own patch.

My memory of what followed is, well, patchy in another sense. I seem to recall a municipal reception evolving into a long drinking and singing session in a local hotel. The mayor, the wonderfully named Padge Reck, delivered a fine solo, a balladeer paid musical homage to a local hurling champion, everyone joined in 'Molly Malone', 'Ole Man River' and other numbers, and my wife and I chirruped out something, I quite forget what. The beer, you see, kept on coming, and coming in a way hard to imagine in rule-bound Britain. At about 11.00 pm a forbidding-looking wire mesh came nine-tenths of the way down towards the bar counter, allowing drinks to be slyly slipped beneath it, and at about midnight it came down all the way, meaning that drinks were slipped round it. My wife and I went to bed at about 3.00 am, as did others, dismaying the then drama critic of the *The Irish Times*, David Nowlan. When he was young, he said, people would still be singing at 6.00 am and drinking at 9.00. Had Ireland and its livers gone soft?

Well, Billy certainly hadn't gone soft. That was clear from his characteristically wry, humorous remarks at the symposium. He recalled his time as a potboy in the Roche family pub, the Shamrock, a famously lively and sometimes turbulent waterfront bar that, as he had told me in an interview some months before, 'brought me to manhood with sailors, dockers, lorry-drivers, a fantastic crowd that had seen the world and had stories to tell.' Sadly, it burned down when he was just 20 and was replaced with an anonymous lounge, itself an illustration of the disappearance of an old Wexford he was to chronicle in *Amphibians*, *The Cavalcaders* and other plays. And the reaction of a customer to the Roche family's disaster? As Billy told the symposium, it was 'Sure, I wouldn't mind but I'd left a bit of rope in there.' That's a line that could come from a play by the dramatist's London-based compatriot, Martin McDonagh, and a pre-echo of the unthinking callousness sometimes to be found in Roche's own characters. He's not, repeat not, a sentimental writer.

Nor was he the least sentimental about Wexford itself, telling the symposium that he loved and hated it and had written in spite and not because of its encouragement. And then came his entertainingly anecdotal tour of the town. We took a peek at the tiny terraced house where the Roche children had slept more than one to a bed and walked past the snooker hall he'd frequented, the dance hall into which he'd slipped via a back window, the plaque honouring the famous boxer who was also Billy's grandfather, and the 'hole in the wall', a slit in an old building through which drink could be bought after closing time. And the tour ended on the quay, beside the statue of a famous citizen staring out to sea – 'his arse turned towards Wexford', said Roche in his dry way.

Not that his ambivalence about his home town prevented some trying to exploit the Billy Roche Weekend. One of its unintentionally comic moments came, not from that genial mayor, who cheerfully remembered spending happy hours in the Shamrock, but from the County Manager, who appalled the visiting Dublin intellectuals by quoting a line from *Poor Beast in the Rain*: 'a man without a home town is nothing.' In its context this is highly ironic, a nerdish boast from one of Roche's narrow-minded losers, but not to this particular gentleman. *The Wexford Trilogy*, he claimed, was about the need for everyone to gather 'under the banner of local patriotism.' The plays were about flying the flag, creating jobs and 'participation, involvement and cooperation.' Their message was to 'buy Irish and buy it in Wexford.' To see *Belfry*, it seemed, would leave you disinclined to shop for imports from Taiwan.

Ah well. Fair enough. One of Roche's prime qualities is that he allows people to come to their own conclusions about his plays' significance. He doesn't force his opinions on his audiences. He doesn't moralize, still less sermonize, still less hector, as many English dramatists did in the later 20th century. And you always feel he is giving his characters the freedom to decide what to do and, indeed, what to be. Which is one reason why, from *A Handful of Stars* in 1988 to *On Such As We* in 2001, I've found myself comparing him to some of the great dramatists of the past, starting with Chekhov.

Billy Roche has Chekhov's ability to feel people sympathetically from inside while observing them coolly from outside. As with Chekhov, his plays unforcedly combine humour and pain as he chronicles the confused ebb and flow of everyday existence in ways that are funny, sad, and sometimes both at once. As he said to me in an interview we had in 1991, 'when I think about life I feel sad, but I'm not a sad person. I want to laugh, I want to cry, I want to do both together. In my plays laughter and tears are brother and sister.' And like Chekhov, he has a generosity of spirit that he extends to his more unlovely characters, even finding something to say for Eddie in *On Such As We*, the coarse, selfish goon who does the dirty work for the tycoon destroying Wexford's traditions.

Again, Roche has Chekhov's instinct for subtext, as you see when (for instance) you encounter the initially unexplained bitterness and rage of Molly in *Poor Beast in the Rain* and come to understand that its cause is the ruin of love. Indeed, you can hear the Russian master's voice in an interesting remark he made in an interview with Kevin Kerrane: 'I would always begin a scene where I ask "what do I want to say?" and then proceed not to say it.' And given Roche's verbal energy, his unaffected ability to make a kind of poetry out of street talk, it's almost as if O'Casey has been exhumed to dramatize Chekhov's short stories in a Wexford dialect. He's been accused of plotlessness and shapelessness, as Chekhov was, and, like Chekhov, Roche can answer that he's recording life as he sees and feels it.

Anyway, that's what I found myself feeling and writing after seeing the *Trilogy* and the later Wexford plays. 'Small enough funeral', remarks a mourner after the burial of a mean-minded local tailor in *Belfry*. 'Small enough life' comes the reply. And you could, I suppose, say that Roche is a miniaturist or theatrical microbiologist studying the urban counterpart of a drop of water and finding that it teems with life worth his and our attention. For him, small is often beautiful, always fascinating – and has a significance way beyond its apparent size.

You couldn't have more circumscribed settings than those of the trilogy, *The Cavalcaders* and, later, *On Such As We*: a tacky pool hall, a run-down betting shop, the belfry above the 'queer old whispering world' of a church, a cobblers, a barbers. You couldn't have a more ordinary, more obscure and, it first seems, duller protagonist than Artie, the sacristan in *Belfry* whose twin horizons are the local church and his home, where he looks after his ailing, possessive mother. It's a small life that seems aimed only at the small funeral that will one day be his own. Yet he launches into a love affair with the married woman who tidies the altar and, though their fling ends and she takes up with another man, this parish-pump Lazarus doesn't simply clamber back into his ontological grave. He emotionally grows, rediscovering the father his mother rejected as a 'wild boyo' and in all sorts of ways becoming a bit less unlike him.

So Artie's story illustrates themes that are both larger and of great interest to Billy Roche: loneliness, disappointment, people's often gallant struggles to cope with both of them, and the discovery of manhood in a world that's inclined to mistrust and repress it, no longer allowing men to be men or, indeed, people to become the whole, self-sufficient men and women they were meant to be. But then there's often mountainous meaning in the molehills that Roche so deftly creates. And, of course, much of this emerges from his observation of Wexford itself, aided by his ambivalent feelings about the town that, having felt a fish out of water as an acting student in Dublin and a jobbing worker in Britain, he ruefully accepts as his and his family's once and future home.

It's something I found myself wondering again and again during the Billy Roche Weekend. How many other contemporary dramatists can lay claim to a location that's both authentic and rich enough to keep feeding their work? Well, Brian Friel has Ballybeg in the north of Ireland, but, fruitful though it is, it's an imaginary location that combines aspects of many real ones and, in any case, is more often than not observed at different and even distant times in its history. Roche's Wexford exists here and now, or in the immediate past, and is so well realized that, when you're in the town itself, you catch yourself wondering if the youth swaggering out of the pub isn't Jimmy Brady of *A Handful of Stars*, the would-be bank robber who will be all too recognizable under the stocking he's ineptly shoved over his face – or if that young shop-girl isn't Nuala of *The Cavalcaders*, on her way to an unhappy assignation with the master-cobbler, Terry.

Certainly, Wexford allows Roche to tackle one of the most important subjects of our era. The town gives his characters roots in an increasingly rootless world, but, as he sees and doubtless experiences them himself, roots bring both gain and loss. As is apparent from *Poor Beast in the Rain* in particular, they trap and limit the likes of the cuckolded husband Steven, whose only ambition is to 'slip through life unnoticed', yet their lack is clearly destroying the wife who ran away from Wexford to England and now precariously subsists on tranquillizers. Stay or go, there are pains and problems. Roots bring camaraderie and community and they bring stagnation and an erosive boredom. You sometimes get the feeling that Roche's characters can't live with or without

Wexford, making the town a microcosm for needs and frustrations that extend to Britain, America, almost everywhere in the West.

But the subject of roots is still more complex than this because Wexford is changing and, in Roche's view, not for the better. Community, camaraderie and much else of value is at serious risk. That's especially apparent in the plays that follow the trilogy. In *The Cavalcaders* a traditional cobblers is about to become another glossy high-street emporium, thanks to the new young owner whose mind is on the mouldering footwear cluttering the shelves, but inferentially also on the town and the townspeople, when he declares 'there's going to be no more of this hanging on to stuff for years on end.' In *Amphibians* the last fisherman in a town once reliant on its herring fleet is about to cage himself in the local canning factory, becoming an older version of the lost young men who lounge about its gates, wrangling, cracking sleazy jokes and potting the odd seagull with their catapults. And in *On Such As We* Roche pushes the subject further still, since the rich, go-getting P.J. plans to raze the slum house in which he doesn't want the world to know he was born, turn his own wife's shop into a fast-food joint, and transform as much of Wexford as he can into another neon-lit shopping mall.

I suppose Roche could be accused of a nostalgia for an irreclaimable past that, on occasions, he comes close to idealizing. I remember him telling me, and maybe later telling that weekend symposium, that he felt much of the fun, most of the eccentricity and many of the old 'characters' had left a Wexford modernizing itself according to that County Manager's prescriptions. Yet, as with Chekhov, there's nothing simplistic about his treatment of an issue that's clearly of great moment to him. He's lamenting but not wholly lamenting social change. Lopakhin rules. The cherry orchards are coming down. But there's also something absurd about the people who sentimentalize the old days. For Joe in *Poor Beast in the Rain*, his youthful exploits with the provocatively named Danger Doyle were wild, wicked, almost Homeric in their daring. Actually, they were either banal or untrue, and the Danger who absconded to England with Steven's wife is now a regretful, worried, mature and realistic man who doesn't want himself or his past to be mythologized.

The hold of the past over the present, the emotional power of parents and particularly fathers, the lure of fantasy, the stunting of dreams and thwarting of aspirations are, of course, themes Roche shares with other Irish dramatists, Synge to Friel. And there are others that are more peculiar to his plays, for instance the persistence of decency and resilience of altruism. As he has said, most unusually for a contemporary dramatist, 'people can be very good and kind if you give them half a chance.'

But let's not forget the wonderful concreteness of his plays, his love of the quirky, incongruous and (remembering the return to Wexford of a chastened Danger Doyle) the unexpected yet logical, and the care with which he observes all his characters, central or not so central. Think of Pat, the insecure young priest in *Belfry*, beset by feelings of inadequacy and, when his mischievous altar boy somehow gets the church bells to toll out 'I Can't Get No Satisfaction', terrified that he'll be in trouble with the bishop. Or of Conway in *A Handful of Stars*, whose half-hidden agenda is to ensure the next generation's lives will be as mediocre as his own. Or, of course, Terry in *The Cavalcaders,* who Roche himself has described as guilt-ridden and, though surrounded by love, incapable of embracing it.

If you think Roche is just a bit too warm and kindly a dramatist, consider Terry, perhaps the darkest character he's created, and, in particular the scene in which, after having sex with the much younger Nuala, he rejects her. She naively tries to penetrate his defences, artlessly fishing for the emotional revelations and love-talk that so bitter and aloof a man, walled off with his jealousy and regrets and self-pity, simply cannot offer. Instead, his post-coital tristesse escalates into resentment and rage. Brutal snubs and slurs of frightening cruelty – 'doodle shit, that's all you are to me' – suddenly cannon across the stage. The result is emotional devastation and, not long afterwards, a vulnerable girl's suicide.

Years after seeing the late, great Tony Doyle and the brilliant young Aisling O'Sullivan play that scene, first in Dublin's Peacock Theatre and then at London's Royal Court, I can still recall the horror of that encounter and Nuala's anguished cry as she makes a last, desperate attempt to rekindle the affair: 'It's a terrible lousy thing to do, yeh know Terry, to take someone's love and throw it back in their face like that.' Yet I recall other things too. I remember Marie Mullen, who played the one woman who seems to understand, tolerate and want to help the master-cobbler, coming out at one point with just two words: 'Jaysus, Terry.' I remember trying and failing to think of another contemporary dramatist who could leave me feeling that this simple phrase summed up a couple of seriously misspent lives, his and her own.

I remember Terry, perhaps thinking of the time he and a friend had sex with his uncle's wife and uneasily aware he's becoming a monster, admitting 'I've done some queer things in my time, I mean I've a lot to answer for.' And I remember the reply: 'Show me the man that hasn't.' Though *The Cavalcaders* was written after the trilogy, that's the writer we were celebrating back in Wexford 1993. Dominic Dromgoole, one-time artistic director of the Bush and the person with the real claim to have discovered and encouraged the dramatist, calls Roche's work 'so precise and so strong, so light and so deep, so trivial and so profound.' Also melancholy, ironic, poignant, elegiac, realistic, tough-minded – and forgiving.

# 7 | The Talk of the Town*

Colm Tóibín

While staying at Coole in the summer of 1901, W.B. Yeats had a dream which became the play *Cathleen ní Houlihan*. He dreamed a scene of domestic harmony being disrupted by a force that could not be resisted, that had the power of an Oracle, and could destroy. That force arrived in the shape of an old woman, who represented Ireland, and who would become young again once Ireland had asserted its right to freedom. She would draw the young man out of the house, away from domestic harmony towards some higher, more noble aim.

Yeats could not write ordinary dialogue. Language for him was full of symbolic resonance; he wanted his words to be charged and electric rather than domestic or realistic. Thus in the days that followed, Lady Gregory wrote his play for him. She created a peasant family in a state of material comfort, she allowed them to plan a wedding and worry about getting more land. She kept the play short and simple; the audience could reasonably have expected the drama to arise from a jilted lover or a secret that had not been told. She resisted Yeats' efforts to have some intimation of the final scene earlier in the play. At her insistence, the arrival of the old woman seemed to have nothing strange about it, and thus her transformation was all the more shocking and dramatic and highly charged.

The play was performed in Clarendon Street in Dublin in 1902. Maud Gonne played the title role and the audience was full of zealous and serious young men who had found a drama that matched their own solemnity, lofty principles and anti-materialism. Thus Yeats and Lady Gregory had created the problem which would emerge again and again over the next twenty-five years. Their own essential impulse as dramatists was heroic and idealistic just as their political impulse was anti-materialist. A part of them was to remain in tune with the nationalist movement and its leaders. But the other part of them recognized the genius in the anti-heroic dramas of Synge and O'Casey, and in the few years after the production of *Cathleen ní Houlihan*, they set about realigning their dramatic principles to include Synge. They were not, they insisted, a political theatre; their aim was to produce art, to enact on the stage the true and the beautiful.

Thus began the abiding tension in Irish drama in the twentieth century between a nation whose self-concept was idealistic and heroic and a set of dramatists who viewed this as a sour and elaborate joke, and who set about deflating it or creating an alternative world which had been written out of Ireland's heroic history. The dramatists were lucky: they had not only Pearse's rhetoric to work against, but they also had the entire body of Yeats' and Lady Gregory's dramatic writings, so concerned with myth and symbol and heroism.

The founders of the Abbey Theatre offered Irish dramatists, then, an example not to follow, a powerful influence to evade and avoid and mock and destroy. But stylistically Yeats and Lady Gregory also offered them a powerful example which was to maintain its spell for a hundred years. In the significant work produced in the Irish theatre in the last twenty years of the twentieth century, the writers have played with the sharply realistic and attempted to place around it a halo, or a shining from within, using a real voice but allowing a poetic force to build from within the voice. In these Irish plays there has been a sense of language as mysterious, a sense of speech moving into prayer, a sense of utterance having at its centre the rhythm and power of song. What Yeats and Lady Gregory attempted to do in *Cathleen ní Houlihan* – move the ordinary into the miraculous – comes up many times in the plays written in Ireland between 1980 and 2000, at its most heightened and intense in Brian Friel's *Faith Healer* and Tom Murphy's *The Gigli Concert*, but also in ways more hidden and mysterious, but just as powerfully, in the works of Frank McGuinness, Sebastian Barry, Dermot Bolger, Paul Mercier and Marina Carr. A speech in the work of these writers, or a snatch of dialogue, is produced to move the audience like a song, is poetic in the sense that it unsettles, it hits the nervous system, it works wonders.

In style and tone, then, there has been great continuity in the Irish theatre in the twentieth century. Also, the anti-heroic impulse, the insistence on working against the grain of the national narrative, has remained central. If the national narrative is the father, then each playwright from Synge onwards sought to kill the father. In *Riders to the Sea*, Synge refused to allow any consolation, except for the words themselves, against the harshness and brutality of western life in Ireland. In *The Playboy of the Western World*, Synge offered a version of Irish life at its most pagan and comic and anti-heroic. And once the struggle for Irish freedom became part of the heroic narrative, part of the terrible beauty, many young men from Sean O'Casey to Denis Johnston to Brendan Behan set about undermining the heroics, subverting the narrative. And once Irish freedom had been achieved, the playwrights established the terms of that freedom as tawdry and sad and restrictive and hopeless.

Between 1980 and 2000, a number of playwrights sought to bring the stage one step further by attempting to put a flag up over a narrative of their own, an aspect of the national narrative which had been pushed aside, or erased, or prevented from emerging. Thus the young volunteers in Frank McGuinness's *Observe the Sons of Ulster Marching Towards the Somme* came back into the Irish narrative from which southern Ireland had excluded them. Thus figures with Dublin accents, pushed towards violence and self-destruction, and lacking the music-hall humour of O'Casey and Behan's Dublin characters, appeared in the work of Paul Mercier and Dermot Bolger. And so too characters from the margins of history – religious sects, the old gentry, the soon-to-be-disbanded RIC – had a flag raised over them and they became central in the work of Sebastian Barry. And in the work of Marina Carr, there is an insistence on the old, dark, violent, atavistic forces – Cuchulain at home – just as the national narrative was moving towards a version of Ireland as bright and shiny.

Thus Irish dramatic writing at the end of the twentieth century set about destroying and subverting and replacing and indeed recreating national heroics and idealizations in *Cathleen ní Houlihan*, but also adapted the tension between current speech, poetic rhythms and the possibility of transformation from which the play derived its power. In this context, the five plays by Billy Roche – the *Wexford Trilogy* (1988, 1989, 1991), *Amphibians* (1992, revised 1998) and *Cavalcaders* (1993) – remain pivotal in the Irish theatre of the period and should be placed at the very centre of contemporary Irish theatre.

Billy Roche's Wexford begins as a real place. The speech in his plays begins as a living speech, whose tones and colours and cadences belong to the streets of Wexford alone. There is not a single line in his plays which could not be spoken by real people in a real place. His urge towards transcendence is more muted and modest than most of his contemporaries, but the urge is there nonetheless, hovering at the edge of almost everything said and done in his work.

His Wexford is fading and faded. The port has silted up and the fishing industry is a thing of memory. But the Wexford Billy Roche was brought up in had all the characteristics of a metropolis and some of its energy. A long narrow main street snakes its way from Redmond Square to the Faythe, running parallel to the quays. Most of the shops are small with large plate glass windows. Half the town manages to walk along the main street at some time of the day or other, and everyone in the shops keeps an eye out, recognizing the passersby. There is a great deal of mockery and warm, ebullient talk in Wexford; fellow citizens are sources of great amusement and interest, from their funny walks to certain other distinguishing characteristics. A great deal is known about everyone, from what you did last night to what your grandfather did forty years ago.

The town has a medieval shape and its cultural make-up is unusual in Ireland, being a mixture of Norman and Gaelic, with some English and Hugenot added. The two historical journals, for example, are not divided Catholic-Protestant, or new and old generations, but, in general, one of them has been run by people with Gaelic names and the other by people of Norman ancestry. (The Norman invasion, incidentally, happened in 1169.)

Competing with the quiet way in which these cultures merge and the quiet way the town watches itself is the heroic narrative of county Wexford, its glorious history. All over the county, there are monuments and plaques to the men of 1798; great ballads are dedicated to their memory. With Cromwell's attack on the town, the Rising of 1798 is Wexford's fundamental narrative, it puts everything else in the shade; what story can compete with it for grandeur and bravery and tragedy?

The flag which Billy Roche flies over the town, however, is also an act of rebellion. His flag insists that there is another story that must be told, a narrative which is not heroic, another reality which must be attended to. His flag comes in two colours, two tones. One half of his vision is political: the urge to represent the talk of the town, the disappointed lives, the sense of a haunting not by history, but by the doings of parents and by the parts of the self we seem powerless to control. But the other part of his vision, more than that of any of his contemporaries, is existential. He is prepared to dramatize his Wexford as a Trojan horse with no Troy in sight, no opening available. He is prepared to dramatize the business of existence as raw sadness, uneasy futility, masked by language and then, suddenly, unmasked and left bare by the same words.

He prefers public places. The plays are set in a snooker hall, a betting shop, a church, a factory and a shoe-maker's shop. Only in a few scenes in *Amphibians* does he allow part of a play to be enacted in the classic cauldron of the Irish theatre – the kitchen or living room of a family house. He is especially skilled at dramatizing that central moment in the public life of Wexford – the arrival of a talkative person into a shared space, full of opinions and gossip. Billy Roche's characters are defeated already, or will have their defeat re-enacted on the stage. No one will become a snooker champion or win money at the betting shop. The shoemaker's is about to be modernized, and the fishing has come to an end, and the old beliefs no longer hold. No one in Roche's work, with the exception of Jimmy in *A Handful of Stars*, has huge ambitions, large desires. The plays are set among an artisan class to working class who were born in the town and will stay in the town. No one wants to go to Philadelphia or sing like Gigli; perhaps more important, no one mentions Ireland. Ireland is not a place in Roche's work; there is no nation to fight against or adhere to. And this gives him a freedom to work with his characters, to allow, in spite of his own modesty, his Wexford to stand for the world. It gives his best work, such as his masterpiece *Poor Beast in the Rain*, a strange timelessness and beauty. His lack of a governing myth – Catholicism means nothing in his work – gives the plays a raw power except when he is finally forced to invent one in *Amphibians*. It is then one most understands what it must have taken to free his characters in the other plays, to allow their own trapped longings and bursts of hope and hopelessness to become solid and dramatic enough that no myths or governing structures were required.

All of the plays have characters who are full of talk, funny, accusing, boastful, mocking. Within this talk, there are, in all the plays, moments of pure sadness, or vicious savagery. A line, or a piece of dialogue, without any extra flourish, can stun the audience into silence. This is done with immense subtlety and skill. In *A Handful of Stars*, it comes in Paddy's speech about Jimmy's parents: 'No God I remember when the two of them were only courtin'. She was dyin' alive about that fella. I often saw them up in the Town Hall and they waltzing the legs off one another. They were grand dancers too. He used to be all done up like a dog's dinner I'm not coddin' yeh – great suits on him and all. And she'd be smilin' up into his face all the time. To look at her you'd swear she had just swallowed a handful of stars. Jaysus she was a lovely girl, so she was.'

Paddy normally talks in monosyllables, and Jimmy's father, the dancer, is now in a place for the homeless, having beaten his wife and made her miserable for many years. Paddy has also spoken of Stapler leaving his wife: 'God and Stapler was married to a grand girl.' All the images of happiness here are presented as small half-remembered events that now seem all the more miraculous because of the misery and the treachery that came after. All eight sentences of Paddy's speech have an innocent beauty about them, a sense of wonder. The first seven of them begin with an iambic beat, the last is more muted in its beat and can be spoken wistfully and sadly and because of what the audience knows, it has the possibility of making everyone in the audience hold their breath. But it is not underlined, or specially marked out. Another actor could choose one of the other sentences to do the same work and let the last sentence carry less emotion.

Steven's speech at the end of *Poor Beast in the Rain* has the same power as Paddy's speech. Steven, too, has been mostly silent in the play and his longest speech ends: 'Your Mammy was the very same. She was always wondering what was over the next hill. She was always wonderin' about somethin'. Jukebox fellas and carnival boxes seem to fascinate her. A fancy scarf blowin' in the wind, a tattoo, anythin' the least bit outlandish at all and she was off. I never knew whether I was comin' or goin' with her. I never knew what way I was fixed with her at all to tell you the truth.'

Although the last sentence is the plainest and the least obviously poetic, it is the most expressive. It hits us like a line in a song that seems to have no obvious power. It appears, however, to have a hidden nervous system of its own, all the stronger because you do not know where the emotion is coming from. Sometimes the same emotional weight is carried by a single line rather than a line within a speech. In *The Cavalcaders* Nuala says 'It's a terrible lousy thing to do, yeh know Terry – to take someone's love and throw it back in their face like that.' While the second part of the line could be from a pop song, the first part has a directness about it. There is a sense of real hurt in those first few words that manages to rescue the second part of the sentence from cliché. In *Belfry*, Pat has a line with a similar power: 'This is a queer lonely auld life Artie yeh know.' Or Isaac in *Amphibians* when he says 'What are youse wantin'?'

What Steven's speech and Nuala's line and Pat's line and Isaac's line have in common, and this is central to Roche's work, is they use an understated speech as if to suggest that they themselves are not worth grander phrases than 'I never knew what way I was fixed with her at all to tell you the truth' or 'It's a terrible lousy thing to do, yeh know Terry.' But because the focus of the play has been entirely on them, rather than Irish society or class conflict or a national narrative, there is no distance between them and us, their suffering carries enormous weight, much greater because their language isn't up to it; how they speak is ostensibly as beaten down as they are, and this tension between the poverty of the language and its beauty brings with it a terrible pathos and helplessless.

Paddy in *A Handful of Stars* and Molly in *Poor Beast in the Rain* operate as a sort of chorus, as a warning to the young about hope. They are mostly stoical, but when their stoicism breaks into a narrative of sadness and regret, it takes on a different sort of power. Everyone is these plays is locked into a cycle of moments of hope and possibility followed by years of dull regret and despair. Class conflict is not in these plays to be resolved or even dramatized, it is simply part of the prison in which people are locked. Badness and weakness in *A Handful of Stars* are passed on from father to son. Love is something that may have happened in the past, or be celebrated in the songs which pepper the plays, but here it is to be enacted as longing and rejection as Linda rejects Jimmy in *A Handful of Stars*, as Eileen rejects Georgie in *Poor Beast in the Rain*, as Terry rejects Nuala in *The Cavalcaders*, as Sonia rejects Zak in *Amphibians*. The men who are rejected are the ones with most spirit, most hope. It is that very hope and spirit which makes them oddly unreliable and untrustworthy.

In all of his plays, Billy Roche takes the idea of love one step further. He dramatizes adultery in his work as no other writer does. There is a long tradition of dealing with adultery on the stage. However, it is mostly comedy and it is often farce.

In Pinter's play *Betrayal,* it comes in its full glory as treachery; it is presented as part of the treacherous nature of the society itself, or indeed as part of the treacherous nature of the very words being used to tell the tale. In Billy Roche, adultery is not comedy and not metaphor and not part of a social malaise. It is another way of making his characters sad, or leaving them sad. In *A Handful of Stars,* Stapler's going off with the hairdresser is reduced to treachery by Paddy's line about Stapler's wife as 'a grand girl.' In *Poor Beast in the Rain,* both Steven and his wife have been destroyed by his wife's departure with Danger Doyle. In *Belfry* Donal discovers that his wife Angela has been having an affair with the sacristan: 'I mean to say a man works hard, dreams hard for his wife and family only to come home one day and discover that she's whorin' around with a gobshite like you. A feckin' little mammy's boy, be Jaysus, I wouldn't mind but I gave her everything she ever wanted.' In *The Cavalcaders,* Terry's wife who was 'a queer good lookin' woman', now, having run away with his friend, has found only misery: 'They say she lives like a nun now. I believe she rarely goes out any more.'

*The Cavalcaders* has all the elements of a farce; it is full of exits and entrances and sparkling dialogue and funny songs. As in a classic farce, it is hard to keep tabs on who has been sleeping with whom. Terry's wife has run away with Rogan, the best man at their wedding; Ted is having an affair with Rory's wife; and Terry and Josie have had it off with Terry's uncle's wife. This event is twice described by Josie in the play: 'she was sort of cryin' when I went in though, like, yeh know.' Nuala in the play commits suicide, driven to it by a number of savage scenes with Terry. Josie dies in hospital. Both come back from the dead in the play. And yet despite the abiding sense of loss in the play, by the end Terry has found Breda whose love he has been resisting throughout the play, Rory's wife is expecting a baby with Ted, Rory and his mother are looking after his daughter. There is almost a sense of harmony in Wexford, the completion of a comedy in coupling and symmetry.

This playing with genre, this refusing to write either comedy or tragedy, is as crucial in the work of Billy Roche as his refusal to deal with the national narrative. Every Irish playwright writing during the last two decades of the century except Roche has attempted to write a tragedy, a play in which a hero is caught between conflicting epochs of belief, in which the hero is doomed because of a fundamental change in the forces at work in the world. Some of the plays merely allow tragedy as a possibility; others pursue it for all it is worth. Roche's characters, on the other hand, accept their fate. Jimmy in *A Handful of Stars* will wait for the cops to arrest him. Steven in *Poor Beast in the Rain* does nothing to prevent his daughter leaving. Both Nuala and Josie in *The Cavalcaders* are only too ready to die. No one shakes their fist at God; no one tries to kill their father. Roche's characters accept what is coming: they have no illusions. They live in an age when tragedy is no longer possible, nor comedy either, when drama is merely an acting out of the sadness which small hope brings. Those locked in the Trojan horse are no longer haunted by the possibility that Troy is in sight. They have only themselves to blame and one another to console or amuse or betray. And there is only a limited time.

Ritual for Billy Roche is the same as romance. The rite of passage for Tony in *A Handful of Stars* to the inner sanctum, which is so delicately handled in the play, will become impossible, just as Isaac's rite of passage in *Amphibians* will be rendered meaningless. So too birthdays, weddings, New Year celebrations, hurling matches. All of these will end in misrule. Roche will allow his characters no consoling ceremonies.

His standing alone in Irish drama, refusing to dramatize the conflicts within identity and nation and history in Ireland, and his refusal to work within a genre, does not mean that Roche's plays are not fully alert to certain traditional themes and tropes. He may not have deliberately set out to make *Poor Beast in the Rain* a re-telling of the Electra story, but the connections are there for the audience to make. Eileen has watched her mother kill her father by running away with Danger Doyle. Danger Doyle is both Aegisthus, who has married Electra's mother, and Orestes, her brother who has returned after many years to help her seek vengeance. Eileen, like Electra, is alone with no husband and no children. In Sophocles' play Orestes leaves a sign on the grave of his father to suggest that he has returned, including a lock of his hair. In *Poor Beast in the Rain*, the locket which Eileen receives from her mother has been bought in Wexford, thus suggesting the presence of her mother or her mother's emissary in the town. And what the emissary wants her to do is not to seek revenge as in *Electra* and punish her mother for her crime. He wants her to do something more savage and more disturbing. He wants her to kill her father again, repeat her mother's action rather than seek revenge for it. This is the stark, dramatic choice she is offered. Danger Doyle wants her to come back with him to London and leave her father behind in Wexford as her mother once did. 'It broke my heart', Steven tells his daughter, 'when she ran off on me like that yeh know. It broke my bloody heart so it did.'

In an Afterword to the published version of the *Wexford Trilogy*, Billy Roche describes working on his second play called *Runaway* which eventually became *Poor Beast in the Rain*. It began as the story of Johnny Doran 'who refused to wrap himself up in the flag of his tribe' during the run-up to the All-Ireland Hurling Final. This is essentially what Billy Roche himself has done. His work is closer, in its integrity and its carefully nuanced study of hope and hopelessness, to the early stories in Joyce's *Dubliners* or to certain themes and tones in Tennessee Williams and Arthur Miller than to anything in contemporary Irish theatre. In refusing to deal with national myths and insisting on placing his characters in the time after tragedy, he has bravely followed his own route and created a body of work which has an extraordinary emotional power and intensity.

* This essay originally appeared in the anthology *Druids, Dudes and Beauty Queens*, edited by Dermot Bolger (Dublin: New Island, 2001).

# 8 | Reflections on the Muse

Conor McPherson

I first became aware of Billy Roche in the early nineties when he was interviewed on Ireland's iconic Late Late Show. He was blazing a trail in Britain at the Bush Theatre with his *Wexford Trilogy*. Not only had he bucked the odds by having three plays all running at once in London, but he suddenly concluded the interview by whipping out a guitar and singing a few songs, and I was thinking 'Who *is* this guy?'

I was about twenty and had just started writing plays, putting them on with my friends at UCD where I was a student. Seeing Billy getting his work done out there in the big bad world, having been refused the support of professional Irish theatres, was inspirational. Also impressive, when I finally got to see his plays for myself, was the deceptive modesty of the work. His characters seemed to wander on stage from Wexford's side streets with an insouciance that was beguiling. He wasn't writing about kings and queens, politics, history or Mother Ireland but the audience were ripped apart because, without realizing it, they'd invested so much emotion in what was unfolding. It was clear there was a mythical dramatic structure hidden deep beneath the small town bluster and I was immediately smitten.

Within a few years good fortune led my own path to the door of the Bush Theatre and I began presenting my work there, having also found it impossible to secure professional productions of my work in Ireland.

It was quickly apparent the high regard in which Roche was held at the Bush. On the landing, half way up the stairs to the tiny theatre, where it could not be missed, was a framed Laurence Olivier Award nomination for Outstanding Contribution to London Theatre in recognition of the *Wexford Trilogy*. Amongst the staff his plays were spoken of with fondness and awe.

We finally got to meet when I was making a feature film called *Saltwater* in Dublin. Our casting director suggested we offer a role to Billy. I was like, 'What? He acts as well?'

And indeed he did. Back in the late eighties he'd been forced to stand in for a few performances as Stapler in his own play, *A Handful of Stars,* in London and he'd intermittently continued acting both in his own work and the plays of others. And so we got to spend time together during *Saltwater's* production, talking about writing and the lonely world of trying to make dreams come alive in the theatre. And I consider myself fortunate because our conversations since then have given me insights not only into Billy's writing practice but the art of writing itself.

In a scene from his 1993 play *The Cavalcaders*, some amateur musicians are sucking their pencils, wondering what they might write a song about, when one of them springs up and proclaims in exasperation, 'Take a look out the window any day of the week and you'll find somethin' to write about. A whole universe of stuff out there and he's wonderin' what we're goin' to write about.' Talking with Billy I began to see that this is how he views his environment when he creates a play; he evokes a world. By 'world' I mean a place which has its own internal logic, where all hangs together cogently, even if that world is alien to us. This sense of completeness, of oneness, of rightness – even when what's happening is 'wrong' – is the bed of fertile drama, and creating it is not as easy as it may appear because its parameters are often beyond language. The theatre demands a world of feelings before even the simplest idea may be uttered. Billy insists however that this cannot happen unless the writer feels truly inspired at the moment of creation. This is perhaps the most salutary lesson any aspiring writer can take from a traveller who has been to the territory.

I got the opportunity to direct one of Billy's greatest plays, *Poor Beast in the Rain*, at Dublin's Gate Theatre in 2005. I found that no matter how many times I read the play it pulled me into its spell, challenged and intrigued me. I must have read it about sixty times in preparation, but once I got into the rehearsal room with the cast, it opened up again, further, deeper, almost taunting the actors. Frighteningly, the play could take as much as they had to give and then would demand more. For the actor who is prepared to go to a place so emotionally bare, unadorned and open as to almost just be themselves on stage, Billy's work is a dream to perform. For the actor who wants to rely on habits, tricks or let the audience do the work, his plays are a nightmare because there is nowhere to hide. You cannot fake the emotion in Billy's plays. Try this exchange between Georgie and Eileen in the amazing long night of the second act: Georgie, so lost and in love with Eileen, unleashes his feelings for her in a way that can only destroy their relationship. I always found it impossible to be unmoved at the sudden loss of their whole future as close friends if nothing else.

> **EILEEN.** .... Jaysus, and I thought I could depend on you.
> **GEORGIE.** Yeah well that was before I found out what you were made of wasn't it? That was before I found out that you were just like your Ma – a real skeet goin' round.
> **EILEEN.** What are you tryin' to do boy, scorch the ground from under us or somethin'?
> **GEORGIE.** You're the one who's done all the scorchin' Eileen, not me. For the past few days my heart's been down in my shoes or somewhere over you girl ... Yeh keep me hangin' on all the time Eileen so that I don't know whether I'm comin' or goin' with yeh. I mean I don't know what I'm supposed to do. What am I supposed to do?
> **EILEEN.** I'm sorry, Georgie. I didn't know yeh felt like that. It was never supposed to be like that between you and me.
> **GEORGIE.** Ah forget it. I don't think you'll be seein' a whole lot of me around here any more anyway. I wouldn't lower meself to tell yeh nothin' but the truth.

It seems so simple, yet because Billy has painted their relationship so stealthily all the way through the play – a charming mixture of youthful innocence and flirtation – to witness its certain death is just one of the play's devastating moments. And it's impossible to 'act' this stuff. You either get to that place – and the play can take you to that place every night – or you might as well forget it. This is because Billy, like one of his playwriting heroes, Tom Murphy, can only write from a place of reality. If he can't feel it, he won't write it. And this is where the muse comes into it.

Billy has a healthily old-fashioned, almost romantic view of writing. He truly believes that the muse comes to visit a writer and without it, try as you may, you are ploughing fallow ground. Yes, when one is re-writing a play, it's possible to spend days on end in the 'office' crafting and redrafting, but without that initial electric current which only the muse can provide, you will have nothing worth redrafting. This is the shocking truth that many people who try to write will discover. Self-consciousness will kill you stone dead. You have to write from a place where you are not even aware of yourself. You must see the world of the play in your mind and observe what is happening there rather than 'create' it. This is the trance-like domain of true inspiration, a realm into which only the muse may admit you.

I plugged into the electric current of Billy's muse and found I was powered enough for the five years it took us to adapt one of his short stories into a movie called *The Eclipse*. Although the struggle to get this film made was immense, I never got bored or gave up because every time I returned to the work I was invited into that world, to look around, to explore it, to live there even – because it actually *existed*.

This process began when Billy was writing his celebrated book of short stories, *Tales from Rainwater Pond*. I was lucky enough to see these stories as Billy completed them when he was looking for people to throw an objective eye across them. We decided that one of the stories, 'Table Manners', might make the basis for a screenplay and we began working on it. True to form, it took absolutely everything we had, and then some, but no matter how much we pulled and prodded and coerced the story, its heart never packed in because its mythical structure was so sound.

It's the story of a frustrated male writer who falls for a female poet who comes to visit Wexford for a literary festival. What he doesn't know is that she has only come at the behest of a successful novelist who is trying to reignite an affair they previously shared. This spine of the story never changed through twenty drafts of the screenplay and finally when I got to shoot the film, I remember looking down the lens of the camera and still truly believing I was looking into the world of the story.

From a fellow writer's point of view I think it's possible to view some of Billy's work in recent years as precisely a reflection on the relationship between the artist and the muse. However, as with the hidden soul in all of his work, this reflection is secreted so deep beneath the surface it might hardly register on first glance.

This concern is perhaps most evident in 'Table Manners', because for the first time Billy actually writes about writers and writing. There are ostensibly three writers at the centre of the story, but it is also possible to view them as three sides of the divided self of any writer.

First we have Michael Farr, a teacher, festival volunteer and amateur writer, who has never managed to fulfil his potential. He feels like a failure. This is the dogging ghost every writer lives with. You wake in the morning (or in the middle of the night) with a dream which you know will compel you to face the blank page until somehow you have managed to recreate a facsimile of its feeling. But this task is fraught with danger. You now have to face your shortcomings on a level so personal you start to believe you must have been mad or stupid to commence this venture.

Tom Murphy once said that writing teaches a person true humility because you are forced to consider your failings over and over until you get to the point of giving up. It is then – and only then – when you have surrendered and walked away, beaten, from your desk, that somehow the work opens up in your mind again, and you are lured back to face down your worst opponent, yourself. It's a fine line between humility and humiliation.

Michael Farr gave up twenty years ago, but the muse is calling him again and he is in turmoil over what this means for him. Kitty Shaw is the poet Michael has been assigned to drive around Wexford for the duration of the festival. She represents the hidden place in every artist that is unknowable even to artists themselves. She seems free and somehow in touch with something elemental, even childlike, yet she evinces a demonstrable darkness and Michael instinctively knows she may lead him to his doom. In that sense, she is the muse.

The third side of the writer is personified by Nicholas Holden. While he is nominally successful and his bestselling books clog up the stands at every airport he flies through, he suspects the price he has paid is that he cannot put any of his real feelings into his work. Like Michael, he longs for Kitty to release something inside him. For this is also the horror of the artist – their past successes will haunt them. While they seek to replicate the holy moment of creation, to repeat oneself in this pursuit is sad and undignified. And yet where does the writer turn when the muse has had what she wants of you?

Inevitably Michael and Nicholas end up on a collision course, and only a violent act by Michael can release him into a new understanding. In the conclusion of the story Billy Roche cannily delivers Michael not to a new world, but back into his old world with new eyes, suggesting artists cannot change the world. They can only change how we see it.

This triangular relationship between the divided self and the muse is also arguably the heartbeat at the centre of Roche's most recently performed play, *Lay Me Down Softly*. Theo Delaney is the ringmaster in a travelling boxing show where all-comers are invited to lay their money down and fight a few rounds with the resident has-beens who never were. The characters are thus caught in a meaningless spiral of inconsequential battles, roaming from town to town. 'I'm good and lost wherever I am', says one of them ruefully.

Theo Delaney is Roche's Prospero, actively conjuring the drama around him yet fearing the emotional storms of parenthood and relishing perpetual exile. The other side of his divided self is the old boxing coach, Peadar, who represents everything Theo isn't. Where Theo is impetuous, boastful and angry, Peadar is cautious, realistic and resigned. Theo may run the show but he cannot function without his old sidekick because Peadar is his conscience, always there to fill the gaps in his psyche. Both men are confronted with their past in the shape of Theo's abandoned daughter, Emer, who unexpectedly arrives looking for her father. And everything changes – because she is the muse, the agent of change or death.

In the sense that each person creates their reality, Theo and Peadar are both artists. Theo is the inveterate dreamer who desperately builds the illusion of control while luring victims into his web of pain. Peadar both sculpts, and keeps in check, the dreams of the boys who get in the boxing ring every night, enabling them to believe their cause is somehow more noble than fighting for pennies. Reflecting the division of the creative self, the audience are induced to suspect that Emer may in fact be Peadar's daughter rather than Theo's.

Like the artist frightened of the pain of creation, Theo grapples to remain unchanged by her presence. He gamely stretches his war stories in an attempt to make himself seem more than a naked loser, but he is gradually revealed as the victim of a neglectful father, crippled by his own suffering and anger, doomed to repeat his past.

Peadar, on the other hand, is invited to face all the agonizing bad faith in his life and make peace with it. He has played second fiddle to Theo's rousing cacophony, never having the courage to step into the sunlight. He abandoned his personal sovereignty by denying his one true love and his child. When Emer arrives he finds himself longing to do the right thing for the first time in his life and be a decent father to her. Yet the play asks the only pertinent question – to whom does the muse belong?

Like all real wisdom, the answer at the end of the play is both surprising yet obvious – she belongs to no one. Emer departs, taking their money and their best fighter. She takes, in fact, all that she is owed. As the muse always must, she has forced a brutal evolution in souls who are never ready.

Billy once told me that the true mark of a Wexford man is that he doesn't believe he comes from a small town. He believes he is from a bustling metropolis where anything is possible. Billy may have been wryly referring to himself. In Wexford he sees a pantheon of colourful, sometimes heartbroken, characters milling around from the high ground at the back of the town, down through its tangle of streets, and on to the quay where the train track mingles with the street, whisking travellers to Rosslare Harbour and on to the wide world. And in between are all the stories a writer could need.

Many of Roche's earlier characters are somehow caught between two worlds, unable to move into a place where their lives make sense, because they are battling the very idea of mortality itself. Thus we find over-the-hill boxers still dreaming of the big time, betting shop boasters who are unable to grow up, hoping their charm will carry them along like lovable children until time inexorably catches up. The early plays are peopled by those who inhabit the cracks in the town's walls, their daily paths so full of delusion that life-altering drama may suddenly descend upon them like thunderous fate itself – and it often does.

But while the early work, like the *Cavalcaders* looking out the window at the 'universe' of their town, laid bare the psychic structure of his place, his world, it is arguable that his more mature work has upped the ante and we are witnessing this most intriguing of writers explore an altogether darker landscape – his own artistic self.

**Figure 2:** Posters from the 'Billy Roche Weekend' (1993), featuring Ingrid Craigie above as Molly with Danger Doyle (Liam Cunningham); below as Angela with Artie O'Leary (Des McAleer). (Photographs by Mark Douet)

# 9 | The White Goddesses: An Interview with Ingrid Craigie

Patrick Burke

Ingrid Craigie, one of Ireland's most distinguished performers, has played major roles in three works by Billy Roche, starting with the last two plays of *The Wexford Trilogy*. She graced early productions of *Poor Beast in the Rain* (as Molly) and *Belfry* (as Angela), and has appeared twice in *The Cavalcaders* (as Breda): opposite Liam Cunningham in 2002 at the Tricycle in London, and opposite Stephen Brennan in 2006 at the Abbey.

Ingrid has starred in plays by almost all major Irish dramatists: George Bernard Shaw, Oscar Wilde, Sean O'Casey, Samuel Beckett, Tom Murphy, Thomas Kilroy, Sebastian Barry, Marina Carr, Conor McPherson, Martin McDonagh, and especially Brian Friel. (In addition to her definitive performances as Grace in two different productions of *Faith Healer*, Ingrid has played all three sisters in various versions of *Aristocrats*.) Beyond the Irish canon, she has appeared in plays by Thornton Wilder, Tennessee Williams, Harold Pinter, Michael Frayn, and Sarah Kane. In 2007 Ingrid was honoured by her peers with a special accolade at the *Irish Times* Theatre Awards.

On screen Ingrid has performed in such films as *The Ballroom of Romance, Widow's Peak, Da, The Railway Station Man, Circle of Friends* – and most notably in *The Dead*, John Huston's adaptation of James Joyce's classic story. In 1993, when Stuart Burge adapted Billy Roche's trilogy for BBC television, she reprised her roles in *Poor Beast in the Rain* and *Belfry*.

After reading English as a student at Trinity College, Dublin, Ingrid joined the Abbey Theatre for five years. Her professional debut came at the Peacock in the role of Emily in Wilder's *Our Town*, which was also director Patrick Mason's first full-scale production. Since then, Ingrid's work has taken her to London, Edinburgh, Montreal, New York, Sydney, and Singapore. The following interview was conducted in Dublin on 28 February 2011. This edited transcript starts with a question about the strong Wexford accent required for virtually all of Billy Roche's plays – but then broadens to reveal an insightful performer's sheer passion for theatre.

**Patrick Burke:** I assume you're not from Wexford.

**Ingrid Craigie:** No, I was born in Cork but I'm from Dublin really.

**PB:** So, doing the *Trilogy*, did you impose the accent or come at it some other way?

**IC:** Actually, the first play I did was *Belfry*, which we rehearsed and played in London, where I couldn't research or work on the accent, but I was surrounded by Wexford people in the company there, so in that instance I just absorbed it from *them*, from the people around me, who were 'the genuine article.'

**PB:** They were 'quare good' [Wexford idiom], weren't they?

**IC:** They were 'quare good'! (*Laughter*) It's a fantastic accent, when you get into it. It's great! Because they were there and could help you, that worked. And Billy is terrific about that: the rhythms of the piece are completely obviously in 'Wexford.' So if you try to read it and you don't know that it's in a Wexford cadence of speech – I don't know how people do it in other countries, I really don't.

**PB:** He writes very well. It sounds so ordinary, but it's crafted.

**IC:** It's wonderful. It's more than a skill to be able to take speech that you hear every day in the street. It isn't just a matter of taking it and putting it down on the page. The art is in making it seem like just what they'd say in the street.

**PB:** When Nuala says to Terry [of their sexual encounters in *Cavalcaders*], 'That was a lousy thing to do', *lousy* is not a word that would come into my mind first, to describe that situation – but then when you examine it, it's the right word.

**IC:** Absolutely.

**PB:** Can I ask about your general approach to playing a role? At what stage do you learn lines? When are you 'off' the script?

**IC:** I think that's changed over the years, maybe with age! People always say to you: 'How do you remember the lines?' That's not really a problem. Usually it's 'How do I *say* the line?' That's much more difficult. When you're young, you learn lines almost automatically – I know *I* did – you go and do it in rehearsal. You'd do the scene a couple of times and it just seemed to 'go in.' When you're younger, you rely probably on your instinct more, and the director, when I was growing up, would give you a lot of input, tell you what to do; it seemed to be quite simple. As you get older, the more you know and the more experience you have, the more you realize what you don't know, and you also become much more aware of the complexities of the work. And maybe the parts, too, as you grow older, become more complex.

**PB:** Not forgetting the difficulty of eye contact, body language, the rich resources of psycho-physicality in the art of acting, if some actors have put the script down and others haven't.

**IC:** In recent years – it started off, I think, when I was doing a production of [Conor McPherson's] *The Weir* – I decided that there was no point in going into rehearsals not knowing it. And that was considered a very old-fashioned idea. I remember Noel Coward used to insist that his company know the lines before they went in; they probably had a very short rehearsal period. And I also think it's really, really important to be absolutely accurate, to pay writers the courtesy of saying the lines that they wrote, and even more so with a good writer. If you say a word incorrectly – if you put in the wrong word in the wrong place, you know it's wrong. The rhythm is wrong. It's like music: they've worked very hard and long, choosing the phrases and the words. So I learnt all of *The Weir*, and I found that wonderful because it gave me then the rehearsal time to work on my performance and with the other actors, as you say, and know the piece thoroughly. I try to become very well acquainted with a play now before I start rehearsals. When I did *Faith* Healer,[1] which I am convinced is one of the greatest world dramas –

**PB:** A masterpiece!

---

[1] Ingrid Craigie has played in two productions of *Faith Healer*: one directed by Jonathan Kent (2006) and the other, following Robin Lefevre, by Michael Colgan (2009).

**IC:** Absolutely, and that was a part I had wanted to play since I had first seen it and thought: 'One day I'd like to play Grace!' And when I got the chance to do it, I learned my monologue beforehand, obviously because it's so difficult and so complex that you have to be on the same level as the director, because if the director is suggesting something, if I don't know the piece as well as he or she does –

**PB:** You can't 'put' it anywhere!

**IC:** I can't put it anywhere, or I can't do anything with what they suggest, or I just accept what they say and it might not be the right suggestion in an equal relationship.

**PB:** In approaching a role, have you any time for Stanislavsky, Strasberg, Sanford Meisner – the 'theory people'?

**IC:** Most actors evolve a kind of a hybrid approach and also what's appropriate to each play. I mean if you're doing Beckett, *Play* say, there's not really much point in doing Stanislavsky-type exercises and things like that. The meaning is in the language and in the playing, and I find it difficult to work with people who are very rigid about working a particular system – and most actors in Ireland *don't* work like that. We work hard, and good actors, I think, do a lot of preparation and a lot of work around what they're doing, but I don't think we all follow 'This is the system, this is what I do', this *actioning* business [derived from Stanislavsky] which I really can't get into at all, although I think it may be useful if you're in trouble in a certain play.

**PB:** And how about improvisations? Are they just idle play?

**IC:** They can help. And sometimes all those games or things, often they're really early on in rehearsals about making a company come together as a group. That's their function and I think they should be left then, because the interesting thing about actors is that we want to work as a company very quickly – you have to form relationships very quickly with the people you're working with, because you have to trust them and also you reveal a lot about yourself as an actor, emotionally and every other way, and if you're a good actor, you *have* to. So you have to shortcut the usual stages of friendships with people and go from one to ten – 'straight in!' – telling things about yourself or revealing yourself.

**PB:** Ingrid, you've worked with some outstanding directors – John Huston, Patrick Mason, Robin Lefevre – on stage and in film. What for you is the most creative relationship with the director in working out an interpretation of a role: what for you is your favourite mode of relationship to a director?

**IC:** Collaboration is my favourite mode. As an actor, I love working with other actors and the director in a collaborative way where you are equals and your opinion is thought to be of equal importance: everyone contributes. I mean there are some actors who will sit back and wait to be told, and some directors would like you to follow instructions. (*hesitates*) That is *not* creative.

All the directors I love working with, it just seems a very natural, organic process. I love people who can stretch you, because I hate lazy directors, who will accept what they're given and think it's fine and not push you towards maybe other possibilities. It's good to work with different directors, because you have to form a relationship again of trust very quickly, and that's difficult if you aren't sure whether you trust *their* judgement, because in the end, although it's an equal relationship, what happens if you have a disagreement with the director about 'I really don't want to do it this way'?

And the strange thing about performance is ... you need *time*. I could know a piece completely and could, theoretically, go in and do it, but actually it takes *time* until you can make it completely your own. And although I can hear things in my head and I know how I want them to sound, or what I can do with the line, it just won't come out until I'm inhabiting it in some strange way, even physically as well. There's that weird transformation until you really inhabit the person you are playing.

**PB:** I remember seeing a very good documentary on Friel around the time of *Wonderful Tennessee* [1993] – in which I thought you were truly exceptional, by the way, as did the director, Patrick Mason.[2] During that documentary he did a kind of a ritual where he got you all to come up, as if at a holy well or something. Was that helpful or was it Patrick acknowledging his educational indebtedness to the Benedictines?

**IC:** Well, the play was full of ritual; this was actually following the idea of a ritual. Now we did it seriously enough, but a bit of you is like the child – remember, we had people like John Kavanagh and Donal McCann in the company [*laughter*] that – I think most actors

---

[2] In this production Ingrid played Berna – a role which, for credible realization, requires a range of acting skills in addition to the verbal.

give most things 'a go', do you know, and *I* used memory of another shrine down in West Cork, those shrines that just pop up, that are pagan really, trees that have things tied on to them and favours on them. And, of course, Donegal's full of them. So, if you haven't done something like that, it is helpful, it can all be helpful.

**PB:** A dangerous question: would you be conscious of notable contrasts in approach between someone like Patrick Mason and certain other directors in Ireland?

**IC:** There are very different types of director, many of whom I love. I recall, some years ago, a conversation with Marion O'Dwyer, facing into a new play to be directed by an allegedly forceful director, and our agreeing that shouting was 'out.' – 'The first time [they] shout, we just tell them, "I'm sorry, we don't do shouting!"' [*laughter.*] I remember playing Nora in Garry Hynes's production of *The Plough and the Stars* [1991], very consciously visually different and, as most people remember, with lots of shaven heads: images, I suppose, of poverty. I remember at one stage doing one of the scenes when Nora comes back, when she's 'looking for Jack' and 'talking', 'doing the lines', 'speaking to the characters who were there with me', and Garry was talking to me *at the same time*; it was like a voice in my head, it came into my head and out of my mouth – she was just suggesting things, not demanding them, and I'll never forget that: it was a wonderful moment: that kind of connection, we were so linked at the time that I could take on board what she was saying and use it immediately, because we'd been working so closely. And Garry makes you feel you can do anything. And when she said 'This is rubbish', she doesn't mean *you* are; she means 'We can all do better than this.'

**PB:** Would Robin Lefevre be the best director of Billy Roche?

**IC:** I suppose he must be. There's something about Robin, his sensibility, but there's a real toughness about Robin as well as a sweetness, which you need for Billy, because you could be sentimental or 'fall off.' Working with Robin on *Belfry* was just wonderful, because he's incredibly sensitive to what's going on. And with Billy's writing – he was a huge presence in Billy's early work.

**PB:** Is it a good or a bad thing to have the author present? I'm thinking primarily of Mr Brian Friel, Mr Tom Murphy and Mr Billy Roche.

**IC:** It can be both – with someone like Billy, he's very easy to have around. Brian has changed how he is: the first play I appeared in was *Aristocrats* [1979], and Brian would appear at the reading and then he'd disappear and then he'd come back for the run-through, quite late on, and give notes to the director.

**PB:** He wouldn't directly address [the actors]?

**IC:** No, very rarely. He might give one tiny, tiny enigmatic note, and if you asked him a question, you'd get an enigmatic answer. However, he's become much more involved in later years. He wasn't at the rehearsals for *Faith Healer,* but he was all the way through at the rehearsals for *Wonderful Tennessee* – and I don't think that was good actually with Brian, because he doesn't trust directors – he doesn't *like* them – and I think that's a mistake, I think it's a big mistake.

And because Brian was in the room all the time, we self-censored ourselves really. And if he writes a stage direction, saying, '*She talks urgently in a low tone*', and Brian is in the room, then you do tend to '*talk urgently in a low tone*', because you're being given the directions from the *writer*. But actually there may be another way to achieve that, that Brian hasn't thought of, and if you surprise him, he's delighted. But you have to surprise him *early:* otherwise, he'll *tell* you to say it '*urgently in a low tone.*'

That balance between a writer letting go to a degree, and the contribution that the actors and the director make, if he's a good director: that makes it theatre, a living thing. Otherwise, it's a piece of literature that you can read at home. Usually, writers are surprised by what they've written. They don't always see things. We're so fortunate and it's extraordinary that we have Brian Friel around, and I love Brian, I've known him for years. After the first reading Brian gave me three notes before we started rehearsals for *Faith Healer,* and he just said three things which were useful to be aware of, and that's fantastic – that's from the horse's mouth – he wasn't speaking the language of *loudly/quietly* but how Grace might *feel.*

**PB:** What about Tom Murphy?[3]

**IC:** Be careful with Tom, because he's very, very clear – and rightly so – on rhythm and the sound of his work: a comma is a comma and

---

3 Ingrid won plaudits for her performance as Mona in Murphy's *The Gigli Concert,* at the Abbey Theatre in 1991.

a full stop is a full stop. The same with Martin McDonagh.[4] Tom
writes in a rhythm and you can't go against it: it takes time to make
the rhythm yours and to believe it. Tom can give directions which
can put actors a bit askew because they take it to mean a whole
performance or a whole theme, whereas he might just mean that
particular small piece. Sometimes you feel a bit inhibited, you want
[the writers] to go away for a while so that you can try things out
and make a mess of it.

You don't want to give a performance [merely] because you want
them to be OK with it. With Billy you never have that, partly because
he's an actor as well, and Billy is much more relaxed about that. He
*trusts* actors and directors.

**PB:** Coming back to the roles you've played in Billy's works – Does
Molly in *Poor Beast in the Rain* still love Danger Doyle?

**IC:** I've been thinking about it, the three women I've played, and
Molly is the least mature woman. She's still a young girl really: she's
still the hurt young girl, who's now older, so she hasn't gone beyond
the time where she was in love with Danger Doyle. And the other
girl, later the wife of the dull but decent Steven, was always number
one, really – when they were younger, she was always turning
people's heads and was a bit wild and took Danger off, as far as
Molly could see – and so she has built up *their* lives to being
something which it isn't.

Steven's wife is a very unhappy woman, and I think Molly is one
of those women who can't let go, can't move on. I mean, I think
there's a choice one can make in life, to say 'That happened. Now
what do I do?' But she won't. She's holding on to her hurt and she's
holding onto that love and kind of fossilized in a way – I mean,
because she's funny and so sharp.

**PB:** Danger is partly there to keep an eye on that, isn't he? And how
does Molly feel about that? Does the characterization need
something at the end, which we haven't seen before? Some hitherto
unrevealed facet of her character?

**IC:** I think at the end, maybe she's grown up, but it's not a happy
grown up. Because when you hold the torch for someone all the
time, you maybe hope they'll come back, some chance that you'll see
him again. He comes back, he comes back for the girl [Eileen], to

---

4 In the week following this interview, Ingrid was scheduled to play in a
   touring production of McDonagh's *The Cripple of Inishmaan.*

bring her back to the mum, and there's nothing. [Danger's] a nice man and he's kind to her, but it's over and she knows it's over. And the saddest thing about her, I thought, is, in a way, it's *all* over for her, because she says, 'What am I goin' to do Danger?' And she's so open about it ...

**PB:** Now in *Belfry*, unlike *Poor Beast* and the later *Cavalcaders*, it is the woman who is the sexual aggressor. So would you say a little about what Angela gets from the relationship with Artie? And what risks is she running?

**IC:** I think Angela is a very interesting woman. She's like a lot of people: [she] found herself (*quiet laugh*) and is not sure how she got there. She made choices and she thought she was making one choice, and I think she found herself in the kind of marriage that she'd never anticipated and never wanted. And she was a bit of a wild girl when she was young: now there's something she keeps looking for. It's dangerous in a way, obviously, to have affairs, and you discover, far into the play, that it's not the first time she's had an affair with someone.

And she's moved on to somebody else she's having an affair with, but I think she is unlike a lot of the men, who are romantic. People usually say that women are romantic. The women are very pragmatic, often, in Billy's plays. They're very grown up and they're very practical – some of them, let's say the middle-aged women – they know this is the way things are. She's married, she has children, she lives in a small town, and – this is some time ago when this was written – she's not going to leave her children. She can't do that, there's no way you can do that, so you take some happiness you can find.

**PB:** Would Donal ever chuck her out?

**IC:** No. He loves her but also he thinks, and maybe he's right, that in some way she needs the stability of their marriage, that she'll always come back to Donal, but she's ruthless with Artie in that once it's found out: 'That's it! It's over!'

And I think Artie has touched her more deeply than other people, and for her it's probably a crisis. And when Donal says, 'one day she's going to really get hurt', I think the damage has been done with Artie, because Artie – it's a bit like [Synge's] *Playboy* in a way: he's liberated by falling in love with her: the language he uses, he becomes a poet almost.

**PB:** Someone who had been a mammy's boy!

**IC:** Exactly. She says, 'I soar in your arms, boy.' It's so beautiful. Oh my goodness, that would have been a perfect relationship, and it's given a lovely, generous embodiment when she appears in the second act, wearing nothing but a surplice – a 'short' surplice![5] That's a kind of wonderful, joyful gift that she gives to Artie, semi-naked except for, if you like, the uniform of a priest. The woman has stolen some of the priest's power by wearing his gear! But for all that, she knows it can't last, and he *doesn't*. I mean, he's completely impractical about it.

**PB:** Billy talks about 'the white goddess' image, that women are capable of nine or ten months and all that nurturing, whereas, at the other side, they can eat you up, they can be monsters. Would you see that as valid for his plays?

**IC:** I think it's in Billy's plays – absolutely, yes, that's Billy's thing, isn't it?

**PB:** But one feels that all his sympathies are on the side of the deviant, the people who've run away, who've loved other men's wives. Who've had torrid affairs. Who break windows in *A Handful of Stars*.

**IC:** Yes. All the transgressors in some way: there's always that in Billy, who opens up the small town and says, 'You should break a few rules here.' The people who are closed and tight and conformist – they're dangerous in the sense of they don't let any light in.

**PB:** They send people to jail!

**IC:** And they send people to jail and they hide the things that are happening.

**PB:** Breda in *Cavalcaders* – to me she's always seemed as much of a mother to Terry as a wife or lover.

**IC:** I find it very interesting, that. I mean they 'are' in development – from Molly, who still is emotionally 'just damaged'; Angela, who has much more of a handle on it, is much more complex. Then there's Breda who has a lot of wisdom: she's not going to die without Terry: she loves him and she knows she's the right woman for him.

---

5 In a delightfully unintended irony, the edition of *Belfry* published by Nick Hern (1993) misspells surplice as surplus!

I remember when I saw the first production [1993]. Marie Mullen, Tony Doyle and Aisling O'Sullivan: I thought that was the best production I've seen – maybe because it was the shock of seeing the play. I saw a dress rehearsal of it, because we were rehearsing *Wonderful Tennessee* at the time and we couldn't see it; we were both opening around the same time. I went round to look at it and I had no idea of anything and they started to sing at the beginning, the boys, and that made me laugh, it was just so fantastic and funny and lads doing their bit of dancing, in the shop. And then there was a wonderful relationship between Tony and Marie which I always thought should be there: it was a strong sexual relationship. And remember he's rubbing her feet; she's in the chair and he's rubbing her feet. And I thought, 'That's a tough one.' There was great flirtiness between them and you just thought: 'These people are right together.' And when Aisling arrived, you think: 'This girl is so dangerous and so damaged' –

**PB:** Dangerous?

**IC:** Dangerous for herself : 'You must leave this girl alone, you'll destroy her, you cannot get involved.' Having the relationship with the girl, this was just screaming at me: 'This is not going to end well. It just can't end well.' And I always felt at the end it shouldn't be that he's 'settling' for Breda, but that he's kind of come back to a kind of sense. It was wrong what he did with that young damaged girl and I think we should feel the age difference should be quite marked, because she's after an older man for whatever reason.

**PB:** And going to an even worse older man, who beats her!

**IC:** Yes, exactly. I don't think you should ever feel, 'Ah, they 're [Terry and Nuala] grand together, and I felt in the production we had [2002], Terry was too young: they *were* fine together – and Breda was a bit 'the old one.'

**PB:** So you're seeing he kind of thinks and feels and senses his way back to you.

**IC:** That's what I got from the first production. That's what I always feel, and I think Breda is a very wise woman. She has her own job, she has her own friends, she can see what's going on, and she has the maturity to say 'I love him', to say: 'This is not [*love*]; this is bad for him.' And Breda is not saying she wants to *mother* him. I think she should get him back because they are right for each other, and not because there's nobody else [for Terry].

**PB:** In terms of structure, Ingrid, *Cavalcaders* has the most elaborate time construction, back and forward, particularly as the play goes on, and then we have the music. What is Billy at? For some people it's an over-elaborate structure. I love it –

**IC:** I love it, too, and I think that's the great thing about theatre that you can play with time, and I think there's a real thrill if an audience just concentrates a little bit. You see a scene and then you're given the back story and that, in retrospect, fills in things that might have been a bit enigmatic and it just deepens the play and then you go on to the next scene and I just think it adds huge richness to it. But audiences can be very determined: they want to start at the beginning and work their way through to the end.

**PB:** And there are some perfectly good plays which can do that –

**IC:** Of course. I remember when we did the *Trilogy* in London, some of the initial expectation – 'What's this?' 'One of the plays set in a church?' – my God, it's such a secular society and (*pause)* they just adored them, they were an extraordinary hit. *Belfry* made a huge impact, the story of people's lives, and even though the lives were very, very different from the lives they were living, what people were experiencing in their own way was not. Billy is such a great story-teller and has such compassion for his characters--

**PB:** He condemns no one.

**IC:** In that it's very like Chekhov!

**PB:** Look at the portrayals of Ted and Rory – how honest, how good a father is Rory, the forgiveness, the skewed friendship of himself and Ted – this is the writing of a man who knows how vulnerable all of us are, how much silent pain there is!

**IC:** Oh, frightful pain! In some ways, the plays remind us that you can be sitting in a car or on a bus and people look ordinary, but we've no idea what they're going through. This is the new form of tragedy, really.

**PB:** Ingrid Craigie, thank you.

**Figure 3:** Ingrid Craigie as Breda, Garrett Lombard as Rory and Stephen Brennan as Terry in *The Cavalcaders* at the Abbey Theatre (2007). (Photograph by Colm Hogan)

**Figure 4:** Cover image for the revised edition of the novel *Tumbling Down* (Tassel Publications, 2008). On the right: Pierce Roche, Billy's father, performs in his pub, The Shamrock. In the mirror, reflected dimly, is 'Useless Island.' (Design by Michael McMullin)

## 10 | A Wexford Musician

Larry Kirwan

Wexford was unique. I don't know if that's still the case, for I'm gone a long time. Still, if the town wasn't etched in my memory I could delve into a volume of Billy Roche's plays and much of its brooding effervescence would come cascading back.

Even as a kid I was never less than aware that I was a temporary tenant. Wexford didn't give a damn about any of us. And why should it? Ptolemy had charted it back in the second century, and in the intervening years a dizzying selection of rogues and marauders had left their psychic footprints all over its narrow streets and back lanes.

The town was totally separate from the county and barely gave a thought to Dublin, let alone such local backwaters as Enniscorthy, Gorey or New Ross. It occasionally tipped its cap to London for we all had relatives in the 'big smoke' and chances were many of us would end up in Cricklewood or Camden Town.

Wexford was by no means homogenous. Each indigenous hive of streets and lanes had its own variant of the townie accent – more Belfast than Dublin, oddly enough – as well as its own customs and mores to be treasured and jealously guarded. Billy and I were from the North End; to the scholar this area would seem to be dominated by Selskar Abbey and haunted by the ghosts of Henry II and Cromwell, but to the great unwashed, the like of us, the Abbey Cinema, replete with swirling visions of Bogie and Marilyn, stood head and shoulders over any old pile of stones no matter what their pedigree.

We were mad about the pictures and it was a rare person – from short-pantsed boy to watch-fobbed granddad – who didn't attend the three local cinemas at least twice a week, while hard-core junkies booted up every night and threw in the occasional matinee fix on the weekends.

When I see Billy's plays I rarely think 'theatah.' The only play I recall making any splash in the Wexford of our youth was John B. Keane's *Sive* – and that only because of the overriding issue of illegitimacy. We were all familiar with the nuts and bolts of this social scourge; there wasn't a street in Wexford that didn't boast of some young lad who'd done a bunk to London after putting some poor unfortunate 'young wan' up the pole.

I don't see much of O'Neill, Miller or Williams in Billy's plays, although Chekhov's keen eye tracks every scene. Neither do I notice the dulling banality of television, the curse of modern playwriting; but I see whole reels of Ford, Huston and Scorsese. And at odd moments I catch glimpses of Cagney, Pacino and DeNiro peeking out from the shadows cast by Billy's characters.

The Abbey Cinema and its flickering visions are long gone, replaced by some blocks of boxy flats that wouldn't even inspire a dry dream. But every time I pass the old site I'm consoled, knowing that some of its ghosts make the occasional short trip down Abbey Street to add their weight to Billy's plays at the Arts Centre or Theatre Royal.

Back in the day there were two types of Wexford men: those who had to go away for economic reasons and the others who fit in one way or the other. Most of the former, like Billy's father, Pierce, worked in London or Dagenham and returned for the Christmas holidays and two glorious weeks in the summer. They inevitably departed on Saturday nights from the North Station aboard the boat train and arrived bleary-eyed and bollocksed in Paddington the following morning. I can still summon up those black and white Saturday scenes of heartbreak, with teary wives, bawling children, and men in their Sunday best affecting nonchalance through the glaze of a couple of bottles of stout.

I recognize that same dry-eyed pain throughout Billy's plays: there are always people coming home or leaving or, at the least, dreaming of escape; someone will get hurt, someone will 'do a runner', invariably things are left unsaid. That's Wexford for you – women cry occasionally, men never; but the tears left unshed inexorably affect the next generation.

Billy's father was what we called 'a character.' He had a big heart and an even bigger smile but I sometimes sensed there was a core of sadness to the man – that he'd let slip some opportunity, regretted it but, in that ineffable Wexford way, chose not to make a fuss about it. Pierce Roche played accordion with a fag drooping from the corner of his mouth; at times he even wore a beret. Picture the insouciant boxman behind Edith Piaf in a Parisian café. He was also a bar owner: The Shamrock on Anne Street was his joint. It was frequented by an unruly, seditious crew – sailors, returned emigrants, gamblers, dreamers, those who fit in nowhere else, many with a barely disguised chip on their shoulder; that pub was anything but staid. Billy went to work there in his mid-teens. What an education! Wexford male society back then was divided into men and boys but the line between was blurred. There were many men of fourteen who looked down on boys of eighteen. Billy became a man early, yet he never lost a certain boyishness. Lucky for him, because a Wexford man's world had little time for music whereas boys thought of little else, except sex, and to many of us they were synonymous. Because of its easy access to London, Wexford was way ahead of the curve in music and fashion. From the mid-50's the town reeked of Rock & Roll. Young townies returned from the big smoke with their Rockabilly 45's – Eddie Cochran, Gene Vincent, Buddy Holly, not to mention sneering Elvis before the army turned him into a moron.

And did they bring home fashions too! Wexford Teddyboys in their multi-coloured drapes, drainpipes and brothel creepers lounged outside Nolan's ice cream parlour while the rebellious sound of reverbed guitars and slapback vocals oozed past them into the narrow Viking streets.

Every boy with a sense of adventure took in the scene from the safety of Johnny Hore's Stores, wishing we were old enough to slouch over and jive or smooch with perfumed Teddygirls in high heels, wide skirts and flashing petticoats, their faces caked with powder and mascara. We longed to be a part of that magic world. Alas, by the time we were old enough the Teds had mostly faded away, their roots rock replaced by Beatles, Stones, Animals and the man himself, Bobby Dylan.

What an effect Mr. Zimmerman had on us – those mystic words and mutinous melodies lashed together by chords that even we could brazen out on cheap acoustic guitars. Dylan made anything seem possible. We knew from Irish ballads that you could tell stories through song, but were our own lives interesting enough? 'Yeah', Dylan drawled back, an eye cocked in bemused assurance. All you needed was a dollop of imagination, a sense of your own well-concealed importance, and the courage to face the inevitable Wexford slagging. I was always aware that Billy had ambitions. I used to watch him brave the stage in cabarets and pubs. Oddly enough, we were never rivals. I guess it was comforting to know that there was someone else banging his head against the wall of Wexford nonchalance. Even then he knew enough to get a crowd going, but I liked to watch him toss in one of his own songs. You did that at your peril, for more than likely this germinating masterpiece would land like a wet blanket on the booze and good times, and be met with groans and shouts of 'Play somethin' we all know, for the love of Jaysus!' I remember nuking many the night myself with hyper-sensitive laments and odes to seventeen year old virgins who didn't even know my name and most definitely wouldn't give me the time of day if they did.

Later on when I had moved to Dublin I didn't notice Billy's absence from Wexford. Years later he told me he had gone to England to 'make it' playing the folk clubs. He never hid the fact that those were hard times. England can be one hell of a lonely place, and folk Nazis are formidable people when you're alone and wrestling with your own demons of shyness and underconfidence.

By the time I got back from my first years in the U.S., Billy was back home. I remember a night out in his cottage just past Carcur in Wexford. I was there with his cousin, Pierce Turner, while the guitar was being swapped around way past the midnight hour. He sang 'Dainty Valerie' in honour of his daughter. There was a delicacy to the song that still wings its way around my brain.

Having a wife and a little girl was something that set Billy apart. Turner and I were footloose and fancy free, living 'the life' in New York. But Billy was really living life. He hadn't, in any sense, caved on his ambitions but they were forced to co-exist with regular Wexford dreams like raising a family with all the attendant joy and heartbreak. Whereas to us a wife and child seemed like an Everest of a load to carry, Billy knew better: he had found his soul companion in Patti, without whom he would never have achieved what he since has.

The Man Who Wouldn't Work, I once heard Billy described. But the guy did slave away, in factories and bars or wherever a shilling was to be made. It's just that these jobs were never some golden grail unto themselves, merely a means to an end. They kept food on the table while the artist, with silence and cunning, was learning his trade and honing his creative instincts.

I was a big fan of the Roach Band – as much for the fact that they were local lads kicking up a storm as for the exuberant angular music they pumped out. They weren't unlike The Rats but without Geldof's attitude. In retrospect, that was the only thing they were missing – for in the end, 'tude' is as important as talent. The couple of singles you might track down don't do them justice; real-deal bands always sound better live. But just take it from me, they could have easily made a dent, mostly because of Billy's zany presence. Even in music, the movies were close to hand. I can't remember now whether it was intentional or not – most of our conversations back then were laced with Southern Comfort – but Billy dressed and acted like a young Chaplin, the tramp careening around the stage in between bursts of quirky pop-punk singing.

But the music business is a bitch and keeping a band together is harder than sedating a sack full of kittens. Besides there was a family to be raised, the girls to be looked after, with Patti in a full time job at Hassetts the Chemists. She was always the first person I'd drop in to see on jet-lagged mornings. To this day she has a beautiful presence that soothes jangled nerves and makes you glad to be home.

Inevitably, though, there comes a time when you store your guitar under the bed, look around at the world and wonder if there isn't a saner way of exploring the human condition. The transition is often hard. I remember one day driving down the Brooklyn Queens Expressway on some dumb delivery job and hearing 'So You Want To Be A Rock & Roll Star' by The Byrds; I almost had to pull over from the pain and loss. I'm sure Billy had such moments in those rocky early 80's. And then came *Tumbling Down*. I haven't read it in twenty-five years and yet there are passages still clear as spring water. Perhaps because it shone a light on a world and a town that I knew too well but had never totally come to terms with. In certain ways that book ensured that I wouldn't be coming home.

I knew the story of the *Boker Poker Club* long before it became *A Handful of Stars*. Many Wexford people did because Billy wrestled publicly with the play, knowing no one else would ever give a voice to the many Wexford adolescents who batter and bruise their way to manhood down the narrow streets and back lanes. What a blast then to hear that the script had been retrieved from a slush pile at The

Bush, and given a production that unleashed a prolific playwright on the world.

There are times during *Poor Beast in the Rain, Belfry,* and *The Cavalcaders* when I fancy I see real people from the past flit across the stage and merge with the characters. On such occasions I often flash back to a slim, dark haired boy lugging crates of bottles around cliques of men in the Shamrock, all the time picking up words and images that later would become the currency of these plays.

What a university The Shamrock must have been! No one gave a thought back then to attending college – that was for other people, the sons of solicitors or doctors.

Becoming a playwright was an even more distant dream not to be shared with anyone for fear of ridicule. It makes you wonder if the college years of eighteen to twenty-two are too precious to be wasted conforming to fashion and convention, intellectual or otherwise. No, there were far more nuggets to be mined in the human quarries of The Shamrock or on the bloody boards of the CYMS ballroom dodging the swinging fists of drunken delinquents while sizing up sweaty Woolworths' girls jiving with their sultry sisters.

The last thing Billy needed was some academic riding herd over his first hesitant lines and chapters. Artistic judgment, discipline and craft come from long periods of gestation and secret striving. Billy has long ago read and digested O'Neill, Miller and Williams. But he didn't really need to. As family was O'Neill's crucible, so the narrow streets of Wexford were Billy's. Willy Loman's existential terror was a dime a dozen in the back lanes of Billy's youth. The renegade women he saw braving The Shamrock might have had different accents than Blanche DuBois, but they were only too familiar with her fading beauty and frenetic courage.

In the heel of the hunt, though, it's the ability to look inside the souls of people that makes a great playwright. This quality set Billy apart as a boy and sustains him as a man. I've experienced it many times down the years but none like the day I followed my father's coffin down the aisle of Rowe Street Church. As I was lost in a haze of self-recrimination for my long absences, Billy took me to one side and whispered, 'Whatever you do, don't let this stop you coming home in the future, okay?' It was quintessential Billy, simple and to the point. He knew I needed the old town more than it needed me.

For Wexford is a unique inheritance and has need of treasuring. Its claustrophobic streets and piss-stained back lanes throb with memories, customs, accents and all the other indefinable elements that go into the creation of a singular essence.

How lucky we are to have a poet who has tracked and measured its DNA so that even when far away, literally or figuratively, we can summon it up through his sentences!

Take care of yourself, brother, and thanks for the laughs and the memories. I'll see you soon.

# 11 | *Tumbling Down* and *Dubliners*: Tales of Two Cities

Alexander McKee

Critics commonly assume that Billy Roche has abandoned the traditional concerns of nationality and religion that continue to preoccupy so many contemporary Irish playwrights. As Mary Carr puts it, 'Roche has emerged as an almost frightening bearer of an Ireland without historical or religious resonances.'[1] Similarly, in an essay reprinted in this collection, Colm Tóibín argues that Roche's best work achieves 'a strange timelessness and beauty' precisely because it remains unburdened by national issues. To some extent, these writers are simply affirming Roche's self-proclaimed desire to dramatize 'a universal story' in his work for the stage.[2] By highlighting the mythic quality of Roche's plays, Carr and Tóibín follow a pattern set by James Joyce's original promoters, who generally ignored Joyce's relation to Irish politics as they made their case for his broader significance. But if Joyce is best understood as a product of his times, as recent critics have suggested,[3] then Roche should also be read as an historically situated artist.

Just as Joyce set all of his books in Dublin during the first decade of the twentieth century, Roche writes almost exclusively about

---

[1] Mary Carr, 'The Plays of Billy Roche', *Journal of the Irish Theatre Forum* 1.1 (Summer 1997), <http://www.ucd.ie/irthfrm/-firstiss.htm#mcarr>.

[2] Quoted in Aileen Donohoe, 'The Pull of the Past', *Fortnight* 358 (Feb. 1997): 31.

[3] During the 1990s, many prominent scholars worked to historicize Joyce as an Irish writer, including Seamus Deane, Enda Duffy, James Fairhall, Thomas Hofheinz, Robert Spoo, and Joseph Valente.

Wexford in the 1960s. He took up this material for the first time in *Tumbling Down* (1986), the autobiographical novel that launched his literary career. At first glance, *Tumbling Down* might seem to be the work of an apprentice struggling to find a voice, as it alternates a bit awkwardly between the first and the third person. But the novel remains central in any consideration of Roche's career, because it introduces many of his ongoing concerns. As the author himself observes, 'all the themes I was writing about in that novel would come back to haunt my plays.'[4] Roche is understandably fond of his first book, and in 2008 he took the unusual step of publishing a substantially revised edition. This new version of *Tumbling Down* makes the novel's thematic and stylistic debts to *Dubliners* even clearer.

Roche has often cited *Dubliners* as a source of inspiration, and he recently described the short stories in his own collection, *Tales from Rainwater Pond*, as 'Joycean, because all the tales circle around the pond as a mirror of the characters in the town. *Dubliners* would be the baby for me. I love that book.'[5] Underscoring the structural similarities between Joyce's book and his own, Roche employs the same mirror metaphor that Joyce used to articulate his purposes in *Dubliners*: to give 'the Irish people ... one good look at themselves in my nicely polished looking glass.'[6] Critically surveying the cultural, economic, political, and religious forces affecting his countrymen in colonial Ireland, Joyce portrayed middle-class Dubliners as impoverished spiritually as well as materially, with few resources to overcome their oppressive circumstances. He explained: 'My intention was to write a chapter of the moral history of my country and I chose Dublin for the scene because that city seemed to me the centre of paralysis.'[7]

Roche does not comment so directly upon the social implications of his own work, but he clearly follows Joyce's example by presenting the Wexford of *Tumbling Down* as an Irish microcosm. Set in the mid-sixties, shortly before the Republic of Ireland gained entry into the European Economic Community, Roche's novel

---

[4] Quoted in Kevin Kerrane, 'The Poetry of the Street: An Interview with Billy Roche', *Irish Studies Review* 14.3 (2006): 373.

[5] Kerrane: 377.

[6] *Letters of James Joyce*, Volume 1, ed. Stuart Gilbert (New York: Viking Press, 1957): 63-64.

[7] *Letters of James Joyce*, Volume II, ed. Richard Ellmann (New York: Viking Press, 1966): 134.

depicts an historic point when the constraining ideologies that dominated national life following independence finally gave way to the modernizing efforts enacted by the Fianna Fáil government of Seán Lemass. *Tumbling Down* captures a certain ambivalence about the economic and social improvements of that time because it focuses primarily on provincial people who were not always prepared to embrace the consumerist values of a rapidly industrializing and urbanizing society. Perhaps for this reason, the inhabitants of Roche's Wexford resemble the denizens of Joyce's Dublin in remaining stubbornly resistant to change.

Roche introduces a theme of paralysis in the very first paragraph of *Tumbling Down,* which describes Wexford as 'a topsy-turvy town that rose up and tumbled down into rows and rows of gardenless houses, streets filled with people whose main ambition was to live until they died.'[8] After personifying Wexford as a tipsy man who cannot find his feet, the opening pages depict The Shamrock bar as 'a tall, lean, drunken building with crumbling walls and moss-filled chutes' (4). This unprepossessing public house, which provides the backdrop for much of the novel's action, is a place of refuge for Roche's characters, a bulwark against the seas of change rising all around them. They go to The Shamrock to sing the familiar songs of their youth and to complain about modernizing efforts like the one-way street system that has been proposed 'due to the increase in traffic over the last few years and the constant dilemma that drivers have to face on the narrow, impassable Main Street' (93-94).[9]

Paddy Wolfe, the proprietor of The Shamrock, happily caters to the nostalgic tastes of his clientele by playing traditional Irish music as well as popular standards. He does particularly good business during the summer tourist season, when visiting customers feel a need to connect with their Irish roots. The protagonist Davy Wolfe, Paddy's son, explains: 'They were mainly returned exiles, living all year long for this fortnight when they could come back home and

---

[8] Billy Roche, *Tumbling Down* (Wexford: Tassel Publications, 2008): 1. Subsequent quotations from *Tumbling Down*, unless otherwise specified, are from this revised text, and page numbers will appear parenthetically.

[9] Wexford's 'increase in traffic' during this period of economic revival typified changes throughout the country. Terence Brown notes that between 1958 and 1961 car registrations rose by 29.5 percent in Ireland. See Brown's *Ireland: A Social and Cultural History* (London: Harper Perennial, 2004): 230.

see my father perform' (72). These deracinated visitors clearly
regard The Shamrock as a link to their lost homeland, and their
annual pilgrimage to Wexford helps them to maintain an Irish
identity.

Of course, Davy Wolfe is so determined to escape from Wexford
himself that he cannot understand why anyone would want to
return. It makes no sense to him that Joe Crofton moved back to
town after spending time abroad. He ponders Joe's decision (36):

> When I said that it was a wonder someone wouldn't build a
> casino or something out on Useless Island Joe Crofton gave the
> idea some thought and kind of smiled at my ingenuity. I
> secretly wondered if he ever felt trapped here. He'd been
> around, I knew that. He had worked on the buildings in
> London ... in the early days. I'd often heard him mention The
> Elephant and Castle and the Edgware Road and all the rest of
> it. One day, when I had saved enough money, I would break
> away from here too. I'd take my guitar and go away and come
> back rich and famous and cocksure of myself. I'd buy up
> Useless Island and build that casino. Casino Blue, I'd call it. Or
> The Lady Luck Café maybe.

Embracing the modernizing impulse that has swept across the
nation, Davy imagines developing the rocky outcrop that sits 'alone
and unused in the middle of this shipless harbour, an island of stone
and clay that looked like it must have sprung from the sea centuries
ago' (1). He is unimpressed by the 'ghostly, enchanted air' that
surrounds this ancient place, which seems to him hopelessly
removed from the modern world, like traditional Ireland itself. In
fact, Davy wants so badly to share Joe's firsthand knowledge of
cosmopolitan London that he plans to import that experience to
Wexford: he daydreams about building a casino on Useless Island
because it would give him and his fellow townspeople immediate
access to modernity in one of its most exciting and seductive forms.
The casino is especially meant to contravene the authorities, both
cultural and religious, who tried to forestall change in Ireland
during the 1960s.

Davy further rebels against these conservative forces by listening
to popular music from Great Britain and the United States. This
does not mean that he turns his back upon the Irish tradition that
his father upholds as the leader of regular sessions at The Shamrock,
and he is especially keen to observe the impromptu performance of
Johnny Sligo, the itinerant street singer who is 'the last of a dying
breed' (40). In this regard, Davy's taste reflects that of many young

people in Ireland in the 1960s and 1970s whose interest in traditional music flowered even as they responded to the new sounds coming over radio and television.[10] Gerry Smyth speaks directly to Davy's situation when he describes the musical revolution that took place in Ireland during the 1960s: 'It would have been difficult for any young musician to play traditional music in the received ways once they had heard, say, Jimi Hendrix play the electric guitar.'[11]

Davy not only wants to play guitar like his rock idols; he also wants to look like them in every possible way. For this reason, he adopts the hairstyle and boots made famous by the Beatles, provoking the conservative Mr. Martin to lecture him about 'Manners, morals and respect' (53-54). Although Davy cannot attend performances by the best-known British and American acts, he regularly gets to see Irish bands like The Freshmen, The Greenbeats, and the Miami Showband perform covers of the latest hits (49).[12] Noel McLaughlin and Martin McLoone underscore the importance of such groups, which 'brought to the youth of rural and provincial Ireland the same kind of liberating hedonism that was associated with other imported forms of popular culture.'[13] As he watches The Freshmen play live at the Parish Hall, Davy dreams of making it big as a rock musician and leaving Wexford for good.

Davy articulates his desire to escape from Wexford during a conversation with Kathy, a girl he meets at a party. Once again, he vows to 'break away from here one day' and to 'take my guitar and sing my way around the world' (65). But Kathy knows better than Davy what it means to leave home, because she has already spent time working in Dublin.[14] She questions his naïve aspirations when

---

[10] Brown: 262. The year 1962 marked the debut of Telefís Éireann, and the first pop music chart was broadcast on Radio Éireann during the same year.

[11] Gerry Smyth, *Music in Irish Cultural History* (Dublin: Irish Academic Press, 2009): 94.

[12] Gerry Smyth addresses the impact that such bands had upon Irish culture and society in the 1960s. See *Noisy Island: A Short History of Irish Popular Music* (Cork: Cork University Press, 2005): 9-45.

[13] Noel McLaughlin and Martin McLoone, 'Hybridity and National Musics: The Case of Irish Rock Music', *Popular Music* 19.2 (May 2000): 188.

[14] Kathy is part of a larger demographic shift that was taking place in Ireland during this period of modernization. As Terence Brown notes, 'In 1926 only 32.27 percent of the population had lived in

she characterizes herself as 'a small town girl running back to the hostel every night and lying awake in her bed listening to the lonesome sound of the city' (65). Having experienced firsthand the alienating effects of life in the big city, Kathy has come to appreciate the values of traditional Ireland that are being threatened by Irish urbanization, and for this reason she makes Davy promise that he will not destroy Useless Island once he becomes rich and famous: 'She said that everybody needed a Useless Island, something that wouldn't change or go away the minute you turned your back on it, and I gave her my word that when I was rich and famous I wouldn't change a thing' (90).

Despite his bold predictions, Davy does not entirely believe that he can 'make a run for it before this small town boy [becomes] a small town man' (139). Roche makes this clear in the first edition of *Tumbling Down* by permitting Davy to wonder openly 'where in the name of God was I going to get the courage to say goodbye to Wexford.'[15] But he works to expose his protagonist's doubts in the second edition of the novel as well. Catching a glimpse of himself in a shop window, Davy suddenly realizes that, 'My face looked real ordinary. ... It certainly didn't look like the face of a bloke who was going to travel the world and come back rich and famous and tattooed and cocksure of himself, but still the same old Davy Wolfe at the back of it all' (139). In this brief moment of epiphany, Davy seems to recognize the absurdity of his rock-star ambitions. Like the title character in 'Eveline', the first story of adolescence from Joyce's *Dubliners*, Davy finds himself paralyzed by indecision as he questions his ability to realize his dreams.[16]

Whereas Davy has only just begun to suspect that he may never be able to leave Wexford, Captain Crunch understands all too well that there is no prospect of escape for him. This 'grizzled old sea-

---

towns of over 1,500 persons. By 1951 that figure had risen to 41.44 percent, by 1966 it was 49.20 percent, and in 1971 it topped the halfway mark at 52.25 percent.' See *Ireland: A Social and Cultural History*: 245.

[15] This sentence appeared in the original edition of *Tumbling Down* (Dublin: Wolfhound Press, 1986): 63. It was excised in the revised edition.

[16] Joyce organized the stories in *Dubliners* to focus progressively upon four different stages of life (i.e., childhood, adolescence, maturity, and public life). Somewhat less systematically, Roche explores the last three of these stages in *Tumbling Down*.

dog' has basically given up on life, and he spends most of the novel drinking himself into a stupor (7). Like the cultural nationalists who glorified Ireland's past, Crunch has created a heroic backstory for himself. Davy's wanderlust makes him naturally susceptible to Crunch's romantic tales of his seagoing days, 'dangerous stories of blades flashing on the waterfront as two men fought to the death ... down some salty avenue in Amsterdam or somewhere; and beautiful women lapping at his feet on the sunlit shores of Mombassa' (16). Davy particularly likes to hear Crunch talk about Indio – 'a woman of great savage beauty with jet black hair ... and voluptuous breasts' (17) – who was born from his imagination.

But Davy can easily tell that his friend is out of step with the times. Crunch is disturbed by the changes taking place around him, as demonstrated by his response to the busy tourist season in Wexford. [17] 'Crunch hated this time of year, everyone acting so efficient all of a sudden,' Roche writes. 'Even The Shamrock had acquired a business-like manner. ... Nobody had time to talk anymore. What's more, and worse again in his book, nobody had time to listen' (70). As if to protest the frenetic pace of life in modern Ireland, Crunch maintains a dissolute lifestyle and happily embraces the stereotypical role of the binge-drinking and riotous Irishman that was a continuing source of embarrassment to the architects of Ireland's economic resurgence in the 1960s.[18]

Roche calls further attention to Crunch's conflict with modernity in the most recent version of *Tumbling Down* by developing the crucial scene that takes place in Crunch's 'dingy second floor flat' after his short-lived attempt to escape Wexford (84). Like Joyce's protagonist in 'A Little Cloud', Crunch desperately wants to believe

---

[17] R. F. Foster describes the tourist boom that took place in Ireland during the 1960s: '[F]rom the late 1950s, Bord Fáilte approached the matter of marketing Ireland with more finesse, and to greater purpose. The development of Shannon Airport led to a huge American influx; the coach-tour industry took over ... By 1967 receipts from tourism had passed £80,000,000, and a new "industry" was well-established.' See *Modern Ireland, 1600-1972* (London: Penguin Books, 1989): 581-582.

[18] See Joe Cleary, 'The Pogues and the Spirit of Capitalism', *Outrageous Fortune: Capital and Culture in Modern Ireland* (Dublin: Field Day Publications, 2007): 264. Captain Crunch is obviously at odds with what Cleary calls the 'more desirable images of modernizing improvement, ... industrial discipline or cosmopolitan sophistication.'

that it is not 'too late for him to try to live bravely.'[19] Ignoring the
infirmities of his decrepit body, therefore, he briefly proposes to go
back to sea, and to the incredulous Davy he makes a solemn
promise: 'if ever I do get down around Valparaiso you'll never see
Captain Crunch again. I'll stay there. I'll stay with Indio' (77).
Almost immediately, Crunch is forced to concede that he can never
reclaim his former glory. Drunk and demoralized, he retreats to his
rented room, only to find himself haunted by a 'faraway,
mesmerizing tune' that gradually takes hold of his consciousness
(84). Working to place this 'wild fairground melody', Crunch
identifies it with both the Tornados' 'Telstar' and the String-A-
Longs' 'Wheels' (84). The reference to 'Telstar' proves most relevant
here, because the Tornados' signature song was named for a
telecommunications satellite that was launched in July 1962.
Crunch is understandably threatened by this novelty record, which
challenges him on two levels: as both a rock-and-roll anthem and a
paean to the space age. The futuristic track is more than just an
affront to his traditional musical tastes; it also serves to remind him
that, at a time of great change, he remains trapped in the past.

Besides exploring the theme of paralysis as entrapment, Roche
evokes the meditations on mortality which are threaded through
*Dubliners* – from the opening story, 'The Sisters', to the powerful
conclusion, 'The Dead.' Davy spends much of *Tumbling Down*
processing the loss of his childhood friend, Mickey Fury, who 'ran
away to sea' and subsequently drowned. Because Mickey's body was
never recovered, Davy initially holds out hope that he might still be
alive. But he finally comes to accept Mickey's death when he attends
the funeral of Johnny, the owner of a shoe-repair shop and a regular
at the Shamrock (131):

> I was feeling kind of mixed up to say the least – sad, angry,
> confused, take your pick. I had been at funerals before, mainly
> relatives – aunts and uncles and grannies for the most part –
> but this was different. Johnny had come into my life a stranger.
> I was not compelled to love him or to feel sorry at his death. He
> had earned my love. He had wooed and won my respect, the
> same as Mickey Fury had done all those years ago. And now the
> terrible finality of it all was brought home to me: Mickey Fury
> would not be coming back; he would not turn up out of the blue
> someday, bronzed and bearded; he did not swim ashore to

---

[19] James Joyce, *Dubliners* (New York: Viking Press, 1961): 83.

some primitive island when his ship went down off the coast of Galatz.

Whether or not Roche meant to recall the character of Michael Furey from the final story of *Dubliners*, it is impossible to ignore the resonances between *Tumbling Down* and 'The Dead.' Certainly, Roche's Mickey Fury bears more than a passing resemblance to Joyce's Michael Furey as a gallant young man who dies prematurely under dramatic circumstances. Even more importantly, these characters serve much the same function in their texts, as they force the protagonists to recognize their own limitations. Contemplating the romantic figure of Michael Furey, Gabriel Conroy comes to the sad realization that none of his passions has ever matched that of the youth who once loved Gretta. In a similar way, Davy Wolfe effectively acknowledges the futility of his own dreams when he finally admits that Mickey Fury will never return. He is no more prepared than Gabriel to 'pass boldly into that other world, in the full glory of some passion.'[20] Compared to the ill-fated dreamers they admire so much, these characters are unable to effect real change in their own lives.

The parallels between *Tumbling Down* and *Dubliners* are stylistic as well as thematic. Aiming to produce an accurate picture of his countrymen, Joyce wrote his stories 'in a style of scrupulous meanness and with the conviction that he is a very bold man who dares to alter in the presentment, still more to deform, whatever he has seen and heard.'[21] This uncompromising attitude turned many Irish readers against Joyce both during and after his lifetime. His work was not officially banned under the Censorship of Publications Act (1929), which was intended to protect the conservative values of Catholic Ireland, but many anecdotes suggest that Joyce's books were unofficially blacklisted in Ireland until the late 1960s. The novelist Brian Moore recalls that 'My father, who was a great reader, said to me once, "James Joyce is a sewer." He never read him, but that was the attitude.'[22] Roche dramatizes much the same attitude through Mr. Martin, the retired civil servant who regards Joyce as 'offensive' because he dwells so much upon 'human weaknesses'

---

[20] *Dubliners*: 223.

[21] *Letters of James Joyce*, Volume II: 134.

[22] Quoted in Joseph Brooker, *Joyce's Critics: Transitions in Reading and Culture* (Madison: University of Wisconsin Press, 2004): 188. Brooker provides a succinct history of Joyce's reception in Ireland: 183-231.

(38). Yet *Tumbling Down* itself shows that Roche appreciates Joyce's lifelong effort to move beyond the imaginative idealism of the Irish Literary Revival in order to explore Irish reality more objectively.

Undoubtedly, it was Roche's dedication to Joyce's 'style of scrupulous meanness' that encouraged him to cut some of the more sentimental and humorous passages from his book when he revised *Tumbling Down*. For example, he removed the wistful description of Rowdy Row's young and innocent dreamers that originally appeared at the start of Chapter Three, focusing instead on the grim realities of life for Wexford's 'Lean hungry-looking children' (47). Similarly, he deleted an entire paragraph about 'Heart of My Heart', a nostalgic song that encourages Davy to think about 'how it must have been in old Wexford' and to invent a heroic, golden age of 'rugged gangs laughing and jeering each other' for his unremarkable home town.[23] Roche also eliminated the bumbling detective named Benny Boyle who was featured prominently in the original Chapter Five as a cartoonlike figure. Because of such changes, *Tumbling Down* reads even more like *Dubliners* than it did before.

Despite his own 'scrupulous meanness', however, Roche demonstrates an undeniable affection for his characters. His sympathy is particularly clear in the final paragraph of *Tumbling Down* as Davy describes his sense of devastation after The Shamrock burns to the ground:

> For me it was all over then I'm afraid, and in no time at all the boys vanished from my life like ghost ships in the night. All except Crunch that is, good old El Cruncho. He's still around – a walking, breathing Useless Island. ... I spied him the other day drinking in The Cape of Good Hope, surrounded by a bunch of denim clad jokers. He was painting them a picture of Valparaiso and talking about Indio, running out of hands and words to describe her build. And when he glanced my way his mischievous grin invited me to relive it all again – the love and the loss and the pain, and that awful feeling of being alone for the first time in my life as I stood there, lost in the rain, watching the walls of The Shamrock come tumbling down. (153)

It is tempting to read the fiery demise of The Shamrock as a symbolic precursor of the political crisis that would shortly engulf Ireland, especially because this dramatic event takes place on St.

---

[23] *Tumbling Down* (Dublin: Wolfhound Press, 1986): 56.

Patrick's Day. As R. F. Foster points out, 'the 1960s would end in a conflagration' with the sudden eruption of sectarian violence in Northern Ireland. [24] But Roche does not spell out such broad implications in his climactic scene, nor does he zoom out as far as Joyce does in the denouement of 'The Dead': whereas Gabriel Conroy ends up thronged by 'the vast hosts of the dead', Davy Wolfe ultimately feels abandoned and alone. If he is haunted, it is only by the affectionate figure of 'good old El Cruncho.' Forced to confront the actuality of change within his own life, Davy cannot help but sympathize with the older residents of Wexford who remain resistant to change.

In the end, Roche's sympathy for his characters is hardly surprising, because he is writing about people he came to know personally when he worked at his father's pub as a teenager. The author has always been happy to acknowledge that characters like Forty Winks, Joe Crofton, and Captain Crunch come directly from life, and he made no effort to disguise the autobiographical nature of his novel when he originally submitted it for publication: 'In the first draft of *Tumbling Down* I used real names for the characters, even for Patti and me, but I was calling the town "Slaneyside." Then somehow when the town became Wexford it felt right to change the characters' names and give myself license to create.' [25] Although Roche ultimately altered some details of his experience, he was reluctant to stray too far from the basic facts. The personal element is still obvious in the revised version of *Tumbling Down*: the book's cover features an old photograph of Billy's father, the publican Pierce Roche, playing an accordion – presumably as a representation of Paddy Wolfe.

As an autobiographical coming-of-age story, *Tumbling Down* undoubtedly owes as much to Joyce's *A Portrait of the Artist as a Young Man* as it does to *Dubliners*. Roche could not easily ignore Joyce's first novel, which Eve Patten calls the 'defining text in the development of the twentieth-century Irish autobiographical aesthetic.' [26] But the elegiac tone and realistic style that Roche employs in *Tumbling Down* point to *Dubliners* as the genuine precursor text. Davy Wolfe may very well share the desire of

---

[24] Foster, *Modern Ireland, 1600-1972*: 582.

[25] Quoted in Kerrane: 373.

[26] Eve Patten, '"Life Purified and Reprojected": Autobiography and the Modern Irish Novel', *Modern Irish Autobiography: Self, Nation and Society*, ed. Liam Harte (New York: Palgrave Macmillan, 2007): 53.

Stephen Dedalus to fly by the metaphorical nets that are at the soul in Ireland 'to hold it back from flight.' Davy certainly bristles at the narrow-minded opinions expressed by many of his customers at The Shamrock, the 'begrudging bastards [who] wanted everyone to be tarred with the one brush' (56), and he defies the dictates of the church by rejecting the moral exhortations of two proselytizing priests as 'voodoo' (145). Roche establishes a kinship between Davy and Stephen by having his protagonist utter such rebellious declarations. But he does not try to update the triumphant narrative of the Dedalean artist who manages to overcome the constraints of nationality and religion. Ultimately, therefore, Roche diverges from Joyce by underscoring the historical realities that helped to keep such an escape tantalizingly out of reach for many Irish people during the 1960s, despite the modernizing, liberalizing agenda that was put into place during this period.

## 12 | Billy Roche's *Wexford Trilogy*: Place, Space, Critique*

Christopher Murray

Seamus Heaney, quoting Carson McCullers, says in his essay 'The Sense of Place' that 'to know who you are, you have to have a place to come from.'[1] Irish writing in general is saturated with a sense of place, a topic which formed the theme of a successful IASIL conference in Galway, the *Acta* of which were edited by Andrew Carpenter.[2] The topic has by now probably become something of a cliché. Not only has Hollywood got into the act with such films as *The Field* (1991), based on John B. Keane's play of that name, but virtually every county in Ireland has its anthem celebrating its local landscape in the lyrical hyperbole of the travel brochure. Place has become a marketable commodity. Moreover, the sporting rivalry masterfully exploited by the Gaelic Athletic Association (the GAA) at local, county, and provincial levels throughout the thirty-two counties of Ireland has succeeded over the years in instilling a peculiar loyalty to place indistinguishable in kind from old-fashioned patriotism.

The interesting thing about Billy Roche in this regard is his theatricalizing of place so that it becomes *lieu* in a double sense. On the one hand there is the actual place in mimesis; on the other hand there is place in the theatrical sense *qua* space, which, as Peter Brook says, is only a 'tool' in effecting the transformation of which

---

[1] *Preoccupations: Selected Prose 1968-1978* (London and Boston: Faber and Faber, 1980): 135.

[2] Andrew Carpenter, ed., *Place, Personality and the Irish Writer* (Gerrards Cross: Colin Smythe, 1977).

theatre is capable.[3] The empty space can become the representation of an actual place. Roche plays variations on the two meanings until they interlock in irony, compassion and defiance, interrogating and celebrating small-town life at the same time. It is highly ironic that Roche should have been fêted by Wexford as if he were copywriter to the local branch of Bord Fáilte, since all three plays find fault with the town in which the trilogy is set. In short, Roche proposes social criticism by astute manipulation of synecdoche: the setting within the setting, the part for the whole, the pool hall for the town and the town for the nation. Any small town might have served, as it has served Irish playwrights from Lady Gregory to Frank McGuinness, Conor McPherson, and Eugene O'Brien, but Roche is different in the way he chooses to define his locale. The distance required for detachment was supplied by the actual ('real') setting of the plays in London: their popularity in London was bound up with their neutrality there, where they could be seen as narratives of entrapment. But once that invisible London setting is removed, the plays may be viewed among the long line of expositions and assessments of Irish life which characterizes the Irish tradition.

In what follows I shall examine each of the plays in *The Wexford Trilogy* in turn, emphasizing the continuity of theme and place and examining their interdependence. I shall then attempt a brief assessment, necessarily limited in view of Roche's subsequent work, and a contextualizing of the plays in relation to contemporary Irish drama before the year 2000.

In *A Handful of Stars* we are given a portrait of a teenage rebel, Jimmy Brady, who gets into trouble with the police and is destroyed. Placed in a narrow working-class milieu, Jimmy is shown to have very little room to manoeuvre. An attempt to get a job at the local factory exposes him to the inauthenticity of his surroundings. A seasoned worker in the factory, Conway, immediately accuses Jimmy of currying favour with the management when Jimmy had merely mistaken his interviewer. Conway tells him that this man is not at all what he seemed and is suspected of theft but protected by the management. Since Conway is himself a despicable character who knows how to exploit his position at the factory, Jimmy sees that this is what he himself might become. He looks for ways to be free: he steals to impress Linda, a girl who seems to believe in him

---

[3] Peter Brook, *The Shifting Point: Forty Years of Theatrical Exploration 1946-1987* (London: Methuen, 1988): 147.

for a time, but soon his reckless, lawless ways lead to his being barred entry to dance hall, cinemas and pubs. As society puts on the squeeze, Linda breaks off their relationship and Jimmy goes off the rails.

Staying within the confines of naturalism, where environment counts for a great deal in locating the roots of tragic action, Roche also makes use of heredity. People in the town say that Jimmy takes after his father, a waster and drunkard who is thrown out of his own home and (in disgrace) lives in a dosshouse. He has Jimmy's sympathy. Jimmy sees his father's fate as prognostic of his own. It is that future he rebels against. He mourns, too, how the conditions of time and circumstance have eroded the love and beauty which once his parents' mutual love manifested; he has memories of them dancing happily around the kitchen. Of course, given the conventionality of the culture, Jimmy is overwhelmed with guilt over his mother's sufferings: 'She never says anythin' yeh know. But you can see the torment in her eyes if you look close. She never says a word. She just sort of broods.'[4] This was the woman whom old Paddy recalls as radiantly in love with Jimmy's father: 'To look at her you'd swear she had just swallowed a handful of stars' (50). Hopelessly, Jimmy tries to bring back those stars again.

Undoubtedly, there is a romantic element to Jimmy's attitude. He is a self-dramatizer. An older man, Stapler, who is himself a non-conformist, points out the excess: 'Most of us wage war on the wrong people Jimmy. I do it meself all the time. But you beat the bun altogether ... You wage war on everybody' (64). Stapler is able to accommodate to the moral pressures of a narrow-minded society: he rolls with the punches and goes his own way. But Jimmy feels more keenly Stapler's defeat in a local boxing contest: Stapler is ageing and will be ground down like Jimmy's father. Jimmy looks at his young friend Tony, facing a loveless marriage to a girl who is pregnant, and he despairs. Tony's lot, as Jimmy sees it, is to join the living dead. In contrast, Jimmy goes on a rampage with a shotgun, settles a few scores, does one more robbery, and wrecks the pool hall. All of this is gestural: 'Yeh see that's the difference between me and Conway. He tiptoes around. I'm screamin'' (60). In his afterword, Roche relates Jimmy to the films he (Roche) saw as a

---

[4] *The Wexford Trilogy: A Handful of Stars, Poor Beast in the Rain, Belfry* (London: Nick Hern Books, 1993): 65. Subsequent quotes from the *Trilogy* plays refer to this edition.

young man and to such icons of rebellion as Marlon Brando, James Dean, Steve McQueen, and all the wild ones 'who unknowingly sacrificed themselves so that the rest of us could be set free' (187). The romanticism in the vision is undercut by the word 'unknowingly': Marlon Brando and James Dean could hardly have been aware that they were liberating Wexford.

Roche's point of view is given sharper focus when the stage setting and use of space are taken into account. He confines the action to a snooker hall or poolroom. This move away from the family as setting is significant. To be sure, Tom Murphy, Brian Friel and Tom Kilroy all at various times have forsaken the familiar Irish setting of kitchen, tenement or drawing room, but never without transforming the space into a version of the home. It is as if they all agreed with Arthur Miller when he said in 'The Family in Modern Drama' that the fundamental question to be tackled by the dramatist is, 'How may man make for himself a home in the vastness of strangers and how may he transform that vastness into a home?'[5] The disjunction between home and world is far wider in Roche's work than in any preceding Irish playwright. To that end he chooses settings which are in their ways anti-family: places of gambling, male preserves, places hostile to domestic values. The unit set for *A Handful of Stars* is to an important degree metaphoric. It is a place of play, a club, a lure for the young and a refuge for the middle-aged. With its slot machine, juke box and pool tables, its imagery is obvious. It is significant that when Jimmy brings Linda to the club late at night to do their lovemaking (he breaks in through a window) she soon feels alien: 'I'd prefer to be somewhere else that's all' (38). It is not a setting which Roche wants to transform in any way, as Murphy transforms the church into a home in *Sanctuary Lamp* (1975) or as McGuinness transforms the factory office into a home in *Factory Girls* (1982). The stage space remains doggedly a 'real' pool hall. To the policeman Swan, whose unsympathetic character is a key to the play's criticism of bourgeois order, the pool hall is a school for scoundrels, a 'little den of rogues', an image of a 'waste of a lifetime': only a 'mental pygmy' would frequent such a place (55). Swan scoffs at the name the hall has acquired locally, The Rio Grande, derived no doubt from a diet of cowboy films; he is blind to

---

5 Arthur Miller, 'The Family in Modern Drama', in *The Theater Essays of Arthur Miller*, ed. Robert A. Martin (New York: Viking/Penguin): 85.

the association of the name with a border into Mexico, a safe haven from the law.

The hall is divided in two and the division is important. There is a door upstage leading into a private room to which access is allowed only to members. This is an inner sanctum where, according to the opening stage direction, 'the older, privileged members go'. Inside there is another, unseen, pool table. Young Tony often leaves the outer pool table when he and Jimmy are in a game, to look longingly through the glass panel of the door leading into this 'shrine', as Jimmy mockingly calls it (56). Paddy the caretaker blocks Jimmy's attempt to enter, as if 'it was Fort Knox or somethin'' (24). The area comes to represent society's delusion of progress. It is where the likes of Conway hold sway. Yet, despite his contempt for Conway, Jimmy perceives the inner room as for 'the élite' (33). Such is the mimicry of hierarchical levels provided by this working class construction. There is a similar experience in *Tumbling Down*, where the seventeen-year-old hero perceives the entrance to the private area of a pool hall as 'the forbidden door.'[6] Such doors are shut to Jimmy all over town, even though all there is on the other side is one more pool table.

It is significant that when Jimmy goes berserk, following Linda's rejection of him as a hopeless case, and goes on a rampage around the town with a shotgun, he returns to the pool hall in the middle of the night and wrecks the inner sanctum. In scrawling his name in chalk over the door he tried to find his identity in a society which has branded him an outcast. He always knew that he did not 'belong in there' (34), but the fact is he belongs nowhere but in prison. And yet Jimmy tries to show that the inner sanctum is itself a prison. Ireland's a prison. Point made.

As social comment *A Handful of Stars* could probably be called naïve. Its appeal, however, comes from the youth of the protagonist in conflict with his community over the question of his 'place' within it. As a version of the 'playboy' figure in Irish drama Jimmy Brady is a tragic loser: if he has style it derives from transgression. To an extent he resembles that other Jimmy, that strident rebel of Osborne's *Look Back in Anger* (1956), but he is far more vulnerable, less intellectual, and less articulate. Jimmy Brady's isolation is the most terrible thing about him because his lapse into criminality is a

---

6 Billy Roche, *Tumbling Down*, revised edition (Wexford: Tassel Publications, 2008: 100.

form of suicide. Inevitably, his fate proposes a strong attack on Irish social structures.

Thus what may appear at first sight in Roche's drama to be entirely banal and mimetic, by accumulation and focus of images becomes metaphoric and even symbolic. His realism may be seen to be artfully constructed. The second play in the trilogy, *Poor Beast in the Rain*, bears out this claim. Here the setting is a betting shop, once more a metaphor for play, gaming, or chance. Once more the location is a public resort of somewhat dubious relation to domestic norms. As in the earlier play, a unit set is maintained: all the action, even some unlikely scenes on a Sunday night (when such a shop, especially in the days before Sunday horse-racing began in Ireland, would not be open), takes place in this environment. The action, further, occurs at a time publicly marked as a sporting occasion, the weekend of the All-Ireland hurling final, in which Wexford is competing. The ritual and carnival elements associated with this annual, nationalistic event are used to highlight certain themes Roche explores here, as he expands his concerns beyond the narrow focus of *A Handful of Stars*: heroism, loyalty and freedom.

The plot centres on the return to Wexford of Danger Doyle after ten years to take away the daughter of the woman with whom he illicitly ran away to London. This daughter, Eileen, works in her father Steven's betting shop where the play is set. Much of the earlier part of the play is occupied with the plans by Steven, Joe and Georgie to travel to Dublin for the big game. On Sunday evening, after the game, Danger comes into the shop amid celebrations over Wexford's victory and has to confront many old friends and enemies. Danger is a hero to those who perceive him as a hero, especially to Joe, a former friend who let him down once and caused Danger to be arrested for petty theft but who now basks in nostalgic and fantastic recreations of the past. Danger Doyle is clearly related to an offstage character, Johnny Doran, close kin in turn to Jimmy in *A Handful of Stars*: 'wild' and 'different.' Doran ran away with a carnival troupe and left a girl pregnant: Danger simply ran away with another man's wife. The plot thus concerns the conflict between a subversive and the community.

Somehow the community projects onto Danger Doyle the need for a hero, a theme in Irish drama ever since Synge's *Playboy* (1907). Roche shows the desperation within the community which lives vicariously through such charismatic figures, who, however, bring destruction of one kind or another with them. Reified by the needs of the community, Danger is correlated to the much-talked-about Big Red O'Neill, a fictional Wexford champion hurler of mythic proportions, and the two men are spoken of in the same terms as film stars, e.g. Paul Newman, Jack Nicholson, Robert Redford and Montgomery Clift. A song in praise of Big Red O'Neill grants him heroic status; when Georgie displays Red's team jersey its gigantic size is a source of wonder: 'You'd want to be Charles Atlas to lift it nearly. He'll [Georgie] be a fine fella when that fits him won't he' (93). Danger tries to assure Georgie that it does not matter if he never grows big enough to fill the jersey, that the important thing is to be true to himself, but Georgie is not ready yet to progress to this self-acceptance. Indeed, he confuses the status of his two heroes and is unable to cope with Doyle's honesty over his past weakness.

After the hurling team's victory, Big Red O'Neill, who remains an off-stage character, is accorded almost god-like status. Joe, Steven and Georgie drunkenly identify with his prowess, as if they themselves had somehow beaten the opposition. But Molly forces the recognition that Big Red's supporters are mere parasites. It is interesting that Roche confers on the woman the voice of outspoken honesty which tears away the falsity of public posturing; in Irish drama – in Murphy's iconoclastic plays for example – this role is resoundingly male. To Roche the delusion of heroism is a male construct; its deconstruction is by women's common sense. When Molly turns to Danger Doyle to square accounts, however, she encounters a man who has already seen through the illusory nature of heroism.

Danger Doyle, in this regard, is a most interesting characterization. He comes ready-made, with his lessons learned. He has discovered that relocation in London had changed nothing; the pain of exile and the memory of wrongs done have forged a necessary humility. He is sure of his own identity but cannot help the disabled. On his return he perceives the folly of his exposure to those who will feed off his strength. He compares himself to Óisín (son of Fionn) in the Ulster cycle of Irish sagas, who left Ireland with Niamh of the Golden Hair to live in the Land of Youth (or Promise) for three hundred years. When he pined to see family and friends again in Ireland, Niamh gave him her magic horse but warned Óisín not to dismount or set foot on the soil. Having reached Ireland, Óisín found vast changes, the Fianna all dead and the new race of men puny and Christianized. Stooping to assist some men to lift a huge stone, Óisín fell from his horse and was changed instantly into a blind and withered old man.[7] In his Afterword to The *Wexford Trilogy* Roche comments that the whole of *Poor Beast in the Rain* is 'held together by an ancient Irish Myth as Danger Doyle returns like Óisín to the place of his birth' (188). The play is therefore a reckoning, a coming to terms with the past and a confrontation with the state of exile. Danger Doyle's return is ambivalent to a town which regards him as wrongdoer as well as hero. Doyle is able to discount the heroic badge and accept the role of wrongdoer. In that guise he makes no attempt to address moral issues. It is as if confronting established Christianity (as Óisín confronted Saint Patrick) Danger Doyle is wise enough to avoid criteria which in Ireland can only lead to victory for the Establishment. Of course, Óisín was a poet (as Yeats well knew, for example) and therefore opposed to Saint Patrick's one-dimensional masculinity. Thus Danger Doyle is on the same side as Molly and against the world of graven images, hero worship and doctrinal certainty.

Doyle survives because of his self-awareness; he knows the myth of Óisín. He is careful not to touch the ground, although Molly angrily orders him to 'climb down off of your high horse there mister' (117). He has come single-mindedly for Eileen, who is needed by her mother, ironically as heartbroken in London as Molly is in Wexford. Molly's sense of desolation, her sense that Doyle forgot about her 'like some poor beast that had been left out too long in the rain' (121), is paralleled by the picture of the tearful woman in London (Land of Promise) who is on tranquillizers. Doyle has no cure for the society which produced such casualties. He will not get involved. The most poignant moment in the play occurs when Molly, having moved from expressions of hate to admission of enduring love, puts a final question before exiting: 'What am I goin' to do Danger?' (122). Her life stretches before her bleakly. Danger remains silent and Molly leaves. Dramatically, it is a wonderful exchange. Roche seems to echo the line at the end of Brecht's *The Life of Galileo*: 'Unhappy the land that is in need of heroes.'[8] In Roche's scenario heroes are but fantasies, seeds of emotional pain and disaster.

---

[7] See Peter Berresford Ellis, *A Dictionary of Irish Mythology* (London: Constable, 1987): 188-190.

[8] Bertolt Brecht, *The Life of Galileo*, trans., Desmond I. Vesey (London: Methuen, 1963): 108.

Further, Roche's critique of the community is presented by means of a critique of loyalty. There is an unresolved contradiction here. On the one hand Eileen's mother was justified in running away from Steven, a burnt-out case described among the town's graffiti as a eunuch. Yet Danger Doyle's last words indicate her loyalty to Steven: 'She's still terrible fond of you, yeh know Steven. She'd never let anyone say nothin' against yeh now nor nothin'" (123). Likewise, loyalty to the local hurling team is paraded as a form of patriotism, though it is also a form of evasion of responsibility. Joe, the most foolish offender in this regard, utters the slogan, 'A man without a hometown is nothin'" (108). Steven agrees and adds that such a man is lost. Earlier, Steven had urged, 'Get behind your team. Get behind your town' (86). But by the end of the play, after Molly has nakedly exposed Steven's real disgrace over his wife's leaving him, Steven comments mournfully, 'This town'll be the death of me yet' (122). That is closer to the truth. Roche reveals the pride and the folly of local heroism and easy loyalty.

When Molly asks Danger why he returned to Wexford, he replies: 'I just came back to kiss the cross they hung me on Molly. Or maybe I came back to set you free' (121). Here the question of freedom raises itself. In Roche's analysis, in *A Handful of Stars* and in the plays which follow, there is a determinism governing human affairs which cannot be altered. Jimmy agrees when Tony says towards the end of *A Handful of Stars* that 'it's nobody's fault' what happened to Jimmy, 'Maybe that's just the way it is.' Yet it is, Jimmy insists, both nobody's and everybody's fault: 'Everyone's to blame' (60). The same sentiment governs the action of *Poor Beast in the Rain*. To bring Eileen with him, Danger Doyle must cause her father Steven more pain; to set Molly free he must let her be. Young Georgie is liberated from his adolescent crush on Eileen but not without disillusion. Freedom is entirely relative, and the oscillation between Wexford and London indicates its nature as a no-man's-land. 'Maybe that's just the way it is.' To be sure, this jettisons analysis and mystifies suffering. Yet we have to bear in mind that Danger Doyle is free to return to London, and he goes with Eileen in the end. That space for movement is something Jimmy Brady never had. In imagining that space, Roche is preserving a balance between Synge and Friel, between the playboy's romantic liberation and the Faith Healer's tragic surrender of the urge to intervene.

The third play in the trilogy, *Belfry*, more openly confronts the crisis which Roche accepts as lying at the heart of contemporary

Irish life. *Belfry* is set in a church – thereby recalling Murphy's *Sanctuary Lamp* – and uses two spaces within it, vestry and belfry, to interrogate the forms which permit or destroy fulfilment today. The play marks a considerable advance in complexity over its predecessors, as it uses a narrator to address the audience and manipulates time freely and flexibly. The narrator-hero, Artie, a sacristan, tells the story of his love affair with Angela, a married woman who helps in the church. He tells the story retrospectively, one year after the affair, and thereafter appears within scenes relating to the affair and its consequences, while from time to time breaking the illusion to act once again as chorus. Although the technique is far from novel, it is worth recalling that *Belfry* quickly succeeds *Dancing at Lughnasa* (1990) and is considerably more adept technically than that other Irish play set in a belfry, Michael Harding's *Misogynist* (1990). Roche's play, while addressing a sexual theme in a church setting, avoids metaphysics and/or theological neuroses, the very stuff of Irish plays with priests in them, and explores instead man's place in society (if the class question is taken as settled) and, secondly, the question of freedom, in a larger context than Roche had so far established.

The classless society is noteworthy in *Belfry*. Nobody pulls rank; there is no hierarchical register of language: all speech is demotic. Instead of the priest being in the role of moral superior to all around him, as was conventional in Irish drama before the 1990s, or instead of his perceiving himself in that role and thereby assuming social superiority also, Father Pat is acutely aware of something bogus in his position. Yet when he tries to express this sense of alienation his language belies his experience (165):

> I mean to say Artie nobody talks natural when I'm around in this get up. What am I talkin' about I don't talk normal meself when I'm around. I'm like an auld fella so I am. The things I come out with sometimes I'm not coddin' yeh. Methuselah has nothin' on me I swear. Hello Missus, how are all the care? ... No I'm just not cut out for it Artie. It don't suit me at all sure.

We never hear Father Pat use any other diction than the kind recorded here. It is not the idiom or the vocabulary but the formality and lack of intimacy of which he is aware. His desire to be closer to the people has nothing fundamentally to do with gaucheness; it is not something a crash course in modern communication could put to rights. Essentially, Father Pat, like the Abbot in Brian Moore's novella *Catholics* (1972), has lost what used to be called his vocation. It disturbs him that he has no answers for a dying man so overwhelmed by suffering that 'He was like a man with no soul inside of him' (146). He regrets not having a woman and children in his life: 'I mean it's a queer auld lonely life boy' (165). These confessions are made to Artie, his own sacristan, *servus servorum*. Change places and, handy dandy, which is the sacristan, which is the priest? Indeed, Father Pat puts the question, 'Fancy tradin' places with me Artie ... , no?' (146). 'Places' in this sense is a vocational and not a class concept. Dramatically, Roche does change 'places': he de-centres the priest and makes the sacristan the centre of attention in this play. We are asked to see Father Pat as trapped in the same way as most of the characters in the play. When he takes to drink in Act 2 we are informed that this has happened before, and that it is Artie's role to care for him and bring him through the crisis. Roche makes it clear that the crisis is chronic, signifying a society in transition towards greater secularism. As to the question of freedom, it must be emphasized that Artie's sexual awakening, which forms the plot of the play, exists in an amoral atmosphere. Neither guilt nor reprobation comes into the picture. Artie is not judged. Father Pat makes no comment on the affair, although it is clear in the last scene that he knows about it. The focus is instead on Artie's Laurentian (as in D.H. Lawrence's novels) release in middle age through sex with Angela: this release creates his re-birth, as Artie tells Angela (161). Oddly enough, the long-term effects of the affair have to do with Artie's initiation into the life of snooker halls, betting shops and card games. These are, perhaps, macho pursuits and so represent the wimpish Artie's self-realization; more importantly, they are the pursuits for which Artie's mother specifically condemned his absent father: 'He was a corner boy of the highest order' (174). By adopting and indeed mastering his father's unapproved life style, Artie liberates himself from his mother's influence. The fact that she is kept offstage, a conscious alteration of the first draft of the play, is noteworthy, according to Roche's comment in his Afterword (188). She is dying and this, too, is significant. Roche is celebrating the enfeebling of the matriarchal power structure, including that of mother church, in Irish society.

Angela's part in this process is less obvious. She is clearly a modern, liberated woman. It is she who seduces Artie in the belfry, a profane space, then, atop a sacred one. She it is, too, who declares the affair at an end in spite of Artie's protestations. There is a reversal here of conventional characterization (in Irish drama at this time), as the woman is empowered both to initiate and to terminate a sexual relationship. But Angela's motive in ending the affair leaves an open question. Once her husband Donal finds out, she puts an end to the romance with Artie. Her reaction is detached and unfeeling: 'We got caught Artie and now it's over. I thought you understood that' (161). Since her husband later tells Artie that she has begun another affair, one has to see Angela as promiscuous, and yet Roche will not have her judged. He simply reverses the stereotype of the sex-driven male. Donal's attitude is protective; he sees his role, finally, as ensuring that Angela has 'somewhere to come home to' (82). This is certainly a new note in Irish literature: one could compare John B. Keane's *The Change in Mame Fadden* (1971), for a more conventional depiction of reception of women's sexual/familial problems in Irish society. By retaining Angela within the social structure, however precariously, Roche calls for a tolerance and a liberation from traditional mores. But he shows at the same time how Angela is both free and conventionally trapped, a Miss Julie of rural Ireland.

It is necessary to clarify here the means by which the secret love affair is disclosed to Donal. Roche candidly makes use of the old-fashioned device of the anonymous letter. He often uses newspapers' reports, letters, photographs and diary records in his plays and they have the effect of installing characters in some kind of historical existence. For example, Jimmy Brady has by heart a newspaper account of one of his adventures with the police in *A Handful of Stars*; he pins up a copy in the pool hall. His identity, the one he tries to create for himself, hangs on that piece of paper. As it happens, the anonymous letter in *Belfry* serves to enable Artie also to create his new identity. When he eventually sees the incriminating letter, he recognizes the handwriting as his mother's, and the discovery reinforces his determination to seek out his father. In the attic at home (i.e. off-stage) Artie finds a letter from his father asking his mother to join him in England and to marry him there, which she refused to do. The two letters are brought into alignment as Artie subsequently contacts his father and, after his mother's death, arranges to meet him in England. Likewise, the two spaces, belfry and attic, correspond as sites of secrecy, ambivalently presented as places of storage and of love. When Donal gives Artie the anonymous letter, he looks out of the window of the belfry at the world below: 'A Town Without Pity! Did yeh ever see that picture Artie? Kirk Douglas. It was good' (181). The audience, too, sees the town without pity, yet it also sees the belfry as the site of Artie's rebirth.

The politics of *Belfry* are brought more sharply into focus through the character of Dominic, a slightly retarded teenager, who is an eccentric altar boy in the church. His mental state gives him the licence of a jester to speak home truths openly. He has no sense of awe before priest, sacristan or woman. He is the voice of vulnerability within a society which decides to lock him up in a special school. It is interesting that there is a somewhat similar character in Jim Nolan's *Moonshine* (1991), staged by the Red Kettle Company in Waterford. In that play Michael is accorded an innocence at odds with the deception and death all around him, and through his involvement in a production of *A Midsummer Night's Dream* he assumes a voice articulating the darkness. He works, paradoxically, to bring light and hope into the lives of the main characters in *Moonshine*. Where priests fail, such characters supply spiritual illumination in recent Irish drama. In *Belfry*, Dominic dies accidentally and absurdly, killed by a passing car when he runs away from the special school. Yet he, too, is a catalyst. His place in society reflects on Artie. Dominic, like Artie, is illegitimate; he too is in search of some degree of happiness. It is interesting, recalling Arthur Miller's essay once again, that Dominic tries to make a home in the belfry and that his proudest possession is a massive key to the church. But Artie needs the belfry himself for his love-nest, and Artie unforgivably beats Dominic violently and cruelly in the belfry when he believes it was he who sent the anonymous letter to Angela's husband. So, like Michael in *Moonshine*, Dominic knows the darkness in the lives and hearts of those who are supposed to care for him.

Dominic loves to go up to the belfry to play the bells (workable properties on stage), which Artie allows him to do. On one occasion, however, Dominic causes trouble when instead of a standard hymn he rings out a Rolling Stones number, 'I Can't Get No Satisfaction.'[9] It is the one occasion when Father Pat loses his temper, as if his own position in the community has been undermined. Dominic's choice of tune, however, forms a keynote not just to *Belfry* but indeed for the trilogy as a whole. The characters can get no 'satisfaction',

---

[9] Because of copyright issues, the song was later changed, both in performance and in subsequent published versions of the play, to 'The House of the Rising Sun.'

although yearning for it in many forms. Dominic further expands on this need. He describes a trip which the school arranged to a hotel to hear a comedian: 'My job here today, says he, is to make you people happy.' Dominic decides that when he grows up he too will make people happy, and he describes how (177):

> Easy. I'll get them all in a big room, right. And I'll say to them, 'My job is to make you people happy. What do yez want?' And when they tell me what they want I'll give it to them and I'll say to them, 'Now are yez happy?' And when they say yes I'll give them all what they want again. I'll do that about ten times boy. I'm not coddin' yeh I'll sicken them all so I will. They'll never want to be happy again.

Beckett could hardly have put it better. If we take Dominic's voice to be, paradoxically, the voice of sanity in the play, we can conclude that Roche is saying that happiness in the popular sense of the word is an illusion. His plays are less soft-centred than may at first appear. One may contrast, of course, the politically concerned playwrights in Britain since the time of Osborne, and by such a standard find Roche lacking in political attack. Howard Brenton, after all, entitled one of his plays *Weapons of Happiness* (1976), and he has made no secret of his belief that drama should indeed be a weapon. [10] Roche, on the other hand, does not regard drama as instrumental for social change, or as a weapon of happiness: 'I worry about the vulgarity of political banner waving.'[11] *Belfry*, like its two predecessors in *The Wexford Trilogy*, makes its points in non-political terms, but it would be foolish at the same time to deflect the social and political implications of all three plays.

Indeed, to say that Roche is not overtly a political playwright is to say that he is entirely in tune with contemporary Irish dramatists. Apart from Frank McGuinness, Michael Harding and, more recently, Gary Mitchell, playwrights in Ireland today are cultivating a style of drama which turns away from specific problems, such as Northern Ireland. Young writers in particular, Sebastian Barry, Dermot Bolger, Declan Hughes, Paul Mercier, Marina Carr, Jim Nolan, are mining material which avoids directly topical or political issues. Martin McDonagh is probably a special case, a parodist, a

---

[10] Howard Brenton, 'Petrol Bombs through the Proscenium Arch', in *New Theatre Voices of the Seventies*, ed., Simon Trussler (London and New York: Methuen, 1981): 85-97.

[11] 'Tumbling Down to London: Claudia Woolgar Talks to Billy Roche about His Plays', *Theatre Ireland*, 29 (Autumn 1992): 6.

subversive, and yet *his* trilogy – *The Beauty Queen of Leenane* (1996), *A Skull in Connemara* (1997), and *The Lonesome West* (1997) – shows signs of familiarity with Roche's. What interests these writers is the confusion in which they find themselves emotionally and culturally. They shy away from politics as from a pit that has ensnared the past generation of writers. If the young writers address topical questions it is in terms of satire only, as Gerry Stembridge packed out the Project with his send-up of the abortion debate, *Love Child* (1992) and his irreverent hunting of sacred elephants in *The Gay Detective* (1996). Mostly, this current generation of playwrights is bored stiff with Mother Machree, Cathleen ní Houlihan, her four green fields and all the rest of it. Their appeal is to audiences, equally young and disaffected, who can respond to a search for new ways of regarding experience, far from the religious orthodoxies and political concerns of their parents. In turning inward on their own sense of being lost and betrayed, contemporary dramatists are creating new narratives of Ireland's shifting place in the world.

Although slightly older than the latest crop of successful writers, Roche is part of this new movement in Irish drama. *The Wexford Trilogy* encapsulates new attempts to define a sense of place, to use stage space, and to define freedom and identity yet again in terms divorced from those used by Friel, Murphy, Kilroy and others. Technically, Roche's plays display a rapid development towards masterly control over theme and stage. Indeed, he is the master of extra-familial space in the Irish theatre. *Amphibians* shows Roche continuing to experiment in this regard: the controlling image is of evolution and its pains, the pains of growth towards some kind of maturity. Here and in the trilogy Roche acknowledges that he is dramatizing social transition. There is certainly nothing utopian about his depiction of contemporary Ireland. Even though the plays all have a basis in popular sentiments, and revel in the non-intellectual, they focus firmly on existential and spiritual dislocation. Roche recognizes and articulates the crisis of spirit Ireland is now undergoing. His interrogation of notions of heroism and freedom in a setting historically associated with the rising of 1798 and 'The Boys of Wexford' has reverberations which extend far beyond local significance.

It is ironic, finally, to note Roche's own reaction to his public reception in Wexford in January 1993. 'I grew up in spite of this town, not because of it. I received no encouragement in my writing.

You love the place you come from, and hate it, because you have a stake in it.' [12] In *The Wexford Trilogy* we have thus a quiet revaluation of our much-vaunted sense of place.

* A slightly longer version of this essay first appeared in *Études Irlandaises*, and I would like to thank the editor of that journal, Jacqueline Genet, for the permission to republish it. The original version was also included in *Theatre Stuff: Critical Essays on Contemporary Irish Theatre*, ed. Eamonn Jordan (Dublin: Carysfort Press, 2000).

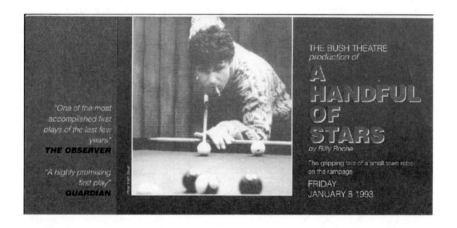

**Figure 5:** Poster from the 'Billy Roche Weekend' (1993), featuring Aiden Gillen as Tony, friend and foil to Jimmy Brady. Photograph by Mark Douet.

---

[12] Quoted by Paddy Woodworth, 'Wexford Celebrates the Work of Local Playwright', *Irish Times*, 11 January 1993.

## 13 | Nearly Never Reaches: Male Friendship in the *Wexford Trilogy*

Belinda McKeon

In certain productions of Sean O'Casey's *Juno and the Paycock*, there is a moment, unscripted by the playwright, which starkly reveals the true nature of the friendship between 'Captain' Jack Boyle and his constant companion, Joxer Daly. In the play's final scene, as the two men emerge from the pub in a state of extreme drunkenness to stagger their way back to the Captain's tenement flat, the Captain fumbles a coin from the pocket of his trousers, but is too far gone to notice. He is too far gone, also, to realize that this is his last coin, and that he has now lost everything, for not only is his home stripped of all its furnishings, but his wife Juno and daughter Mary have walked out on him, and his only son, Johnny, has been killed for betraying a fellow member of the IRA. When Joxer sees the coin fall, he waits for his moment, waits until the Captain's back is turned, and then he pounces, pocketing the money with a sly grin. The message to us is clear: Boyle may be in the company of his only friend, his 'butty', but he is truly alone. His wife and daughter have also found themselves in a grim predicament at the close of the play; not only is Johnny dead, but Mary is pregnant with the child of a man who has abandoned her. 'My poor little child that'll have no father', she wails to her mother. 'It'll have what's far better', Juno responds. 'It'll have two mothers.' Against the vision of such a defiantly united front in the face of hardship, the Captain's situation looks even more desolate still. But he has brought it on himself. He and Joxer have attempted to live in a kind of Tír na nÓg – the mythical land of eternal youth – evading responsibility, drinking the hours away, refusing to follow up on offers of work when they come. Now, like Óisín in the legend of Tír na nÓg, they must let their feet touch the hard ground of reality, and deal with the consequences. In this, the two old friends are unlikely to be of much comfort to one another.

For the men of Billy Roche's *Wexford Trilogy*, too, the business of being a man is a lonesome one, no matter how many men there are around. The first play in the Trilogy, *A Handful of Stars* (1988), enacts a moment reminiscent of Joxer's theft of the Captain's last coin, and this moment becomes a microcosm of the subtle and nuanced consideration of male friendship which Roche sets up in the Trilogy as a whole. Jimmy, the young tearaway in *A Handful of Stars*, has gone on a drunken stealing spree, and comes into the pool hall in which the play is set, more money in his pockets than he knows how to handle; he scatters coins all over the floor.[1] Two older characters see these coins, each at a different moment, and they pick them up, each in a different way; the obnoxious Conway grins to himself with more malice than Joxer could ever have mustered, while old Paddy, the caretaker of the pool hall, helps himself to some of the coins with no obvious pleasure. Within this moment, we see the twin poles of how men will most overtly relate to one another in the Trilogy: a gleeful one-upmanship or a grim passivity. One man delights at taking advantage of the younger man; the other man does what will be done, recognizing the inevitability of it but not finding it anything to grin about. Roche's plays create a dynamic in which older men know the world, and watch as younger men stumble into the mistakes which will eventually, painfully, bring them to a form of that same knowledge. But there can be nothing as simple as teaching and learning. There can be nothing as simple as returning to the young man the coins he has scattered. He must discover their loss, and the lack of them, for himself. Roche's men must find their own way. Their scattered coins are not handed back to them.

The plays of the Trilogy take place in territories which in some sense recall the situation in which we leave the Captain: dilapidated spaces in which men are largely left to their own devices, with only rare female intervention, and with a forced and often desperate sense of conviviality. In these territories – the shabby pool hall of *A Handful of Stars*, the betting shop of *Poor Beast in the Rain* (1989),

---

[1] Billy Roche, *The Wexford Trilogy*, revised edition (London: Nick Hern, 2000): 23. Subsequent references to the plays are drawn from this edition.

and even the church belfry in *Belfry* (1991) – men gather to try and escape the world outside. Within these spaces, they try to make and control a world of their own. 'I mean, I come in here to get away from women', Jimmy, the young rebel in *A Handful of Stars,* says to his girlfriend Linda when she visits him in the pool hall. 'And look at the state of poor Paddy with yeh. He's nearly after havin' a hernia in there. I mean to say Paddy don't even like lads with long hair comin' in here, never mind girls' (16). Paddy, the old man who acts as caretaker in the pool hall, certainly does seem to react negatively to the appearance of the play's only female character; he watches her with 'a vexed expression', we are told, and frowns, too, on a later visit, 'condemning her presence' (48). In *Poor Beast in the Rain,* meanwhile, the hapless Joe, who spends all his time backing horses and reminiscing about his glory days with his own old 'butty', Danger Doyle, voices his dissatisfaction at the fact that women, as well as men, are this year travelling on the bus which has been organized to take local people to see Wexford play in the All-Ireland Hurling Final. ' ... when you and me were runnin' the show we had none of this auld codology did we?' he says to Steven, the owner of the betting shop. 'It was strictly a money on the counter, men only affair' (72). As for the belfry of the Trilogy's final play, it cannot be argued that this is a place in which women are entirely unwelcome; the life of middle-aged Artie is brightened beyond measure when he begins an affair with Angela, the married woman who does the church flowers, but it's very clear that her entrance into this space has changed the accepted order in a manner which can only cause upheaval. 'Little did poor auld Boyle the tailor realize that the day would come when a woman would be ringin' his funeral bell', says Artie, and Angela responds with a comment which, for a man who describes himself as 'the poor little sacristan with the candle grease on his sleeve' (127), is likely a little too close to the bone: 'It was probably the nearest he ever got to a woman in his life' (136).

Logically, then, these men should be content when they are left alone with one another in their men-only clubs. But they are not. The belfry offers something like sanctuary to the 'simple-minded' altar boy, Dominic, to the troubled, alcoholic priest, Father Pat – even, for a while, to Angela's husband, Donal – but when the good-natured banter and chat of these men is examined more closely, it seems to consist only of hackneyed phrases, of cheap jokes and stories (171-172):

**DONAL.** A man, a fox, a dog and a cat had to get to the other side of this river, right. But the man only had a small raft and so he could only take one of them at a time. How did he do it? ... Bearin' in mind now that the dog'll ate the cat and the fox'll kill the dog if he leaves them alone together. How did he do it? The fox and the cat won't touch one another now.
**DOMINIC.** Well he brought the fox over first, right.
**DONAL.** Yeah and the dog'll ate the cat on him!
**DOMINIC.** Oh yeah, I forgot about that! (...)
**PAT.** *(Chuckling.)* That's a good one Donal.
**DONAL.** What? (Donal looks at Pat and laughs.)
**DOMINIC.** Alright I'll ask you one. What did the monkey say when he sat on the razor blade? And they're off! Do yeah get it? They're off! *(He laughs.)*

Father Pat knows more than anyone else how little sustenance there is to be gained from artificial conversation, and it is no coincidence that he is mired in perhaps the most exclusively male territory of all. Late in the play, when he loses his resolve and begins to drink again, Father Pat comes to Artie desperate for help, actually ringing the church bell as 'a sort of an S.O.S' (165):

**ARTIE.** What's wrong with yeh now?
**PAT.** This is a queer lonely auld life Artie yeh know.
**ARTIE.** I know.
**PAT.** I've no friends or anythin'.
**ARTIE.** What are yeh talkin' about? You've lashin's of friends.
**PAT.** No. I've lashin's of acquaintances yeah. No friends though. Thanks to this garb here. I mean to say Artie nobody talks natural when I'm around in this get-up. What am I talkin ' about, I don't talk normal myself when I'm around. I'm like an auld fella so I am. The things I come out with sometimes I'm not coddin' yeh. Methuselah has nothin' on me I swear. Hello missus, how are all the care?

The priest is drunk when he turns to Artie with his worries, but that he feels able to do so is significant nonetheless, and this scene taps into a vein of compassion which runs deep in Roche's dramatic vision. Yet for the characters of his *Trilogy*, compassion is badly needed, and hard won. The titles of two of the plays may stem from the emotional states of women – *A Handful of Stars* from the lost happiness of Jimmy's mother, and *Poor Beast in the Rain* from the cleaning woman Molly's grief at having been abandoned years previously by Danger Doyle – but what the *Trilogy* depicts most powerfully is the loneliness of men. Roche's men need one another, in ways which they find difficult to admit; in ways they find more difficult still to negotiate. As Molly tells Danger Doyle of the impact his sudden departure made on his old friend Joe: 'Yeah well Joe woke up one mornin' to find that there was a great big hole in his life yeh see. He's been tryin' to fill it up ever since' (96). What Roche's men discover, often painfully, is that it is not just the absence of a sidekick that leaves 'a great big hole' in life; such a chasm can be glimpsed and felt, too, even in the midst of apparent camaraderie. Roche's male characters can nearly trust one another, can nearly rely on each other; no more than that. But 'nearly never reaches', as young Georgie says in *Poor Beast in the Rain*, when the horse he has backed fails to make it first to the finish line (69).

Sweetly smitten with Eileen, the girl who works in her father's betting shop, Georgie in *Poor Beast* is a character whose vulnerability is very clear. He is not yet a man, and though they do so fondly, the older characters do not hesitate to remind him of this fact at every turn. At a previous hurling match, Georgie was lucky enough to catch the discarded jersey of the legendary Big Red O'Neill, and he carries it with him like a kind of talisman. 'By Jaysus you'll be a fine fella when that fits yeh', says Molly (84). Georgie is not as innocent as Dominic, the young altar boy in *Belfry* whom the stage directions actually describe as 'simple-minded' (128), but like Dominic, who constantly repeats phrases and stories of Artie's, Georgie is something of a sponge for the views and verdicts of those around him, even where his self-image is concerned: 'I'll be a fine fella when that fits me won't I?' he says to Steven, a few moments after Molly has teased him about the jersey. And that he believes everything he is told by other people is key to his eventual disappointment. Instead of disregarding Molly when she drops petty hints about Eileen's past relationship, Georgie turns to an older man, Joe, for clarification (91):

> **GEORGIE.** Don't mind me askin' yeh Joe, but what's Molly always hintin' at about Eileen? (...)
> **JOE.** Ah yeh know Molly. She's probably tryin' to make out that Eileen is the same as her ma at the back of it – a bit of a skeet goin' around.
> **GEORGIE.** How can she say that Joe?

Joe, barely paying attention to what he is saying, reveals that Eileen is believed to have had sex with her previous boyfriend; he then returns to his own preoccupation with the arrival of the bus to Croke Park. But Georgie, we're told, is 'devastated' by what he has heard, and for the remainder of the play, he will be a darker, more troubled person. Joe's shrugging attempt at a disclaimer – 'Anyway it was just a rumour' – is very far from the kind of guidance and advice Georgie needs from the older man; the next day, when Georgie, drunk and distressed, turns once more to Joe for guidance, physically reaching for him and saying 'This is important', Joe is just as casual, telling him merely to 'Forget about Eileen ... Forget about her', before pulling himself away from Georgie's grip (113). At the close of the play, Georgie, the boy who gazed wistfully at Eileen in the opening scenes, is shouting in the street and 'laughing manically.' His sensitivity has been replaced by a coarseness which sees him mock another man, Danger Doyle, for once having shown emotion: 'the big hard man cryin' his eyes out up in the courtroom' (120). He has been cruel, too, to Eileen, and she has made her decision to leave for England.

Georgie's disadvantage may be that he has no boy his own age to knock about with, in the way that Joe and Danger Doyle knocked about the neighbourhood in their day. And yet the companionship of a peer seems to be of negligible advantage to the younger men in *A Handful of Stars*, Jimmy and Tony, whom we meet in the play's first scene, fighting over the pool hall's one good cue. Jimmy is clearly the more dominant of the boys, easily winning the struggle (4):

> **JIMMY.** Look stop whingein' and fire.
> **TONY.** I don't see why I should always end up with the bad cue.

Jimmy's goading of his friend continues as we watch the two boys interact; he forces Tony to claim miscued shots and then steals shots of his own, and when Tony expresses a desire to go to a new film in the local cinema, Jimmy ruins the ending for him – 'He gets shot right between the eyes in the end' (7).

And yet there is more to Jimmy's behaviour than mere meanness, or casual cruelty; there are signs that an insecurity about losing his friend, and a jealousy that is in its way almost romantic, may well be the true motive for Jimmy's selfish spoiling of Tony's film. Jimmy insists, not once but three times, that he and Tony have already seen it together, something denied by Tony, who likely wants to see the film with his new girlfriend, Mary. At a later point in the play, Jimmy exhibits a similarly childish jealousy when Tony – who is now in fact engaged to Mary, having gotten her pregnant – needs to run wedding-related errands instead of spending time with his friend in the pool hall. In fact, learning that Tony needs to meet his fiancée for an hour, Jimmy goes into a rage, sweeping the snooker balls from the table, 'ending the game prematurely' (49). He may be a tearaway in general, but such conduct still comes across as extreme; clearly, the prospect of losing his right-hand man affects him deeply. When Jimmy goes off the rails in the latter part of the play, robbing local stores and rampaging with a shotgun, the break-up of his relationship with Linda stands as the most obvious trigger; but the loss of Tony is arguably just as much of a crisis for him. When Jimmy knows that he is cornered, Tony is the only person he will trust to go to the police for him: 'I want you to go up to the barracks and tell them where to find me' (54). He needs and indeed demands Tony's help, and insists that he will not drag Tony down with him (57):

> **JIMMY**. (*Jimmy eyes his woebegone friend.*) Look if you're worried about gettin' the blame for this don't. I'll tell them that you had nothin' to do with it. Okay?
> **TONY**. That doesn't matter.
> **JIMMY**. It does matter.

Of course, what Tony knows is that the favour Jimmy has asked of him is one that might potentially bring as much trouble for him, Tony, as it will for the fugitive Jimmy; Tony knows that there is a good chance that he will be implicated, or beaten, at the very least held in a cell for the night, by the detective Swan and his cronies, and with his wedding in the morning, this is not an attractive prospect for Tony. But Jimmy cannot see the nuances of the predicament; like a frightened child, he merely wants what he wants – and indeed what he wants, he confesses in a moving moment, is for his estranged parents to speak to one another again, something which he believes his rampage might bring about: 'But sure maybe this'll get them talkin' again if nothing else. It'd be gas wouldn't it?' (65). Asking the help of either parent is not an option; his friend is the only person to whom Jimmy feels able to turn. Roche, however, does not close *A Handful of Stars* with any easy or sentimental resolution of the tension in which the young friends thus find themselves locked; an older man, Stapler, enters the scene and, reading the situation, volunteers to go to the barracks himself. Tony and Jimmy's goodbye is muted and ambiguous; indeed, it is not clear at the play's end whether Jimmy truly intends to wait for the police or is instead intending to make another dramatic move, possibly involving the shotgun he has hidden. Only one thing is for certain: as he crouches by the jukebox in the half-light of the club, lighting another cigarette, he is utterly alone.

But if his younger men are drifting, Roche's older characters in the Trilogy are for the most part truly at sea. The mythic friendship of Danger Doyle and Joe is central to the tragicomic energy at the heart of *Poor Beast in the Rain*; with his highly embellished stories of their glory days, Joe recalls Synge's *Playboy* and the 'great gap between a gallous story and a dirty deed' (76):

> **JOE.** Poor auld Danger. We made fellas hop around here me and him I don't mind tellin' yeh. Me and Danger. We were the kingpins in this town at the time so we were. Danger and me. Yes, the kingpins we were ...

In Joe's mind, he and Danger were a duo of cinematic stature: 'Butch Cassidy and the Sundance Kid.' And, he tells Georgie, he feels sure that Danger looks back on their reign with the same affection: ' ... not blowin' me own trumpet or anything, but I think I can safely say that he wouldn't mind seein' me again either' (77). However, when Danger makes an unexpected return after a decade's absence from the town, it's no great surprise to learn that his own memories of Joe's cherished days are very different; to Danger, those days were hardly worth remarking on at all, except for the betrayal by Joe which occurred when they attempted to break into the betting shop together (93-94):

> **DANGER.** You were outside keepin' nix. Or supposed to be keepin' nix I should say. ... next thing I know I've set off some sort of an alarm and there was cops swarmin' all over me. No sign of your man here at all of course.
> **JOE.** I whistled out to yeh Danger.
> **DANGER.** Yes yeh did yeah. Yeh must have whistled under your breath then because I never heard yeh.

Although Joe wants to insist that the legend of Danger still endures, Danger is a realist. He knows that the fallout from his reason for leaving the town – he ran away with Eileen's mother, Steven's wife – will have been significant, and there are signs, too, that in the intervening years he has learned that manhood is not just a matter of outward swagger and rebellion. In a Trilogy so deeply preoccupied with notions of masculinity, a very significant moment occurs when Danger readily admits to having wept in the courtroom as he was charged with the betting shop break-in all those years ago. Joe seems to want to protect Danger, still, from the truth about this unmanful display, believing, perhaps, that to betray him in this would be a far worse betrayal than that which occurred under the betting shop window (94):

**JOE.** I'll never forget that boy. Danger gettin' led in with a great pair of handcuffs on him and he nearly cryin'. It was queer funny.
**DANGER.** What do yeh mean nearly cryin'? I was cryin'.

It is hard not to attribute some significance, too, to Joe's use of the adjective 'queer' in this context, since it is not a word he uses elsewhere in the play. Outright homophobia, or indeed outright homoeroticism, have a very subtle presence in the *Trilogy*, but, inevitably in plays so intimately concerned with male relationships, they are present, and in each case that presence tends to arise where emotion is being displayed more openly or more fully than these men would prefer or with which these men would feel comfortable. Hence, to Joe it was not merely funny but 'queer funny' that Danger cried in court (94). Meanwhile, the general euphoria and excitement of Wexford's victory in the All-Ireland Hurling Final are such, it seems, that certain distancing jokes have to be made: Joe quips that all those heading up to Dublin on the bus 'will probably end up sleepin' in the one bed' (72), and later says of Red O'Brien's winning goal that it was so 'deadly' that 'Meself and Mickey Morris kissed and hugged one another so hard that people started wonderin' about us' (107). In *A Handful of Stars*, a more sneering hint of homophobia emerges, as Jimmy comments on Conway's apparent obsequiousness at work: 'When I was in there havin' the interview Conway's tongue came slidin' in under the door. Quick as yeh can says O'Brien to me, get your back to the wall.' (18). Meanwhile, Jimmy's apparent jealousy in relation to Tony's approaching marriage and his departure from the tight knot of their own dynamic surfaces in a physical struggle which seems to have something of a sexual charge: '*As Tony bends to take his shot Jimmy springs up behind him and rams the cue between his legs so that Tony is raised up and suspended in mid air. ... Jimmy throws himself on top of Tony, climbing up on him, throwing his leg over him as Tony tries halfheartedly to fight him off*' (45).

If the business of being a man is a lonely one, the business of being able to call oneself a man is one over which Roche's characters obsess, even when they have ostensibly long since reached that milestone. But for the younger characters, there exists an enormous preoccupation with the achievement of becoming a man. Dominic, in *Belfry*, is much more obviously a child and, out of sympathy for his nature, the older characters allow him to remain that way; but in the other two plays, the fact that Jimmy, Tony and Georgie are still boys provides the older characters with ammunition to use against them. Stapler, Paddy and Conway insist on calling them names like 'boy' and 'son', while Molly calls Georgie a 'little get' (84) and Joe largely dismisses his affection for Eileen. But it matters hugely to these young men that they would be able to frame themselves as men. To Tony, such an accolade would seem to come along with admission to the private members' room in the snooker club; he longs for this. Jimmy's anger is easily sparked when he is reminded that his youth renders him somehow less of a man than his older counterparts. He mouths off about making a bet with Conway, but Conway effortlessly gains the upper hand, because he has the money to make the bet and Jimmy does not (14). There is a sense that, when Jimmy goes on his rampage, stealing from local shops, it is as much to have the money to place this bet as for the reason he states, which is to bring his girlfriend on a date.

Jimmy, though, is at the same time conscious of having ammunition of his own; his youth may hold him back, but it also renders him physically superior to the older men around him. When Conway pries into Jimmy's reasons for having visited the factory earlier that day, belittling his chances of getting a job or of impressing Linda, Jimmy is ready for him with a retort with which Conway can hardly argue (12-13):

> **JIMMY**. I took one good look out the window and I saw all these grown men walkin' around dressed up like peasants and I decided there and then that it wasn't for the likes of me after all. (*Conway opens up his overcoat to reveal his overalls.*)
> **CONWAY.** It takes a good man to fill one of these boy and don't you ever forget it. (*Jimmy reaches across and tugs roughly at Conway's overalls around the groin area.*)
> **JIMMY**. I'd say it's a queer long time since you went next or near to fillin' that up then is it?
> **CONWAY.** Hey, don't let the grey hairs fool yeh poor man.
> **JIMMY**. It's not just the grey hairs Conway. It's the bags under the eyes and the green teeth and the fat belly ...

Callow and reckless, Jimmy ribs Conway cruelly about the many signs of ageing which the older man is already exhibiting, even though he is only in his mid-thirties. He will be cruel in this way to a still older man, Paddy: he teases him about his underwear showing – 'Supposin' a couple of young ones walked in here now. You'd drive them into a frenzy, so you would' (22). Later he tells Paddy: 'don't give your heart a hernia' (24). Jimmy hits a nerve with these remarks to Conway and Paddy, and he knows it; the fact of their growing older is something with which Conway and Stapler, in particular, have not made peace. Paddy may not care that he is old now, but Conway and Stapler do. Stapler competes in a boxing match in which he has no chance, and later, after he has been badly beaten by a much younger man, Conway remarks to the detective, Swan, that Stapler is now too physically deteriorated: 'you'd want to be a young lad for that game' (30). In *Belfry*, Donal, the married man who is in the same age group as Conway and Stapler, is beaten by a younger man in a handball game and sinks into a depression: 'Donal is still down in the dumps over that auld handball match', says Angela. 'The young fella ran rings around him I heard. He won't go out nor nothin' now. He just mopes around the house all day drinkin' mugs of tay. I think he feels it's the end of an era or somethin'. And maybe he's right. ' (141).

But if it's the end of an era for Donal and men like him, it's the waste of an era for Jimmy, Tony and Georgie, as well as for the ultimately tragic Dominic; these are young men on the thresholds of their lives, right on the cusp of what life might offer, and in each case, it would seem, they destroy any chance to better themselves, to pull themselves out of the dingy, all-male ruts in which they are already stuck. Jimmy will go to jail; Tony must marry his pregnant girlfriend; Georgie loses the girl he loves and seems to have become an altogether angrier, less pleasant person, and Dominic, by *Belfry*'s end, has been struck by a car on yet another attempt to escape the industrial school to which he has been sent. Of the four characters, of course, Dominic has had the least chance of all, but Artie truly believes that a year or two in the industrial school will enable him to get a job. Instead, he dies when he is barely a teenager, let alone a man. For him, as for the others, it's hard not to see a metaphor in the scene in *Poor Beast* in which Eileen crosses the non-runners off the board, or in the mentions of things – cribs, suits – being acquired on the 'never never.' Nearly never reaches, as Georgie says. And these young men will never reach what they might.

Stapler, in *A Handful of Stars*, knows why a situation of this sort might arise; it's not as though he and his peers provide any great role models for boys like Jimmy and Tony (51-52):

> **STAPLER.** I mean yeh can't blame young fellas for goin' off the rails either can yeh?
> **CONWAY.** How do yeh mean Stapler?
> **STAPLER.** Well let's face it, if a young lad takes a good look around him what do he see? He sees a crowd of big shots and

hob-nobbers grabbin' and takin' all before him. But as soon as a young lad knocks off a few bob out of a poor box or somewhere they're all down on him like a ton of bricks.

Stapler tries to be something of a father-figure to Jimmy and Tony – but it doesn't work out so well, perhaps because Stapler himself, with his attempt to keep boxing even when he is physically no longer up to it, has clearly not fully grown up, either. Jimmy is more conscious of Stapler's efforts in this respect than is Tony, and reacts with resentment, perhaps because of the difficult situation with his own father; as Stapler tries to give Tony advice, Jimmy says 'Let him play his own game' (9), indicating that it really is and should be every man for himself in this situation, with nobody helping anybody else out.

But Stapler tries; unlike Conway, who dismisses Jimmy as 'a bad 'erb' (50), he cares. When he hears that Tony is getting married, his face saddens at the news (11), since he feels that Tony is too young and is being trapped, perhaps in a way in which Stapler himself has been trapped in his own youth. When the other thirty-something man, Conway, mocks Tony for having cried in the canteen on the morning he realized he had no choice but to marry his pregnant girlfriend, Stapler recalls Danger Doyle as he responds to this image of the boy crying: 'Sure, that's no harm' (12). In *Poor Beast in the Rain*, the character who seems least fitted to be paternal – Danger, who has in the past stolen a woman away from her husband Steven and young daughter, Eileen – is in fact the character who dispenses the thing closest to paternal advice. We might expect him to be angry with Georgie when the latter, drunk and distressed over rumours he has heard about Eileen, goes shouting in the street about how Danger cried in the courtroom all those years ago. Danger is not annoyed; nor is he embarrassed. 'That's it Georgie boy, you shout it from the rooftops son', he says (121), and in this case, unlike in *A Handful of Stars*, the word 'son' is not derogatory or designed to put the younger man in his place; rather, it is almost tender. And indeed there is 'calmness and tenderness' in his face, the stage directions tell us of this scene as it develops, with Molly attacking Danger verbally when he refuses to show anger or disappointment (121). We are reminded of Stapler, looking at young Tony with fondness even as he boxed him in an early scene (8). Danger also gives Georgie permission to ignore the pressure to be a man before he is ready; while the others tease him about filling Big

Red's jersey, Danger takes a different, and again a calmer, stance (97):

> **DANGER**. I'm goin' back tomorrow evenin' Georgie, and I'm goin' to tell yeh one thing but it'll be a queer long time before you see me again boy ... you'll be well after fillin' out that jersey by then so yeh will.
> **GEORGIE.** We'll have a long wait for that I think.
> **DANGER**. But sure what harm if yeh never fill it out Georgie. Aren't yeh big enough?

In *Belfry*, it is to Artie that all the men ultimately come, despite themselves, needing some kind of fatherly guidance; even the cuckolded husband, Donal, comes to him for a chat in the end. But much about Artie, including his very decision to make his living working in the church, indicates that he may need a paternal figure himself; as a boy, he was abandoned by his own father, and an image from a photograph of him being carried on his father's shoulders haunts him like something he has lost and desperately wants to regain (147):

> **ARTIE**. Is that what I was tryin' to do for Dominic when I brought him to live with me – carry him on my shoulders to a place where he'd never been before? Is that why I organized the party for him? Who knows? Deep and meaningless questions hah! Yeh know whenever I remember that party I don't think of Dominic at all now. It's meself and Angela that I see. In fact sometimes I have to wonder who was carrying who!

Companionship is tough. It's never clear who's carrying who, and nor is the notion of being carried at all one with which Roche's men can allow themselves to be comfortable. In *Poor Beast in the Rain*, Molly – a character with a flawless radar for people's deepest vulnerabilities – homes in on this question when she attacks Joe's sense of belonging to the Wexford team purely by virtue of being a supporter (107-108):

> **MOLLY.** What do yeh mean 'we'? ( ... ) How many goals did you score today ... How many balls did Georgie there put over the bar? The way you're talkin' anyone'd think that you had somethin' to do with Big Red's goal. You had nothin' to do with it boy ( ... )
> **JOE.** I was there to cheer him on anyway. More than you were ( ... ) I'm a Wexfordman and he's a Wexfordman ( ... ) When he scores I score. Or we score I should say.
> **MOLLY.** ( ... ) Big Red O'Neill must be browned off carryin' you crowd of eejits on his back everywhere he goes. It's a

wonder some of yeh wouldn't get down and walk a bit of the
way once in a while.

Can these men ever admit to carrying each other and to being
carried? The legend of Tír na nÓg ends with Óisín leaning down
from his horse to help some weak men lift a huge rock; as soon as
his feet touch the ground, however, he withers in old age and dies
instantly; what is left of his body must be lifted up by the younger
men. In a Trilogy so pervaded with the tensions of male friendship,
with its strivings and its flaws, the most striking moment of all is
perhaps the moment in which Danger Doyle tells Molly that he
doesn't believe Óisín, in the legend, would possibly have given up
that magical land of youth for something so slight as friendship
(117):

> **DANGER.** I'll never forget the first mornin' the Christian
> Brother told us about that and I couldn't help thinkin' at the
> time that a man'd want to be a bit soft in the head or somethin'
> to come back from a land of eternal youth just because he
> wanted to see his auld mates again ... He must have had
> somethin' else on his mind Molly, hah?

Danger has done an Óisín; he has left the place of his birth and
has had the chance to reinvent himself elsewhere. Whether it is
possible to achieve such a reinvention is another matter, and the
returned Danger remains sufficiently closed that we never discover
how successful he has been; there are hints, though, that life in Tír
na nÓg is far from perfect. Danger Doyle insists on standing apart
from his 'auld mates.' When a local row erupts, he provides a
rebuttal to the famous final line of Patrick Kavanagh's 'Epic' – 'Gods
make their own importance' – with a line to rival Kavanagh's:
'Among yeh be it' (117). To break out of the insularity of a small town
brings an objectivity that makes everything clearer. It also brings a
loneliness. But as Roche's men know, it's lonely on the inside, too.

# 14 | Harvest Fires and Angry Saints: Theatrical Appropriations of Celtic Festivals*

Martin W. Walsh

Irish dramatists have often tapped into the rich heritage of their folklore and folkways, but Billy Roche's *Amphibians* is unusual in centring on a major feast of the old Celtic calendar: St. Martin's Eve. Commissioned by the Royal Shakespeare Company in 1992, the play premiered at the Barbican Pit in London, directed by Michael Attenborough. Six years later Roche himself directed a lightly revised version of *Amphibians* in his native Wexford. In this production Roche also played the role of Dribbler, an older friend of the family at the centre of the play. Dribbler serves as a kind of chorus figure, a Wexford fisherman of the old school who is a supporter if not an active practitioner of traditional folkways. Chief among these is the rite of passage of a fisherman's son, staged at a prominent seasonal marker.

The aboriginal calendar was also put to dramatic use in a better known play of the early 1990s, Brian Friel's *Dancing at Lughnasa*. The dates in question are archaic Irish festivals which bracket the harvest season: Lughnasa, commencing August 1, is the initial harvest festival; St. Martin's Eve, November 10, marks the end of the harvest season and the onset of winter. Both playwrights draw on ethnographic materials, but both also *invent* traditions for dramatic purposes, demonstrating their attraction to a past that is hypothetically 'pagan.' Both dramatize the archaic rituals as liberating forces in small-town Irish life, but both also present them as dangerously transgressive. Both practice what I call an 'ambivalent nostalgia', and Roche in particular devises an elaborate ritual performance upon folkloric material and its calendar base.

*Dancing at Lughnasa* (1990) has already achieved the status of a classic, with numerous international productions and awards as well as a major motion picture treatment in 1998. As an autobiographical 'memory play', it centres on the five Mundy sisters and their recently returned missionary brother who live near the fictional village of Ballybeg (Irish for 'small town') in Donegal – a thinly disguised version of Friel's own home town of Glenties in the southwest portion of the county. Michael Mundy, Friel's narrator, begins the play by recalling the summer of 1936 when he was seven. He introduces the festival of Lughnasa by means of the family's newfangled wireless set:

> And because it arrived as August was about to begin, my Aunt Maggie – she was the joker of the family – she suggested we give it a name. She wanted to call it Lugh after the old Celtic God of the Harvest. Because in the old days August the First was Lá Lughnasa, the feast day of the pagan god, Lugh; and the days and weeks of harvesting that followed were called the Festival of Lughnasa. But Aunt Kate – she was a national schoolteacher and a very proper woman – she said it would be sinful to christen an inanimate object with any kind of name, not to talk of a pagan god.[1]

Thus Friel establishes one of his favorite themes: narrow, puritanical Irish Catholicism vs. an older 'paganism', loosely defined, which is played out as well in the person of Father Jack who has succumbed to African animistic spirituality after twenty-five years in Uganda.

---

[1] Brian Friel, *Dancing at Lughnasa* (London: Faber and Faber, 1990): 1. There is already a considerable body of criticism on the play, for example in the monographs by F. C. McGrath, *Brian Friel's (Post)Colonial Drama: Language, Illusion, and Politics* (Syracuse: Syracuse University Press, 1999) and Richard Pine, *The Diviner: The Art of Brian* Friel (Dublin: University College Press, 1999). Major articles include: Prapassaree Kramer, '*Dancing at Lughnasa*: Unexcused Absence', *Modern Drama* 43 (2000): 171-181 and Richard Allen Cave, 'Questing for Ritual and Ceremony in a Godforsaken World: *Dancing at Lughnasa* and *Wonderful Tennessee*', *Hungarian Journal of English and American Studies* 5 (1999): 109-126. Despite its title, the latter article includes no discussion of the old 'pagan' festival of Lughnasa.

What does not fit into a strictly autobiographical framework is that for Glenties and environs *Lá Lughnasa* was just as foreign a notion as it was for audiences in Dublin, London or New York. After the play premiered, Dr. Malachy McCloskey, one of the older residents of Friel's hometown, was quoted as saying: 'I never heard of the festival of Lughnasa in me life.' Marie Clare O'Donnell, a supervisor in the town's co-op added: 'And we wouldn't be dancing round fires or anything like that. Not in my time, or my mother's.' To a large extent, Friel has constructed a festival for his theatrical environment.[2]

But if the stage *Lá Lughnasa* is not part of the playwright's own living tradition, it is hardly an invention out of whole cloth. Friel almost certainly availed himself of a major, indeed the definitive work published in 1962 by the Irish Folklore Commission, Máire MacNeill's *The Festival of Lughnasa: A Study of the Survival of the Celtic Festival of the Beginning of Harvest.* There is much in MacNeill's massive study that Friel would have found useful. For instance, she lists ten locations in Donegal as 'festive heights' for communal assembly where young people picnicked, danced and lit bonfires.[3] Although most of these are in the far north of the county (the nearest some forty kilometres from Glenties), the references establish a strong case for the survival of Lughnasa in the county as a whole. One of the distinguishing traits of the ancient festival for MacNeill is the communal picking and consuming of bilberries. Lughnasa indeed was called 'Bilberry Sunday' (*Domhnach na bhFraochóg*) in many locations. Although bilberry-picking in the play is simply a family economic activity on the part of sisters Agnes and Rose, it also serves as the excuse for Rose's romantic tryst up in Loch Anna in the 'back hills', and thus lines up with the broader, erotic connotations of the festival.

In the play Lughnasa provides three concentric circles of festive energy, expanding outward from the confining Mundy household: first, the Marconi radio set (a.k.a. Lugh), the maddeningly

---

[2] Delaney, Paul, ed. *Brian Friel in Conversion* (Ann Arbor: University of Michigan Press, 2000): 229-30. Friel's dramatic latitude here might be compared to the way he turns his own apparently normal missionary uncle (normal apart from recurring malaria) into the addled apostate Father Jack.

[3] Máire MacNeill, *The Festival of Lughnasa: A Study of the Survival of the Celtic Festival of the Beginning of Harvest* (Oxford: Oxford University Press, 1962): 140-148.

intermittent source for dance music in the home itself; second, an organized harvest dance in Ballybeg; and third, the troubling 'pagan' festival in the back hills.

The Marconi set comes fully to life midway through Act 1 leading to the most famous scene in Irish drama of the past half century, based on two pages of detailed stage directions. The temperamental radio goes from 'scarcely audible' to loud *ceili* dance music with traditional tunes such as 'The Mason's Apron.' Maggie, the fun-loving iconoclast, is the first of the sisters to abandon her routine household task, kneading dough, to respond to the beat (21):

> *She is breathing deeply, rapidly. Now her features become animated by a look of defiance, of aggression; a crude mask of happiness. Now she spreads her fingers (which are covered with flour), pushes her hair back from her face, pulls her hands down her cheeks and patterns her faces with an instant mask. At the same time she opens her mouth and emits a wild, raucous 'Yaaaah!' – and immediately begins to dance, arms, legs, hair, long bootlaces flying.*

Maggie's enthusiasm is immediately communicated to the simple sister, Rose, whose wellingtons pound out their own 'erratic rhythm', and then to Agnes who, of all the sisters, moves 'most gracefully, most sensuously.' The mania spreads to unwed mother Chris who is folding Father Jack's laundry. She merrily dons his white surplice to join the dance, much to Kate's chagrin. The four sisters now create 'a dance that is almost recognizable. They meet – they retreat. They form a circle and wheel round and round.'

Friel repeatedly emphasizes the 'grotesque' elements of this performance: 'the sound is too loud; and the beat is too fast. ... instead of holding hands, they have their arms around one another's neck, around one another's waist.' In a superbly managed dramatic moment, the stiff matriarch Kate finally succumbs to the energies released on stage, but unlike her sisters, she dances alone and in silence, 'totally concentrated, totally private, a movement that is simultaneously controlled and frantic' (22). And then the overheated Marconi set fails and the revel collapses.

Critics often use the term 'Dionysian' approvingly for this spontaneous release by the Irish maiden ladies. It certainly creates an exhilarating moment for the theatre audience. Indeed, the film version transposes the dance to the climactic moment of the piece, making it a final release of all the pent-up energies of the summer and simultaneously a demonstration of sisterly bonding before the family tragically disintegrates. But the film version omits all of Friel's grotesque elements: Maggie's flour mask, Chris's parody vestment, the wrestle holds.[4] Such Dionysian energy is dangerous and disturbing as well as celebratory, as Agave and her fellow Bacchantes discover at the end of Euripides' play. Notice the reaction of the sisters themselves after their intense experience of choreomania (22): '*They look at each other obliquely; avoid looking at each other; half smile in embarrassment; feel and look slightly ashamed and slightly defiant.*' Michael's opening monologue had already problematized the event for us (2): 'I had witnessed Marconi's voodoo derange those kind, sensible women and transform them into shrieking strangers.'

In marked contrast to this early Dionysian outbreak, the majority of the dancing in the play is done to Broadway and Hollywood musical numbers (particularly 'Dancing in the Dark' and Cole Porter's 'Anything Goes'), which have a much less ambiguous connotation and are the principal vehicle for Michael's warm memories of his parents and maiden aunts. For both kinds of dancing, however, the women are dependent on the fickle radio set to provide the musical cultures, pop or folk, which they cannot reproduce themselves. They remain, as ever, severely limited in expressive ability as well as in expressive opportunity.

Immediately prior to the Dionysian scene, the sisters had briefly entertained the possibility of attending once more the local harvest dance, an organized, commercial event. In Maggie's description of such an event from a previous decade, a ballroom-dancing competition was part of the festivities (20). Enthusiasm for the idea spreads and builds through the group of women despite the elder Kate's warning against 'all the riff-raff of the countryside' who will dominate the event. But Agnes does not care 'how young they are, how drunk and dirty and sweaty they are ... It's the Festival of Lughnasa. I'm only thirty-five. I want to dance' (12-13). Kate is almost swept away by her sisters' enthusiasm, but in the end she reminds them all of their age and social position (they are sisters of a priest, after all), and the idea is ultimately quashed, as many such initiatives in the past had been, we would assume. In many ways this early passage serves to foreshadow the Dionysian scene and

---

4 See Joan Fitzpatrick Dean, *Dancing at Lughnasa: Ireland into Film 7* (Cork: Cork University Press, 2003).

effectively demonstrates the power of puritanical repression, with its mixture of natural reserve, fear, and self-importance within the family structure.

Although the term 'pagan' can refer to make-up, pop songs or cigarettes in matriarch Kate's strict moral lexicon, there is a sense of a real, if residual paganism up in those back hills where *Lá Lughnasa* is full of very troubling energies indeed. We have the report of Young Sweeney dying of third-degree burns from some sort of bonfire accident. The simple sister, Rose, seems to have inside information (16):

> It was last Sunday week, the first night of the Festival of Lughnasa. And they were doing what they do every year there in the back hills ... First they light a bonfire beside a spring well. Then they dance round it. Then they drive their cattle through the flames to banish the devil out of them ... And this year there was an extra big crowd of boys and girls. And they were off their heads with drink. And young Sweeney's trousers caught fire and he went up like a torch ... That's what happened ... they do it every Lughnasa. I'm telling you.

This description reflects materials that MacNeill collected for nineteenth and early twentieth-century Lughnasa gatherings – apart from the odd detail of the cattle purification which seems temporally displaced, a ritual act more typical of St. John's Eve (that is, at the beginning rather than the end of the summer season). It is clear, however, that Friel wants the back hills event to remain deliberately out-of-focus with an intriguing, distant pagan allure.

As the stresses of the play mount, Kate lets out a bit of second-hand information she had evidently meant to suppress (35):

> That young Sweeney boy from the back hills – the boy who was anointed [given the sacrament of Extreme Unction] – his trousers didn't catch fire, as Rose said. They were doing some devilish thing with a goat – some sort of sacrifice for the Lughnasa Festival; and Sweeney was so drunk he toppled over into the middle of the bonfire. Don't know why that came into my head.[5]

---

[5] MacNeill does list some instances of roasting beef in association with Lughnasa, and goats were prominently displayed and even crowned at the Lughnasa-associated Puck Fair at Killorglin, County Kerry and the Ram Fair at Greencastle, County Down. But there is nothing like Kate's goat sacrifice in the record. Perhaps the character's classical

In the final reference to young Sweeney, however, the tragic implications recede and the violent Lughnasa ritual shrinks back into a simple drunken accident. As Rose reports after returning from her tryst with Danny Bradley up at Loch Anna: 'The boy who got burned, the boy you said was dying. Well, he's on the mend ... His legs will be scarred but he'll be alright' (59). The full Lughnasa festival thus remains tantalizingly out of sight.[6]

It seems clear that Friel wants to imbue a sense of the pagan past and its vital, ambiguous energies in his Lughnasa festival, but he is not ready to commit any of his early twentieth-century Irishmen to an actual *faith*, even in the wild back hills. What the playwright achieves, then, is a subtle, dramatically useful tension between the suppressed and the liberating, the 'Catholic' and the 'pagan.'

With Billy Roche's *Amphibians* (1992, revised 1998) we move from the far northwest of Donegal to the far southeast of Wexford, and from the beginning of the harvest season to its endpoint, Martinmas. Roche acknowledges a heavy debt to Friel, and his festival of St. Martin's Eve functions theatrically in a similar way to Lughnasa. The title of Roche's play refers to the Wexford fisher folk who, sadly, are losing their intimate connections with the sea. In his prose works Roche assigns them to a neighborhood he calls 'Rowdy Row.' All but the independent-minded Eagle are now employed in the local cannery, the Menapia Seafood Factory.[7] They no longer

---

education, some recollection of the 'goat-song' of tragedy, has influenced her interpretation of the 'pagan' goings-on.

[6] Friel employed a similar process of demystification in an early play, *The Enemy Within* (1962), where St. Columba receives a disturbing report that the 'Picts in Cromarty' have relapsed, 'reviving old Druidical practices in the mountains there' (24). Toward the end of the play, however, it is reported that in fact 'not a trace of an organized revival' was to be found in Cromarty (47). As might be expected in a film treatment of *Dancing at Lughnasa*, the mysterious festival up in the back hills had too much visual potential to be kept tantalizingly in the background. In becoming concrete, however, the festival loses almost all of the creative ambiguity the play manages to create around it. The Lughnasa bonfires of the 1998 film are merely unpleasant, like an out-of-control fraternity party.

[7] The Menapii were an ancient Celtic tribe mentioned by Caesar as living in the Rhine delta and to whom Ptolemy the geographer attributed a colony on the coast of Leinster (that is, County Wexford). Roche's use of the name for a grubby seafood factory may

fish themselves but are reduced to gathering and processing the local shellfish. Eagle's somewhat odd nickname suggests a great fisher, and indeed at his first entrance he appears emblematically with '*a salmon in each hand.*'[8] Eagle is determined to keep to the old ways and for his twelve-year-old son, Isaac, he is arranging to revive an old Wexford fishermen's puberty ritual. The boy is to spend a cold night alone on nearby 'Useless Island' in a specially constructed hut. Useless Island is an uninhabited wild place. Rumour has it that a wild boar roams the island, and a mermaid was supposedly sighted off its shores. Eagle's older friend Dribbler recalls (162) 'a great big bull seal' during his own initiation that 'started roarin' and bawlin' in the early hours – frightened the friggin' life out of me.'

Roche's Useless Island is based on a feature in Wexford Harbour called 'The Ballast Bank', an artificial reef created in the nineteenth century from the ballast materials of sailing vessels. Roche frequently evokes Useless Island in his 1986 novel *Tumbling Down*, in many ways a Wexford *Under Milk Wood*. A loved and hated landmark, Useless Island reflects the teenage narrator's melancholic moods or serves as a projection screen for his post-pubescent fantasies. It is often the site of adolescent or extramarital trysts, as in 'One is Not a Number', a story from Roche's 2006 collection *Tales from Rainwater Pond*. Although its barrenness and ugliness are always emphasized – 'an island of stone and clay that looked like it must have sprung up from the sea centuries ago'[9] – Roche occasionally gives Useless Island a bit more acreage, foliage, and distance out to sea than the modest reef of stones in Wexford Harbour might warrant, and he attributes an abundance of sea life to the locale. Seals, perfect oysters, and other abundant shellfish are frequently associated with Useless Island. In Irish folklore since time immemorial, bleak offshore islands were regarded, like burial

---

be a bit ironic, although there are other local Wexford appropriations of the ancient cachet – the 'Menapia Sea Angling Club,' for example, which has its own website. Roche's short story 'Table Manners' in *Tales from Rainwater Pond* focuses on a literary festival being held in Wexford at the fictional Menapia Hotel.

[8] Billy Roche, *The Cavalcaders and Amphibians: Two Plays* (London: Nick Hern Books, 2001): The sea eagle or erne (*Haliacetus albicilla*) is one of the largest and rarest species of raptor in the British Isles.

[9] *Tumbling Down*, revised edition (Wexford: Tassel Publications, 2008): 1.

tumuli and megalithic constructs, as portals to the realms of the *sidhe*. In *Amphibians*, then, it would seem that Roche wishes to lend his local island some of the 'pagan' allure we have seen in Friel's Lughnasa bonfires of the back hills.[10]

When a boy is abandoned on Useless Island, the father carouses back on the mainland with his mates, toasting his son's health and fortune. When the lad is fetched off the island the next morning, the hut is burned behind him, a particularly archaic touch on the part of the playwright. Here is Dribbler describing the end of the ritual to the somewhat anxious Isaac (12):

> I'll never forget the mornin' I was comin' back. I could feel the heat of the fire on the small of me back as I was gettin' into the boat and I could hear the auld crackle of the hut and that yeh know. I was dyin' to turn around and look back at it yeh see. And as we were nearin' the shore I could see all the people comin' out of their houses and down the auld bank to the beach—women and children and auld men and everythin' and they all wavin' and callin' out to me and all. Jaysus it was really a magic feelin' alright though. But sure your Da was the last boy to go out to the island, Isaac, yeh know.

The hut which is to be built for the initiation on Useless Island seems to require a ritual precision with no expense spared. Eagle spends nearly half of the profit from his salmon catch, some twenty-three pounds, on wood for Isaac's hut. Veronica, Eagle's wife, finds this extravagant and ridiculous because the thing will be burned down in any case. They have a row over it, Veronica dismissing the whole business as 'playin' games.' Eagle, obstinate and we may even say obsessive, can only insist on what amounts to his ritual piety (131-32): 'I need special timber for the hut yeh see. 'Cause it all has to be tied together, yeh know. No nails no nothin'? ... The hut has to be built in a certain way and that's all about it.' Later he describes the hut as 'like a little igloo so it is' (145), suggesting his almost aboriginal mind-set.

---

[10] Friel based his *Wonderful Tennessee* (1993) on a mysterious off-shore isle near Ballybeg. The island is just far enough away to be occasionally lost from view in the haze and is thus variously described as the 'disappearing island' ('hard to know what size it is, it keeps shimmering'), the Island of Otherness, or Island of Mystery (*Oilean Draoichta*), in an obvious appropriation of the legendary Hy Brasil of Irish mythology.

The special evening designated for this elaborate initiation ritual, 10 November, is not a very pleasant season for North Atlantic island camping. The Vigil and Feast of St. Martin of Tours, a major festival of the Western Church for well over a millennium, was celebrated widely in Ireland and involved some rather archaic practices, including sacrificing a domestic fowl or larger animal for prophylactic signing with its blood. The jambs and lintels of the house and barns, and even the foreheads of the children of the family were daubed with the Martin's Eve blood.[11] The ritual is no doubt a reflection of Martinmas as a traditional marker for slaughtering the winter's store of meat. In common with many other northern European cultures, Irish Martinmas thus represented the end of harvest season and the onset of winter. In addition, Martinmas was hardly more than a week after All Hallows (*Samhain* in Irish), the ancient Celtic New Year when the otherworld, whether pagan or Christian, was perilously close.[12]

Roche loads his play with several ominous St. Martin's Eves. Eagle's love child with Bridie had been delivered stillborn on that date, a year before Isaac's birth. Marian Brennan, wife of old Mosey and lover of the local factory owner, Edward Taylor, had walked into the sea on 9 November some years before that. Both their graves are part of the set, a headland that faces Useless Island, and are visited

---

[11] Sean Ó Suilleabhain, 'The Feast of St. Martin in Ireland', in *Studies in Folklore in Honor of Stith Thompson*, ed. W. Edson Richmond (Bloomington: Indiana University Press, 1957): 252-61. See also an earlier study by Henry Morris, 'St. Martin's Eve', *Béaloideas* 9 (1939): 230-35. Specifically Wexford Martinmas folkways, such as slaughtering a goose and tossing its head over the house, or sharing the goose broth and meat slices with the poor of the district, can be found in *Folklore of Country Wexford*, ed. Diarmaid Ó Muirithe and Deirdre Nuttal (Dublin: Four Courts Press, 1999): 162 and 169.

[12] Cf. the famous Child ballad 'The Wife of Usher's Well' from the Border country, a ghost story set 'about the Martinmas time' – some eight to ten days after All Souls' Day. Truly terrifying ghosts, as well as multiple decapitations and other bloody deeds, are associated with St. Martin's Eve in several stories in Jeremiah Curtin's *Tales of the Fairies and Ghost World, Collected from Oral Tradition in South-west Munster* (1895). Interestingly, Christy Mahon in *The Playboy of the Western World* (1907) appears to have fled his patricide over the 'eleven long days' from *Samhain* to Martinmas – that is, from the time of the 'walking dead' to the time he experiences Pegeen's interest in him like 'the sunshine of St. Martin's Day.'

by various characters in the course of the play. Evidently on another Martinmas Eve the inseparable Dempsey twins perished. The healthier of the two was rowed out to the island for the initiation, but the 'little lad with the cast in his eye' heard his twin brother desperately calling for him in the middle of the night and attempted to swim to the island, only to find himself exhausted by the effort. His brother, then attempting to rescue him, also drowned (158-59). These were, apparently, near contemporaries of Eagle, and the implication is that their tragedy (indirectly caused by the community's strict interpretation of the ritual) was the reason for the custom lapsing since Eagle's day. A casual remark by Veronica – 'St. Martin's Eve'll be the death of the lot of us, I think' – thus acquires an ominous resonance, as if her son Isaac were destined to be some sort of sacrificial victim of his father's single-minded scheme.[13]

Prior to Isaac's departure for the island the neighbours bring gifts, such as cakes or mementoes, for the young initiate. In the 1992 edition of the play Isaac receives a St. Martin medallion. Then Eagle, after rowing his son over in the early evening of the 10th, initiates Isaac into the manly mysteries of stout-drinking and reveals some darker layers of the tradition (156-157):

> **ISAAC.** There's somethin' kind of special about St. Martin' Eve, Da, ain't there?
> **EAGLE.** Yeah. No self respectin' Wexford fisherman would ever cast a line on St. Martin's Eve.
> **ISAAC.** Why not?
> **EAGLE.** I don't know. They're superstitious about it. It's supposed to be unlucky or somethin'. Sure there's a song written about that and everythin'. 'The Fishermen of Wexford', it's called.

Eagle then sings the ballad for his son – 'There is an old tradition sacred held in Wexford town,/That says: "Upon St. Martin's Eve no net shall be let down" ...' – and concludes:

> That song was written about a disaster that happened here one time. A few fleets decided to disregard that auld tradition and go out fishin' on Martin's Eve. Seventy men were lost that day from this little town alone, boy. That's the last line of the song in fact. 'Seventy Fishers' Corpses Strew the Shores of Wexford Bay.'

---

[13] This line appears only in the original edition: *Amphibians* (London: Warner Chappell Plays, 1992): 87.

In this scene of bonding between father and son, Eagle confesses to having 'once and once only' violated the St. Martin's taboo himself. He vaguely admits to having 'a bit of fire in me belly or somethin' and refused to listen to anyone', resulting in a 'bit of bad luck' (157). This may be a veiled reference to the stillbirth of Bridie's child on St. Martin's Eve thirteen years earlier, and guilt over that event might well be one of the motives driving Eagle's near-obsessive concern over Isaac's initiation. In a later scene of the play, for example, Roche juxtaposes Isaac singing 'The Fisherman of Wexford' to keep up his spirits as he settles in for the night on Useless Island with Eagle *standing over the boy's grave* on the headland, laying a gift, and blessing himself (174-175). Bridie's musical signature, 'I Let My Hair Down', plays under Eagle's tableau. As 'The Fisherman of Wexford' ballad comes to pervade the doings on Useless Island, we have what amounts to a wake for all the 'amphibian' dead, those of the distant as well of the immediate past, intertwined with the young lad's rite of passage. Again, St. Martin's Eve, like its neighbour festival *Samhain*, becomes charged with the ancient polarities of Death and Renewal.

'The Fishermen of Wexford' and its underlying folk tale are at the dramatic heart of *Amphibians*. Personal correspondence with the playwright has revealed that he composed original 'folk' music for a traditional ballad he found in the works of the great Fenian, John Boyle O'Reilly (1844-1890).[14] O'Reilly's creative works, like those of many other nineteenth-century Irish nationalists, are 'processed' folklore at best. 'The Fishermen of Wexford' is a competent, suspenseful art ballad and accurately reflects the weather folklore of Irish Martinmas to be discussed shortly. It is based on a Wexford legend current in the 1820s and probably dating back to at least the eighteenth century. Patrick Kennedy recorded it in his *Banks of Boro, a Wexford Chronicle* in 1867:

> A Wexford legend says that on one recurrence of this festival [St. Martin's Day], November 11, the people in all the boats plying about the Wexford line of coast were warned, by an apparition of the Saint pacing along the waves, to betake themselves to the harbours. All who neglected the advice perished in a storm that ensued the same afternoon. In our youth [pre-Famine era], no Wexford boat would put to sea on

---

14 Jeffrey Roche, ed. *Life of John Boyle O'Reilly together with his Complete Poems and Speeches* (New York: Cassell Publishing, 1891): 544-46.

that Saint's festival, no miller would set his wheel a-going, no housewife would yoke her spinning wheel. Occasionally, when a goat or sheep was ill, and seemed likely to die, its ear was slit, and itself devoted to St. Martin. If it recovered, it was killed and eaten on some subsequent 11th of November. It would not be sold in the interim for ten times its value.[15]

O'Reilly's ballad version proceeds to account for the local superstition – 'No fisherman of Wexford shall, upon that holy day,/ Set sail or cast a line within the scope of Wexford Bay' – by telling of a 'wondrous shoal of herring' entering the bay on a long ago St. Martin's Eve. The fishermen, sorely tempted by the sight, break their long-held taboo and set out to haul in this seeming bounty, despite the shrill warnings of their womenfolk. In dismissing their superstitions, the fishermen even slight the guardian saint: 'And scoffingly they said, 'To-night our nets shall sweep the Bay:/ And take the Saint who guards it, should he come across our way!' Those on shore begin to hear ominous sea winds rising. Then as the fleet is about to let down its nets, a strange apparition appears. It can only be the angry St. Martin:

> ... Lo! the daring boatmen shrink
> With sudden awe and whitened lips and glaring eyes agape,
> For breast-high, threatening, from the sea uprose a Human Shape!
> Beyond them, – in the moonlight, – hand upraised and awful mien,
> Waving back and pointing landward, breast-high in the sea was seen.
> Thrice it waved and thrice it pointed, – then, with clenchéd hand upraised,
> The awful shape went down before the fishers as they gazed!
> Gleaming whitely through the water, fathoms deep they saw its frown, –
> They saw its white hand clenched above it, – sinking slowly down!

The fishermen nevertheless succumb to their 'rebellious greed.' As the enormous herring shoal turns back seaward, they frantically ply their oars after it and cast their nets. Two boats of 'God-fearing men', however, cut their lines and flee shoreward, just in time to escape the sudden tempest which claims seventy lives.

Such fatal miscalculations are not uncommon among subsistence fisherman of northern waters, but the art ballad also reflects a fairly archaic level of Christian folklore in which an important patron saint, like Martin, can take personal vengeance on the blasphemous or 'rebelliously greedy.' It is the kind of thing one finds throughout the works of Gregory of Tours in the sixth century, and was common

---

[15] Patrick Kennedy, *Banks of the Boro, A Wexford Chronicle* (Dublin & London, 1867): 364.

in Catholic folk belief through the Baroque era. St. Martin is here imagined as dwelling under Wexford Bay, a Christian appropriation of the great Irish sea god Manannán Mac Lir. As a traditional marker for the onset of the winter season, Martinmas would have served as a signal for the secession of regular travel on the sea-lanes, a date beyond which certain danger lurked. The bay-dwelling St. Martin thus serves as both a warning apparition and a vengeful storm-raiser, a barely Christianized 'pagan' force.

The massive survey project of the Irish Folklore Commission undertaken in the 1930s and 40s yielded many examples of this strangely aquatic and archaic St. Martin.[16] From County Kerry came

---

[16] Research in the Irish Folklore Archive at University College Dublin was carried out in July 1993 (with special thanks to one of its frequent patrons, Michael Ross). Manuscript numbers refer to the bound questionnaires arranged by county. The prohibition of fishing on St. Martin's was only part of a larger field of perilous activity at that seasonal threshold. For inlanders, no wheels were supposed to turn, especially mill wheels. Likewise, no short cuts or other compromises were to be taken with the blood-sacrifice, under pain of supernatural retribution. The motif of Martin as a protector of seafarers goes back to the fourth century and Sulpicius Severus's *Dialogues*, and was passed down to medieval popular culture through Jacobus de Voragine's *Legenda Aurea*: 'A ship was sinking and a merchant who was not yet a Christian exclaimed: "May the God of Martin save us!" A great calm settled over the sea at once.' *The Golden Legend: Readings on the Saints*. Trans. William Granger Ryan (Princeton: Princeton University Press, 1993), ii: 295. St. Martin was directly invoked in Irish-language prayers against drowning:

> Mary, Christ and the Saints
> between us and harm,
>
> ...
> Patrick with his staff,
> Martin with his mantle,
> Brighid with her hood,
> Michael with his shield.

R. MacCrocaigh, *Prayers of the Gael being a Translation from Irish into English* (London: Sands & Company, 1914): 41. See also the 'Ocean Blessing' from the Gaelic-speaking Hebrides collected by Alexander Carmichael in the nineteenth century, as quoted in *Carmina Gadelica: Charms of the Gaels* (Hudson, NY: Lindisfrane Press, 1992): 121.

the tale of a father and son who went fishing on St. Martin's Day and, finding their boat immobilized, discovered the great Christian saint playing merman – 'He saw the man in the water and he naked and his two hands against the boat, and he stopping the boat and they came home, and all the other boats were drowned' (MS. 674: 247). From County Clare is an account of St. Martin appearing on a white horse riding over the waves to warn a pious fisherman who had been diligent in saying his rosary. He was saved, but his fellow fishermen perished (MS. 675: 122). Closer to Roche's own country is the Waterford story of a fisherman who refused to cast his nets on the saint's day and was ordered, 'Sit up behind me!' by the Wave-Rider, and so was spared (MS. 677: 45). In County Waterford such Martin apparitions were considered the 'sign of a great gale', sometimes called 'St. Martin's Storm' (MS. 677: 91, 158, 161). Similar accounts come from Limerick and Mayo as well. From Wexford itself comes the report of a few survivors of a night-time gale: 'When the storm was at its height they said they saw St Martin and he riding on a white horse. So ever after that night fishermen are afraid to go out on St Martin's night for fear of getting drowned' (MS. 880: 84). It is clear from these modern folklore records that the saint can still, in his archaic, ambivalent *virtu,* be equally saviour or avenger.

With regard to the play *Amphibians,* then, the ominous Martin's Eve material is authentic folklore. Roche had earlier tapped into this tradition in *Tumbling Down* where a very unpleasant character by the name of Dancer viciously mocked the fisher folk of Rowdy Row and defied their 'superstitions' about St. Martin's Eve.[17] On the other hand, Billy Roche has stated (in a personal communication) that his play's detailed initiation ritual, despite its authentic tone and plausibility as a profession-based rite of passage, is a complete invention. Of course, the isolation of young lads in a liminal environment is an essential feature of tribal initiation rites, as Van Gennep's *Rites of Passage* (1909) makes abundantly clear. Roche's constructed ritual maintains the classic tripartite structure: (a) a *rite*

---

On the Feast Day of Michael, the Feast Day of Martin,
The Feast Day of Andrew, band of mercy,
The Feast Day of Bride, day of my choice,
Cast ye the serpent into the ocean,
So that the sea may swallow her up.

[17] *Tumbling Down,* revised edition: 48 and 80.

*de séparation*, the voyage out to the island; (b) a *rite liminaire* resulting in a *stade de marge,* the 'liminal' stage creating a period of marginalization where the boy is outside of normal time and society, homeless and without status – in effect 'useless' like the island on which he camps; and (c) a *rite d'agrégation*, the return voyage, the burning of the initiation hut, and joyous welcome by the community.[18]

Roche's re-creation is indeed one of the most complete representations of a *rite du passage* on the modern stage. Like his character Eagle, the playwright seems to long for a more organic sense of the life-cycle even if it means conjuring up a vengeful saint as storm-deity brooding over the ritual site. But this is always a fragile, self-conscious nostalgia. After Eagle introduces 'The Fisherman of Wexford', the tune is employed through the rest of the play in various modes: celebratory, elegiac, and ultimately ironic. Indeed the play's climax involves the wrecking of Isaac's ritual night by the drunkenly malcontent Broaders Brennan and his cronies, Humpy and Zak – examples of young men with no roots or sense of purpose, who employ the tune sarcastically and irreverently. Broaders, as it turns out, is pathologically jealous of Eagle and his vision for himself and his young son, and has only venomous contempt for the revived initiation on the island and its supporting folklore. Broaders had posed his own sadistic rite of branding his mates with a heated knife-blade in opposition to the Martin's Eve ritual (122): 'I think yez are all gone soft in the head or somethin'. Building huts and settin' fire to them! That all died out years ago! There's what yeh want now. The mark of the crab burnt into your arm.'

In the climactic scene of the play we are in the middle of Isaac's night alone on the island when Broaders suddenly kicks the dying fire aflame. Zak is guzzling drink and Humpy sits on the roof of the hut 'howling like a wolf.' Isaac's store of sandwiches is brusquely commandeered and fed to the seagulls. His medallion is ripped from him. Broaders leads the bullying, tearing down both Isaac's initiation rite and the heroic image of his independent-minded father. After a moment of threatened violence, the somewhat more sympathetic Zak begins to croon the 'Fisherman of Wexford' tune, recalling the celebratory sing-along in the pub, then in progress, that

---

[18] Arnold van Gennep, *Les rites de passage* (Paris: É. Nourry, 1909): 26-27.

provides communal counterpoint to the boy's lonesome vigil. This leads to bitter reminiscences on Broaders' part as the ballad transforms into a fevered recitation accompanied by 'savage' percussion (179-80): '[ZAK] begins to beat out a rhythm on an old wooden box. After a while HUMPY becomes infected and he too begins to beat on an old tin can ... The rhythm climbs to a savage crescendo.'

This is Roche's equivalent of the Mundy sisters' Lughnasa dance. 'Rough music' has long been a folk mechanism for the punishment of social deviance, but here it is dangerously inverted. Broaders, moreover, has a counter-idea for initiating Isaac into the gang: his 'mark of the crab.' He proceeds to heat up his sacrificial knife in the campfire. Isaac escapes this heavily Biblical moment (he is also an Abel to Broaders' Cain) due to the intervention of the trysting lovers Brian and Sonia. Broaders' rage is turned against the wealthy young man, and then against his own crony Zak when Zak attempts to restrain him. Broaders wrecks the initiation hut, which he sarcastically dubs 'our inheritance' in a fit of savage nihilism (185): 'Queer ignorant ain't I? A real savage boy! But yeh see the problem is ... I don't believe in fairy tales like yeh know!' Ultimately, Broaders' self-loathing turns back on himself. He brands his own forehead with the red-hot knife as the 'maimed rites' of St. Martin's Eve come to their warped climax.

Both our playwrights, Friel and Roche, deal in what I would call 'ambivalent nostalgia' in their theatrical re-creation of archaic festival events. Their nostalgia is essentially romantic, a yearning for fuller, more communal and, at the same time, more individually vitalizing ceremonies organically linked to the ancient agricultural year-cycle. But there is ambivalence in this longed for reversion to a simpler, happier paganism. We can see the self-mutilated Broaders as well as young Sweeney, he of the stupid Lughnasa bonfire accident, as collateral damage in their playwrights' theatrically constructed archaic festivals. Major characters do not fare much better. Rose Mundy has definitely come away damaged from her Lughnasa experience. Perhaps she was deflowered by Danny Bradley; perhaps she escaped his drunken lust. Either way her one romance is at an end. Apart from the erotic secret she now holds over her sisters, her life is hardly transformed. Isaac seems to have survived his St. Martin's Eve initiation not much the worse for wear, but there is little hope that the old ritual has been successfully revived. Just as some Wiccan or neo-Druid might attempt to revive 'ancient' traditions, Eagle has cobbled up a 'meaningful' initiation ritual for the benefit of rootless modern youth, but ultimately this proves a narrowly selfish enterprise, and a shambles in practice. The final fragmentary quotation of 'The Fisherman of Wexford' at the fade out of the penultimate scene is intentionally ambiguous, indicating, perhaps, Eagle's sense of his own failure (187):

> **EAGLE.** There is an old tradition Mosey huh?
> **MOSEY**. Yeah. ... Sacred held in Wexford town!

Eagle after all, despite his fierce independence, will soon be joining the workforce in the seafood factory just like everybody else. And while Isaac is one of the most attractive child characters in recent Irish drama, we cannot place a lot of confidence in his chipper twelve-year-old resolve, in the final scene with Dribbler out on the headland, to take up his father's mantle as the 'Lonesome Boatman', the last of the true fishermen of Wexford.

Both Roche and Friel create poignant drama out of their ambivalent nostalgia for St. Martin's Eve and Lughnasa. It is really only the strength of familial love that mollifies the tragic implications of these formerly vital traditions of celebration now overwhelmed, belittled, or distorted by the crass, indifferent modern world and rendered dangerous to their all too vulnerable celebrants.

*An earlier version of this essay, under the title 'Ominous Festivals, Ambivalent Nostalgia: Brian Friel's *Dancing at Lughnasa* and Billy Roche's *Amphibians*', appeared in *New Hibernia Review* 14:1 (2010): 127-41.

## 15 | *The Cavalcaders*: Billy Roche's Signature Play

Kevin Kerrane

To call any work of art a 'signature' piece is to suggest that it embodies the deepest preoccupations and most distinctive techniques of its creator. *The Cavalcaders* is that kind of drama: an iconic reflection of Billy Roche's singular talent. It combines familiar elements from his earlier plays – a public space as the setting, a pattern of sexual betrayal, a fluid sense of time, a subtle use of music, and a secondary cast of unseen characters who seem just as real as those on stage. Roche not only integrates all of these components; he complicates each of them, and may even take one or two to a dramatic breaking point.

As a result, the play demands inventive stagecraft, and so a full discussion of *The Cavalcaders* should take account of its unusual production history. For example, the same director, Robin Lefevre, has overseen all three major runs of the play: 1993 at the Peacock Theatre in Dublin, transferring in January 1994 to the Royal Court in London; 2002 at the Tricycle in London; and 2007 at the Abbey in Dublin. The first two of these featured Billy Roche himself in the role of the exuberant Josie, a singer in the quartet named in the play's title, and a worker in the shoe-repair shop that serves as the play's single setting. The 2007 production was the very first show in the newly configured Abbey, and as an intimate story enhanced by music it provided an ideal showcase for the theatre's improved sightlines and acoustics. *The Cavalcaders* has also been staged in Northern Ireland, Wales, Australia, and the United States – and in a translated version in Japan, where it was given the title of one of the original songs Roche wrote for the play: *Sayonara Street.*

These incarnations and permutations of the script help to clarify its challenges. *The Cavalcaders* can be difficult to stage successfully, partly because of the very qualities that make it a signature work. Benedict Nightingale, who regards the play as a 'near masterwork', has observed that its relatively minor impact at the Royal Court in 1994, after a triumph at the much smaller Peacock in Dublin, resulted from the cast's intimate acting and strong Wexford accents: 'those sitting further back than row D had trouble keeping up with a plot that itself somersaulted disconcertingly through time.'[1] The following analysis, which surveys a few options taken in various performances, has benefitted from personal interviews with Billy Roche and Robin Lefevre, and from the sheer luck – and pleasure – of having seen all three major productions of this most intriguing play.

## Setting

The stage image of an old-fashioned shoe-repair shop establishes a link to the traditional public spaces of Roche's *Wexford Trilogy* (1988-91), whose plays were set in a snooker hall, a betting shop, and a church belfry and sacristy. A later play, *On Such As We* (2001), takes place in a barbershop along a main street where commercial modernization appears to threaten an authentic town culture. (In that play one symptom of unwelcome change is the disappearance from the street of a traditional shoe shop.) *The Cavalcaders* uses modernization as an opening premise: Terry, the former proprietor, stands glumly in the disused shop while Rory, who was once an employee, chatters about his plans to reopen it as a mechanized business. A moment later the audience is looking at the shop as Terry remembers it – about seven years earlier, when it was still a busy place.

The imagined location, at the centre of small-town life, harks back to 'The Shoebox' in Roche's early novel *Tumbling Down*: a small shop at the edge of Wexford's main square, The Bull Ring. The proprietor, Johnny, is a popular figure in the town, and in several respects – his singing skill, his heavy drinking, and his early death – he prefigures the character of Josie in *The Cavalcaders*. Although Johnny is sometimes described working alone at his bench, he is seen only through the front window of The Shoe Box; Roche does

---

[1] Benedict Nightingale, Review of *The Cavalcaders* at the Tricycle Theatre, in *The Times* of London, Wednesday, January 9, 2003.

not take the reader into the shop. Of course *The Cavalcaders* brings the action inside, but a production in a proscenium-arch theatre can also suggest that the picture frame of the stage is like a window facing the street, thus inviting viewers to think of themselves as part of the community.[2]

The effect is heightened in scenes of singing, because the shop space doubles as a rehearsal site for The Cavalcaders. The quartet, led by Terry, works on routines they will perform at local venues. An old piano (positioned against a wall at stage left in all three productions directed by Robin Lefevre) becomes a more crucial prop than any tool of the cobbler's trade, and in fact *The Cavalcaders* barely dramatizes the shop as a business. The bustle comes not from customers but from the four workers, whose banter quickly establishes this setting as an essentially male space. In Roche's plays, such spaces – like the snooker hall in *A Handful of Stars* or the barbershop in *On Such as We* – are always modified subtly by the introduction of female characters. In this play the two women, Breda and Nuala, sometimes come into the shop for the music, but more often for romantic reasons. Each of them loves Terry, and each in her way is frustrated by his inability to receive that love, much less to return it.

As *The Cavalcaders* proceeds to explore Terry's troubled mind, its use of stage space transcends the realism of Roche's other single-set plays. Paula Murphy has suggested that the opening image of the shoe shop – 'small, claustrophobic, and jumbled' – foreshadows the main character's journey into his cluttered psyche. The audience never sees the shop's back room, but in the present action of the play Terry sometimes stares fearfully toward it, as if at a source of hidden traumatic memories, and through that doorway (stage right) the 'ghosts' of his past eventually emerge. In a way, Murphy concludes, 'the shop itself represents a human cranium.'[3]

---

[2] In a 2002 interview Roche also traced the setting of his play to recollections of a real Wexford shoe shop where locals gathered to sing, and 'the sun always seemed to shine.' But he suggested that his memory of a well-lighted place must be false: visiting the now-closed shop, Roche realized that it had only a tiny window: 'The sun couldn't have shone in there. It's like the darkest place you ever saw.' See Jasper Rees, 'A Small Irish Town Shows Us the World', London *Evening Standard*, January 3, 2002.

[3] 'Passages Through a Two-Way Mirror: Billy Roche's *The Cavalcaders* and *Amphibians*', in *Passages: Movements and Moments in Text*

More literally, for all four Cavalcaders the shop is an arena of conflict where moments of unity (joking at work, singing in harmony) are gradually overshadowed by scenes of discord and distress. When Christopher Murray surveyed Irish drama of the 1990s, he was struck by the ways that Roche's plays undercut the notion of 'home' – not only by avoiding the traditional Irish settings of kitchen, drawing room, or tenement, but also by showing characters failing to gain entry to 'some sanctum or state that would appease their sense of dislocation.' This alienation, Murray says, is epitomized in *The Cavalcaders*: 'Roche effectively suggests the possibility of community through a barbershop quartet, but as the play unfolds we see the desperation and history of betrayal beneath this joyous illusion.'[4]

## Adultery

Each installment of the *Wexford Trilogy* had featured a story of sexual betrayal: Stapler's extramarital affair in *A Handful of Stars*, Danger Doyle's theft of Steven's wife in *Poor Beast in the Rain*, and (at the very heart of the drama) Artie's short-lived romance with Angela, Donal's wife, in *Belfry*. In *The Cavalcaders* adultery becomes exponential. Colm Tóibín, in an essay reprinted in this collection, compares the play to a classic farce in which 'it is hard to keep tabs on who has been sleeping with whom.' One way to keep tabs might be to construct a chart like the one on the next page. Any such chart would show, first and foremost, that Terry's story takes place within a tangled web of community life.

Terry's personal history includes three sexual burdens: his illegitimate birth, his intimacy as a teenager with the wife of his beloved Uncle Eamon, and his desertion by his own wife. The audience hears how Terry's wife ran away with his best friend, Rogan – and then sees a similar conflict play out in the dramatic foreground when Rory's wife leaves him for Ted, a fellow Cavalcader. At the centre of the story Terry carries on a doomed affair with Nuala, a much younger and very vulnerable girl – and when Terry rejects her, Nuala becomes the mistress of a married

---

*and Theory*, ed. Maeve Tynan, Maria Beville, and Marita Ryan (Newcastle upon Tyne: Cambridge Scholars Publishing: 2009): 120-27.

[4] 'The State of Play: Irish Theatre in the 'Nineties', in *The State of Play*, ed. Eberhard Bort (Trier : Wissenschaftlicher Verlag Trier, 1996): 16.

## Characters in *The Cavalcaders*

**Mentor:** UNCLE EAMON

**The 6 characters seen on stage:**

|  | 4 Cavalcaders | | Women who love Terry |
|---|---|---|---|
| 2 who die | Josie | | Nuala |
| 3 seen in 'the present' | Rory | TERRY | Breda |
| | Ted | | |

**Dark Presence:** POE

### Recurrent off-stage figures

**Unfaithful spouses:**

Eamon's wife (with Terrry)
Terry's wife (with Rogan)
Rory's wife (with Ted)

**Shadow characters:**

Jacques LePouvier (for Josie)
Rogan (for Terry)
Downtown Munich (for The Cavalcaders)

**Parents:**

Terry's mother
R. Deacon (?)

**The larger community:**

Rory's daughter
Poe's wife ('Morticia')
'Beautiful Bundoran'

. . . and a dozen others

man who abuses her. At one point Josie recalls Terry's wedding ceremony, when Rogan stood at the altar as best man: 'I'm not coddin' yeh, yeh could nearly smell the treachery in the air, boy!'[5] *The Cavalcaders* is so awash in sexual intrigue that Josie's remark could serve as an epigraph for the whole play.

Roche's work generally reflects the increasing liberalism of Irish society, and most of his characters experience little remorse about illicit sex. (In *Belfry* the sacristan Artie and the married Angela consummate their romance in a church tower.) Terry's portrayal is exceptional: the playwright has called him 'my most guilt-ridden character.'[6] This guilt is not grounded in Catholicism. It derives first from shame − the stigma of illegitimacy in a small town. Terry appears to have absorbed some of his mother's feelings of unworthiness; he remembers her almost hiding in her own neighbourhood, peering out from behind a half-door (30):

> The poor crator was so ashamed of herself that she became just
> a little face in that auld dark doorway in the end. Practically
> disappeared, she did ... I mean, if it wasn't for me Uncle Eamon
> I'd've been lost altogether. Yeh know Communions and
> Confirmations and all the rest of it. Sure he worked wonders
> with me when I think of it − considerin' like.

Uncle Eamon was Terry's rescuer and mentor, a surrogate father. Eamon founded the original Cavalcaders and made Terry promise to keep that musical legacy alive. Throughout the play, Terry describes his uncle as a magician as well as a musician (he 'worked wonders'), and Eamon's tuning fork, a recurring prop, is like a wand. If the Camelot story provides the scaffolding for *The Cavalcaders*, as Roche has often said, then Eamon is Merlin.[7] After Eamon composed music for a Mass, Terry says, 'he was like a god around here that time now, yeh know. They'd nearly get off the path for him, man. Until she got her hands on him, of course. By Jaysus, she really sapped the magic out of him alright, boy' (60).

---

5 *The Cavalcaders and Amphibians: Two Plays* (London: Nick Hern
   Books, 2001): 45. All subsequent references to *The Cavalcaders* are
   to this edition and will be inserted parenthetically in the text.
6 Kevin Kerrane, 'The Poetry of the Street: An Interview with Billy
   Roche', *Irish Studies Review*, XIV, 3 (August 2006): 377.
7 Ellen Battersby, 'Dreamer Without the Angst', *The Irish Times*
   Weekend Review, April 7, 2007.

Terry is referring to Eamon's wife, an obviously disturbed personality who might charitably be described as 'sexually unwell.' When the boys were in their teens, she seduced Terry – and then tried to seduce Josie, who was unable to go through with the act when he saw her crying. Years after the event, she suddenly decided to tell Eamon about her liaison with Terry. This sense of primal sin is the second dimension of Terry's guilt; it is apparently the reason he tells Nuala 'I'm not a nice fella. I'm not!' (44). He even seems to feel that he deserved to be cuckolded. When Josie calls Rogan 'a bum', Terry replies: 'what we done and what he done was no different' (50). In an interview Roche has observed that Terry, because of his betrayal of Eamon, 'feels unworthy of love, even though he's surrounded by love. He can't embrace it. That can be an Irish male dilemma, I think.'[8]

All this turmoil in plot and character can create difficulties for the play in performance. The knot of illicit relationships may be less problematic than the main character's demeanour: typically sombre, brooding, and emotionally guarded. On stage Terry sometimes seems like a Hamlet without soliloquies. Even as the script gives the audience a strong rooting interest in him, it challenges the lead actor to convey feelings that the character is trying to repress. And when Terry does emote, the effect can be shocking – especially near the end of Act One, when Nuala's consuming neediness drives Terry to a speech of emotional devastation (45):

> What do I care. I mean I don't care where yeh go, do I. Just go. Back to your Da's farm or somewhere. Back to the funny farm if yeh like. I mean I don't care. It makes no odds to me one way or another where you go or don't go, because you don't mean doodle shit to me like, yeh know. I mean I swear I don't give you one second thought from one end of the day to the next. Yeh know? Doodle shit! That's all you are to me.

Liam Cunningham's performance of this scene in 2002, at the Tricycle Theatre, was intensely physical – as dark and brutal as Artie's whipping of Dominic at the end of Act One in *Belfry*. Yet Michael Billington, reviewing the Tricycle production for *The Guardian*, still complained that the protagonist seemed undramatically passive, merely 'a permanently defeated character with some unappeased sadness in his soul.'[9] Billington wished for a

---

[8] Kerrane, 'The Poetry of the Street': 377.

[9] *The Guardian*, January 9, 2002.

greater dramatic contrast between Terry 'as he is' and 'as he once was' – suggesting another basis of difficulty, at least for some critics, in the time-scheme of the play.

## Time

*The Cavalcaders* maintains two time sequences. Its 'present' frames the play in the first and last scenes, with a few intermittent returns, as Rory is cleaning out the old shoe shop before its modern makeover. In this sequence, covering less than a half hour in the characters' lives, Terry converses with Rory, or ruminates on his own, until Breda joins them in the play's final moments. The 'past' of *The Cavalcaders,* the centre of the story, takes us back about seven years to cover a few months during Terry's relationship with Nuala, when he was in his forties and she was half his age. This sequence occurs inside Terry's mind, and within it the audience sees all six of the play's characters interact – and hears them reminisce or argue about events even further back.

Two-track time schemes are a familiar convention in plays like Tennessee Williams' *The Glass Menagerie* or Brian Friel's *Dancing at Lughnasa*, in which a narrator brings the audience along on a memory trip. Roche himself had done something similar in *Belfry* when his narrator, Artie, haunted by the end of his affair with Angela, started to obsess about the day the affair began, replaying that day from multiple angles, in no obvious order, the way that any heartbroken lover might remain at the mercy of fractured memories.

*The Cavalcaders* complicates this premise by running its two time sequences with no narrator to guide the audience. And in Act Two, under the pressure of Terry's heightened emotions, the flashbacks jump the tracks, commingling or appearing out of sequence. Some reviewers have found these shifts chaotic: in 1994, for example, Paul Taylor quipped that 'whoever erected the signposts on this stretch of memory lane should try a career in maze-making.'[10] By contrast, in 2002 Fintan O'Toole praised 'the rhythmic unfolding of the past through a series of flashbacks that gives the story a wonderfully rich texture.'[11] In Act Two, as time

---

[10] 'Lost in Billy Roche's Wexford', *The Independent*, January 10, 1994. This criticism was echoed by Stephen Dunne in the Sydney *Morning Herald* (April 28, 2003) in reviewing a production of *The Cavalcaders* directed in Sydney by Maeliosa Stafford.

[11] '*The Cavalcaders*; Lyric Theatre, Belfast', *The Irish Times*, October 31, 2002.

becomes psychological rather than chronological, the skills of the lighting designer and of the actor playing Terry become even more essential in making transitions intuitively clear – but the shifts in *The Cavalcaders* do not seem inherently more daunting than those in Arthur Miller's *Death of a Salesman*, which even includes a flashback nested inside another flashback.[12]

Fluid time in *The Cavalcaders* creates several moments of strong irony. After the audience has learned of Nuala's death – a suicide motivated by her married lover's abuse and Terry's final rejection – Terry remembers an intimate moment from an early phase in their relationship. Nuala says: 'Sometimes I feel a bit ashamed of the things I ask you to do to me.' Terry replies: 'I'd do anythin' yeh want me to do. As long as yeh don't ask me to hurt yeh or anythin'.' As the scene ends, Nuala remarks: 'You'll probably do that anyway – in time' (86).

At the conclusion of *The Cavalcaders*, back in the present, it becomes clear that Terry has found stability with Breda, a voice of mature sense in all the prior scenes. Earlier Breda had delivered an ultimatum similar to Nuala's – telling Terry, in effect, *We're both single. So if we're to see each other, why should we sneak around? What are you ashamed of?* Terry was unable to respond. But at the end of the play he and Breda are living together (they may or may not be married), and as they leave the shop she insists that he must stay home until his 'flu' symptoms are gone. The audience understands, of course, that Terry's aches and fever have come from the stress of the evening's memories.

Is this a happy ending? *The Cavalcaders* has not traced out a change in Terry; in fact, by replaying his memories of cruelty to Nuala, the play has dramatized a third dimension of his guilt. According to director Robin Lefevre, 'People who have been damaged, the way Terry thinks he's been damaged, don't change that much. Billy and I agreed from the very first production in 1993

---

[12] In the first act of *Death of a Salesman*, Willy Loman sits in his kitchen reminiscing about a day 17 years earlier when he returned from a sales trip – and within that enacted memory, while chatting with his wife, he remembers and relives his tryst a few days earlier with a woman in his Boston hotel room. As he emerges from this 'interior' flashback, his guilt triggers an angry outburst, and the resulting tumult jars him back to the present.

that we're not in the business of redeeming Terry for an audience. That's who he is. You have to pick the bones out of that.'[13]

Lefevre's directorial strategies have differed in each major production. In 1993 Terry's role was performed with smoldering intensity by the great Tony Doyle. (After Doyle's death in 2000, Roche added a dedication to him in the published version of *The Cavalcaders*.) Doyle was 51 when the play premiered, which made it easier for audiences to appreciate the age gap between Terry and the fragile Nuala (Aisling O'Sullivan). When Liam Cunningham played Terry eight years later, he had just turned 40, and his performance was so sexually charged and physically intimidating that Terry's repeated line 'I'm old and you're young' had less credibility. When Stephen Brennan played Terry in 2007, age was not an issue, but the actor remained more grounded in his character's morose moods, both in past and present scenes, than either Doyle or Cunningham had been. As a result, the other performers took up the slack. Two of them were reprising their roles from 2002 in London – the luminous Ingrid Craigie as Breda, and the gifted musician David Ganly as Ted – while John Kavanagh replaced Billy Roche on stage, adding a different flair to the portrayal of Josie. As a result, the Abbey version became more of an ensemble production. 'It was easier', Lefevre says, 'to pick up on the idea that this wasn't *The Terry-Nuala Show* or *The Terry-Breda Show*. Everybody had something to contribute.'

## Music

In performance some of Terry's rough edges can be smoothed out when The Cavalcaders sing, because the audience now sees and hears him as more expressive and soulful. Roche was a professional musician before he became a writer, and all of his plays teem with music, whether emanating from a jukebox in a snooker hall or chimes in a belfry. But in *The Cavalcaders* music – like adultery – is not just a dramatic element; it's substantive.

The play draws theatrical energy from eight musical passages, four of them original compositions. The first is an old music-hall number made famous by George Formby: 'I'm Leaning on the Lamppost at the Corner of the Street/ Until a Certain Little Lady Comes by.' Early in Act 1, the quartet is in the shop doing vocal

---

[13] Telephone conversation with Robin Lefevre: June 30, 2007. All subsequent quotes by Lefevre come from this interview.

warm-ups. Ted is at the piano in the corner, and when he hits the first note the other Cavalcaders suddenly turn and sing the Formby song toward the audience, momentarily breaking the fourth wall. In every production of the play this moment has elicited surprised laughter or applause as the gap between stage and audience space is suddenly vitiated. The effect was especially striking in 2007 in the reconfigured Abbey. Fintan O'Toole observed that the new design by Jean-Guy Lecat restored the fan-shaped auditorium to its classical roots by 'raking the tiered seating down from where the balcony used to be, so that much of the audience is now level with or a little above the actors.' The result was a 'triumphant' theatrical intimacy, beautifully realized by *The Cavalcaders* in performance.[14] In effect, the 2007 Abbey production restored something of the studio-theatre experience of the original Peacock performances of 1993.

Two of Roche's original compositions dramatize contrasting romantic predicaments: 'One Heart Broken' is a lament by an abandoned lover; 'Sayonara Street' is a fond farewell by a man initiating a breakup. Within the play both songs have been written by Terry, and both express his own conflicts – the continuing ache of having lost his wife to another, and his current struggle to escape Nuala's devouring emotions.

According to Lefevre, 'Billy uses music in this play the way that music should be used in the best musicals. It's in the place of a scene. It's not music tacked on; it actually moves the whole action forward.' A clear example comes in Act One, after the first verse of 'One Heart Broken', when the singers gather at stage left around the piano to practice their four-part harmony by humming very softly, while at centre stage Breda tells Nuala about 'the auld days' in the community, with details (some amusing, some ominous) of Terry's

---

[14] 'Abbey's Seating Rejig Makes for Dramatic Improvement', The *Irish Times* Weekend Review, April 28, 2007. The Abbey production also included a cut-out space above the stage, a vertical rectangle about four feet by eight, that for most of the play showed painted images of traditional small-town rooftops. In a memory scene in Act Two, this cut-out became a frame in which Josie sang 'Smoke Gets in Your Eyes' as if he were a solo singer in a local lounge. In the play's final scene, as Rory tells Terry and Breda about his big plans for a fully modern shop, the Abbey audience saw a new insert with construction cranes in the background. According to Robin Lefevre, he and the set designer (Alan Farquharson) wanted to 'connect Rory to the Celtic Tiger, as a voice of Ireland's incredibly rapid change.'

wedding day. Instead of simple exposition, the scene offers a reverie set to music.

In a drama of shifting moods – humour, passion, pathos – music bridges many gaps, especially in Act 2 when Terry's memories converge. Near the end of the play he hears eight bars of the 'Alleluia' from the Mass written by Uncle Eamon, first as played on the piano by Ted and a moment later as sung by the choir at Eamon's funeral. Both passages stir Terry's guilt even while conveying forgiveness. As it happens, this 'Alleluia' is part of a complete Mass composed by Roche himself: 'I wrote Uncle Eamon's Mass,' he says, 'because I was so immersed in the play. I wondered: 'What would Eamon actually write? How would it sound?' ... And I meant it when I wrote it. I was trying to get to the heart of that little town and what religion meant to them, and the sacredness of life, and the disappointment of being let down.'[15]

Eamon composed his Mass using the piano that is now the play's most important prop. Inside this family heirloom, in the final scene, Rory discovers a small plate engraved with the name of the original tuner, 'R. Deacon', an itinerant who may well have been Terry's father. In any case, when Terry agrees to have the piano moved to the home he now shares with Breda, he is also taking ownership of his own past, with all of its consonance and dissonance.

## Off-stage characters

As the chart of characters indicates, the six people seen on stage in *The Cavalcaders* are far outnumbered by the invisible figures made real for the audience through recurrent reference. Roche's previous plays had included significant unseen characters, with sharp focus on an off-stage mother in each installment of *The Wexford Trilogy*, but *The Cavalcaders* goes much further in summoning up a town's shared life, past and present, good and bad.

Among the off-stage characters, Terry's ex-wife (never given a name), becomes a kind of Guinevere: Josie says that 'she lives like a nun now' (46) as she tends a garden and nurses Rogan. Surprisingly, Terry still idealizes Rogan, and often praises the boxing skills of the friend who betrayed him. In an interview Roche refers to Rogan as 'Terry's younger, more vital self' and 'a shadow, a doppelganger, a spiritual brother.' In this interpretation of off-stage characters, Josie's alter-ego would be Jacques LePouvier, a Frenchman who

---

[15] Kerrane: 378.

used to visit the town, and a formidable boxer in his own right. Jacques is Josie's 'spiritual god', Roche says, 'what he'd love to be, the essential gallant part of him. And at one stage when Terry and Josie fall out, they're arguing about their alter-egos. You can almost feel them leaving their bodies and then coming back.'[16]

These remarks suggest the extent of Roche's debt to depth psychology and myth studies. Besides alluding to Camelot, *The Cavalcaders* draws on one of Roche's favorite books, Robert Graves's *The White Goddess: A Historical Grammar of Poetic Myth*. For example, Nuala's poetry about the rowan tree as her mystical protector alludes to Celtic lore regarding the healing and sustaining powers of the mountain ash. As a representation of the eternal feminine, untamable and capricious, the White Goddess is manifest in references to Terry's wife, but she is also incarnate in the play's on-stage women.[17] When Nuala asks what Terry's wife was like, Breda replies: 'She was a little bit like you – a little bit like me' (29).

The vocabulary of *The White Goddess* is particularly helpful for stressing the complexity of Roche's female characters. At first glance, the play's character-chart appears simply to privilege 'the four lads' while mapping a pattern of female perfidy over the course of three generations – and a few commentators on *The Cavalcaders* have used the word 'misogyny' as if identifying Roche with Terry.[18] A closer look suggests that this drama offers an incisive critique of its male protagonist by developing an off-stage character, a Gothic figure appropriately named Poe, as a projection of Terry's dark side.

Poe is the most disturbingly real of Roche's unseen characters. An undertaker who also manages the local variety shows, he seems a

---

[16] Kerrane: 374.

[17] Graves notes the significance of the rowan tree, and its red berries, in Irish celebrations honouring Brigit ('formerly the White Goddess, the quickening Triple Muse'), as well as in the Cuchulain saga, and the romance of Diarmuid and Grainne. See the emended and enlarged edition of *The White Goddess* (New York: Farrar, Strauss and Giroux, 1975): 167-68. In an interview Roche explained: 'In *The Cavalcaders* the White Goddess is Terry's wife, who ran away with Rogan. We don't see her, but she's also there in the triple guise of Breda, Nuala, and Terry's mother who represents the old crone. Maiden, mother and moon, basically' (Kerrane: 374).

[18] See especially reviews of the Abbey production by Peter Crawley in *The Irish Times* (April 16, 2007: 6) and Tanya Dean in *Irish Theatre Magazine*, VII, 31 (Summer 2007: 121).

harmless cartoon-figure at first. Poe has a big face, described as looking like 'a well-slapped arse' – and when the four Cavalcaders watch through the window as a gorgeous bank clerk ('Beautiful Bundoran') walks down the street, they note that the undertaker is ogling her too: 'he's after catchin' his big chin in the spokes of his bike', Terry says (15). As a concert organizer, Poe frustrates The Cavalcaders with uncertain bookings and unfavourable placement on programs, but he is also unintentionally funny in his role as emcee. Rory quotes him as announcing: 'Frank McCarthy, the well-known memory man and clairvoyant will not be appearin' due to unforeseen circumstances' (32).

Poe's characterization becomes progressively more sinister, and far more vivid than if he were actually seen on stage. 'He's a Poe by name and nature', Josie says – and then suggests that this dour personality may result from Poe's trauma as a young man when he went down to the basement of the funeral home (Rory calls it 'the dungeon') and found his father lying dead after a freak accident (31). Rory refers to Poe's wife as 'Morticia', but the joke turns sour when Terry tells how Poe once cut off all her hair: 'he was goin' off to some convention or somethin', and he was afraid of his life that she'd go out on the rantan while he was away' (35).

The sick side of Poe is most evident when Nuala reveals in Act Two that he has been her secret lover. 'He used to beat me', she tells Terry. 'With his belt. Down in the cellar below his shop ... He told me I was like Eve. He said that Eve came into the Garden and ruined everything' (73). Nuala says that Poe dumped her when she became pregnant, and she tells Terry of a plan for revenge against this Confraternity man, who wears 'his pioneer badge and his fainne and his black diamond on his arm and all the rest of it. Well maybe he won't feel so tall when I spill the beans on him' (72).

Poe may be in the play to represent a pillar of the community who, in reality, is a hypocrite and pervert, but he also expresses the darkness within Terry, just as Uncle Eamon had provided a beacon of grace and benevolence. As the character-chart suggests, these two off-stage figures can be seen as the poles of Terry's personality. When Terry instinctively takes Poe's side by warning Nuala to remain quiet ('That man is a married man with a family'), she responds by equating the two lovers who have turned her away: 'I'll show you. I'll show him too. Because you're nothin' only a pair of lousers, Terry. Dirty lousers, yeh are, the pair of yeh' (74).

Roche also uses off-stage characters comically – for example, by shadowing the quartet itself with a younger singing group called Downtown Munich, who seem to have copied The Cavalcaders' repertoire, including specific musical arrangements and hand movements. Terry says these rivals should be renamed 'Downtown Mimic.'

This other quartet caricatures The Cavalcaders, and even foreshadows their breakup. Early in Act Two, Rory gleefully tells Ted about Downtown Munich's fiasco the night before: 'The big fat lad fell off of the stage and everythin', he was that drunk. They started arguin' in the dressin' room after you were gone Ted, yeh know. The fella with the glasses kneed the big lad in the bollix and all' (54-55). A few moments later Ted admits to Terry that he is having an affair with Rory's wife and has asked her to move in with him. Then Ted leaves the shop, and The Cavalcaders, for good.

Seven years later, in the present time sequence of the play, Rory has custody of his daughter, who is now ready to make her First Communion. His loving description of this child makes her another of the play's compelling off-stage characters (13):

> Oh she's a real little madam now the same one! ... I was lyin' in bed there though Terry yeh know and next I hears her stirrin' inside the other room. She gets out and toddles across the landin' to the bathroom – a little sleepy head on her. I hear her do a little widdle then flush the toilet after her and then she goes runnin' back to her little warm bed again and I think to meself, 'How did I get her this far and all eh?' Yeh know! ... They're deadly little sounds though ... (He *chuckles and basks in the thought of it all.*)

In the world of *The Cavalcaders* such small bits of domestic happiness assume monumental importance, especially as expressed in the everyday poetry of Wexford speech. Rory's loving words also reflect his resilience. Like Terry, he lost his wife to a supposed friend, and near the end of the play he tells Terry of having encountered her, now pregnant, on the street with Ted: 'I just said hello to them and that ... All water under the bridge now' (87). Rory's statement masks profound grief, and yet his pain has not metastasized into bitterness or cruelty. He remains upbeat, or at least tries bravely to seem so. In using Rory to round out the play, Roche provides Terry with a dramatic foil who – unlike Rogan, Poe, or Uncle Eamon – is there to be seen, and admired, on stage.

The ending of *The Cavalcaders* affirms the play's signature status in yet another way: by crystallizing a vision of life – empathetic and forgiving, yet resolutely unsentimental – that underlies all of Roche's work. When Trevor R. Griffiths reviewed the original production at the Royal Court in 1994, he singled out Tony Doyle's 'brilliant' performance as Terry, but gave most consideration to the playwright's generous spirit:

> Billy Roche's skill as a dramatist lies in his ability to show us convincing images of our shared humanity and the ways in which the texture of our lives is made up of quiet desperations and betrayals, minor-key achievements and qualified local victories ... [His play] is an elegantly comic elegiac tribute to ordinary people muddling through and coping with their human failings.[19]

This sense of commonality helps to explain why *The Cavalcaders* has appealed to audiences outside Ireland, from Theatr Clwyd in Wales to Sambyakunin Gekijo in Japan. The play has crossed boundaries of geography as well as genre by transforming Wexford into a universal town.

In *The Cavalcaders* the town's boundaries are broad, and its extended community includes the dead (Josie, Nuala, Uncle Eamon) as well as the living. The town's culture runs deep, layered with music, fisticuffs, magnanimity, gloom, poetry, treachery – and love. This extraordinary range gives *The Cavalcaders* special standing among Billy Roche's artistic achievements. It may be both his darkest and most hopeful play. And no other work so fully dramatizes his core imaginative premise – Wexford as the world.

---

[19] 'Over Barriers', *Herald Scotland*, January 12, 1994: 9.

# 16 | *Trojan Eddie*: The Power of Laughter and Degradation

Katherine Clarke

> 'You're a smirky little bastard. Anyone ever tell you that?'
> 'I've a dirty kind of a smile alright, but sure what harm?'

Near the end of Billy Roche's 1996 film *Trojan Eddie*, Raymie (Sean McGinley), a wheeler-dealer with a penchant for spending money before he earns it, bleeds to death in the muck of a leaky old warehouse. Ginger (Brendan Gleeson), a red-haired thug with the look of a small child in the body of a grown man, has taken a baling hook from its holder on a mud-stained wall and attacked Raymie from behind, plunging the hook deep into his back. As Raymie presses against a now bloodstained mirror, his anguished expression is clearly visible. 'That sure wiped the smile off your face, didn't it?' says Ginger. 'I don't see yeh smilin' now, ya feckin' little prick yeh – laughin' at me! You, laughin' at me! I don't think so!' The brutal killing has been provoked by a casual joke, a hint that Ginger is a cuckold, made by a man unaware of its consequences. The effect of the blow comes as a surprise even to Ginger: as the realization of what he has done kicks in, he makes a run for the door.

The incident illustrates the paramount importance of retaining one's dignity in this tight-knit provincial world, of never letting anyone get a leg up or attain any sort of edge within the social ranks. Though Roche's characters exist far outside big cities or ordered municipalities, their power struggles are no less intense for that. Living within a fiercely hierarchical, yet somewhat fragile, community of Travellers in a muddy small-town landscape, the male characters interact according to what Victor Merriman calls 'the grammar of crime films.' Irish Travellers have regularly been seen within a framework of criminality, a view perpetuated by mainstream media. In popular culture the Traveller is a kind of barbarian sub-species, a social pariah and problem of the state in need of assimilation and supervision. Characteristics of this Mafia-style world, Merriman says, include 'uncompromising adherence to family ties, and respect for elders and tradition.' Such qualities are usually regarded as positive, but on the screen they are represented as 'sinister and threatening to sedentary society ... introverted, primitive and dangerous.'[1]

Presiding over the action of *Trojan Eddie* is John Power, the deeply lonely and insecure alpha-male of the community, played discerningly by Richard Harris as haggard and somewhat burned out. The father of Ginger, Power is a settled Traveller, having broken away from his family when they tried to move on to the next place; yet he remains emotionally hollowed by the death of his wife, a Traveller named Kitty. Although he heads a local trading empire, his small office, positioned at the top of a set of winding rusty stairs, is more like a run-down shed. It connects to a room cluttered with shiny trophies, candlesticks, chandeliers and golden objects for Travellers to marvel over – but through a sort of optical illusion, director Gilles Mackinnon presents a view out the window, and the audience is surprised to see a large whitewashed country home, with ponies in the yard, where a young Traveller girl named Kathleen might finally find a roof over her head.

One of Power's minions, Eddie (Stephen Rea), appears to live a futile, dispassionate existence, working a daily grind ('like a Trojan') while raising two children as a single father. Eddie comes to life in his role as salesman, and the film begins with his dynamic spiel in a warehouse as he gets a crowd bidding eagerly on Power's wares – appliances, apparel, and assorted kitsch. He models himself on Bargain Joe, another salesman who used to come around the village years ago: 'He was a real jingler-boy', says Eddie. 'He could sell yeh somethin' yeh didn't even want ... And the banter he had, fuckin' genius boy.'[2] Out of the bull ring of the sales market, Eddie dreams

---

[1] Victor Merriman, *Because We Are Poor: Irish Theatre in the 1990s* (Dublin: Carysfort Press, 2010): 171-175.

[2] As a fast-talking hawker of goods, Eddie is reminiscent of a character introduced in Roche's novel *Tumbling Down*: 'Cheap Charlie, the most famous and charismatic of all Irish street traders.' Charlie's

of starting up his own business, freeing himself from Power's demands, but he can't seem to find the funds or the momentum to make his way out of this mess or escape the pull of his tightly-bound community. He tells his girlfriend (Brid Brennan): 'It's as if the story's already begun, ya know, and I'm sorta locked into it or something.' For most of the film, Stephen Rea plays Eddie as a passive figure, and Mackinnon provides frequent close-ups of his hangdog expression.

Eddie's morose demeanour harks back to the attitudes of some of Roche's other middle-aged males, like Steven in *Poor Beast in the Rain* or Terry in *The Cavalcaders* – men whose wives, like Eddie's, have abandoned them. 'I thought I was goin' to sneak through life unnoticed', Steven says at the close of his play, finding an odd solace in the sense that he's going nowhere fast.[3] For Eddie, however, the tide may ultimately turn when laughter and mockery disrupt the order of Roche's finely drawn and fragile world. As in the scene with Ginger and Raymie, a snigger behind the back of an enemy or the feeling that the whole village is having a laugh at one's expense often leads to conflict. In fact, Eddie's ultimate emancipation comes only through the collapse of John Power's own dignity and pride.

The fold of the Travellers, as Roche portrays it, is a world of one-upmanship, depending heavily on a delicate balance of power within its ranks. Ginger's bullying is learned behaviour, a paranoid style passed down from his father. 'I mean Jimmy here is strong', Power declares in one scene, 'but he couldn't hold a candle to my Dad ... I mean he couldn't hold a candle to my dad, right?' As the tragic hero of his own twisted story, Power has one fatal weakness: his sadness over the loss of Kitty. Desperately trying to replace her, he looks to Kathleen, a much younger fiery-natured girl with a love of shiny things and the ambition of being settled in a home. 'I don't like the road myself', Kathleen tells Power one afternoon by the river. 'When I get married, I'm wantin' to live in a house with a little orchard out the back and a swing for the children and all. People think the Travellers don't like beautiful things but we do, and they think that we don't feel the cold as well, but that's not true either.' As her would-be rescuer (if somewhat beyond his peak), Power shares her

sales patter (amplified by a megaphone) seems to be a model for Eddie's at the beginning of the film. See *Tumbling Down*, revised edition (Wexford: Tassel Publications, 2008): 69-70.

3 *Poor Beast in the Rain* in *The Wexford Trilogy* (London: Nick Hern Books, 2000): 122.

ambition of domesticity: 'I am a king', he exclaims one evening in the local pub, 'and a king needs a queen.'

The film exoticizes Kathleen's free-spirited ways: she swims naked in the river, golden rings piled on her fingers and red curls blowing in the breeze. To Power she seems a quasi-mythical figure; to the audience she seems more an embodiment of Power's insecurity. As Roche writes in an introduction to the screenplay,

> She reminds him of his late wife. In other ways she represents his youth and vitality. But more than all that she seems to be a link back to the old life that he has forsaken. For, in spite of his riches there in an underlying sadness about him – like a man who has lost his place in the tribe.[4]

Although Kathleen acts in one sense as a mirror reflecting the ever-changing landscape of Power's anxiety, her character is not a merely an instrument of plot, as some critics have suggested. (Mary Burke calls the characterization of Traveller women in the film 'outrageously one-dimensional.'[5]) Like the characters around her, Kathleen is just one figure making up our overall perception of Travellers. Roche's depiction rejects stereotype or reduction of any kind, and Kathleen is a finely shaded individual, especially as portrayed in the film by Aislin McGuckin. Though riddled with doubt, Kathleen possesses an agency of her own, thwarting attempts by others to strip her of it.

Michael Patrick Gillespie observes that Power quite foolishly seeks to reinvent himself through Kathleen. Power tries to construct a viable future by replicating, as closely as possible, the happiest moments from his past, but the relationship is hopeless from the outset.[6] Roche has described Power as the Fionn MacCumhall of the story – and in a striking parallel to the Irish legend of Diarmuid and Grania, Kathleen is in love with Power's nephew (Stuart Townsend), who is named Dermot.

Despite his better judgment, and his previous knowledge of the love between Dermot and Kathleen, Power cannot fight the way he feels and falls headlong into a situation that will ultimately

---

[4] 'Introduction' to *Trojan Eddie: A Screenplay* (London: Methuen, 1997): vi.

[5] Mary M. Burke, *Tinkers: Synge and The Cultural History of the Irish Traveller* (Oxford: Oxford University Press, 2009): 242-245.

[6] Michael Patrick Gillespie, *The Myth of an Irish Cinema: Approaching Irish-Themed Films* (Syracuse, NY: Syracuse University Press, 2008): 99-102.

humiliate him and cost him his place within the community. On her way to the wedding Kathleen emerges from the family caravan clad in a white frilled dress to cheers by the locals, and at the wedding reception Power twirls her around the dance floor, her feet lifting lightly off the floor. But what should be a glorious moment, with grins on the faces of Power and his bride, is transformed for the viewer into a painfully awkward scene as Kathleen's peers avert their eyes and stony-faced older men acknowledge the strangeness of the union with bemused glances.

Later Power sits shamefaced at the wedding table and watches, with tight jaw and sad eyes, as his bride dances in the arms of her much younger lover. Neighbours exchange knowing and pitying looks as a female Traveller (Dolores Keane) sings a cautionary song, 'Love Makes a Fool of You', that Roche composed for the film:

> You think that you're in heaven
> But you haven't got a clue
> Love can take you to the stars
> Then love makes a fool of you.

The grey-haired husband is helpless to regain his power when Kathleen makes a bid for freedom with Dermot, clutching £11,000 in wedding cash contributed by the guests. By the standards of his tribe, Power should react to his new wife's infidelity with rage and a commitment to revenge, but his sadness leads him to a much more honest and humiliating admission. He tells Eddie: 'I'll take her back whenever she wants to come back. I don't care what she's done. I tell you this because I know you'll understand like.'

Power is referring to Eddie's own status (or lack of it) as a cuckold, and a passive one at that. Eddie's embarrassment throughout the story comes not only from being a 'townie', one who does not belong, but also from having accepted his former wife's infidelity and blatant disrespect. As if he will always have Eddie to look down on, Power says: 'Your Missus could be bangin' right in front of yeh and you'd still take her back. 'Cause you're a sucker. I mean we're all suckers when it comes to women. But you take it to the extreme. You're a fuckin' double-decker.'

In turn, Eddie's ex-wife, Shirley (Angeline Ball), demeans him as Power's lap dog: 'Still the good little boy you used to be, coming when you're called.' Eddie bears this too, but finally erupts when Shirley – after hinting that she has just returned from another sexual encounter – threatens to take custody of their two daughters away from Eddie, and even raises the question of whether he is really their father. Eddie's accumulated frustration suddenly bursts forth in physical violence, and the audience may be surprised to find itself rooting for him as he pushes Shirley forcefully against a doorframe, punches her in the mouth, and continues to strike her. Mackinnon's camera keeps a background image in focus: a statue of the Infant of Prague, who seems to be watching everything. Through this sequence the audience is reminded that Eddie, a settled member of an urban community and an outsider within the circle of Travellers, is just as apt to use violence, even against women, as the supposed itinerants or degenerates. The application of extreme force and brutality, the scene shows, is not a measure confined to simply Travellers but a characteristic of society as a whole.

'They are never represented as just themselves but always as Other to the norm of the settled population', writes José Lanters of Traveller representations.[7] But *Trojan Eddie* succeeds in turning this assumption on its head. Though the Travelling community is not in itself the subject of Roche's film, the playwright assumes his role as an observer of this subculture with great fairness, responsibility and a subtle touch, daring to tell the tale from inside their world. In his introduction to the screenplay Roche explains (v-vi):

> Travellers have their own unique culture – their own songs and stories, their own mode of dress, their own language even; which I know as Shelta – one of the secret languages of Ireland. I decided to make them the insiders of my story (they are usually portrayed as 'victims' or as 'outsiders' or worse again as the 'shunned'). In this tale, it is Trojan Eddie, the settled one, who is on the outside.

The Traveller characters revert to Shelta at a key moment in *Trojan Eddie*. In the immediate aftermath of the wedding humiliation, the groom's closest conspirators gather in his tower to plot their next move: they will track down Dermot and Kathleen and take back what belongs to their leader. Power himself languishes in this situation, taking a backseat to his henchmen. They converse in deliberately hushed tones, employing Shelta in order to ostracize Eddie from the discussions, pointing him out as a potential traitor, 'a townie … a real snake in the grass.'

---

[7] José Lanters: *The 'Tinkers' in Irish Literature: Unsettled Subjects and the Construction of Difference* (Dublin: Irish Academic Press, 2008): 154-156.

**Figure 6:** A climactic scene from *Trojan Eddie* (1996), with Richard Harris as John Power and Stephen Rea as Eddie. 'It was a beautiful screenplay, sad and poetical', says director Gilles Mackinnon. (Photograph by John Hession)

Near the conclusion of the story, Eddie and Power come face to face for the first time since Raymie's murder. After friends and relatives have gathered in the graveyard to lay Raymie to rest, Eddie hangs back from the crowd to speak to his former boss, who is leaning against a tree. Power looks exhausted from recent events, including the arrest of his son. His body is limp, his soul crushed; since Kathleen ran away, Power's position as head of the community has been compromised. He has been shamed and has lost the respect and loyalty of the tribe. And he still has not recovered the missing money.

What follows is a conversation reminiscent of the murder scene, a power play in which Eddie triumphs with little effort. 'We used to laugh at you, you made our lives worth living', Power says bitterly. 'What', Eddie responds, and you think no one's laughin' at you or somethin'?' For Power, confirmation that folks have been laughing behind his back is the last straw: summoning up all his remaining ferocity, he grabs Eddie by the collar and threatens to destroy him if he finds that this 'little toerag' played any role in Kathleen's disappearance or the theft of the money. Here Eddie makes his break, simply by wresting free and looking into Power's eyes with 'a certain compassion' before walking away. Power can only hurl insults: 'I know who I am, and what I am, and what I'm worth. But you, you haven't got a clue, not an idea ... "Trojan Eddie" – trojan fucking eejit.' Roche's screenplay specified (76) that Eddie's composed face should fill the foreground, with Power in the background '*jerking and twisting and pointing, his whole body going into abuse.*'

The film's final scenes offer what initially seems to be simple poetic justice. First, Kathleen returns to Power by using Eddie as her intermediary. Dermot 'is after bailing out on me', she says. 'Bad luck may he never shun.' Eddie drives her to Power's property and watches her climb the wooden stairs to his office. (We see Power look up from his newspaper, but the actual reunion is not dramatized; Kathleen has returned to this man more by default than by positive choice.) The next scene shows Eddie brooding in the cluttered flat of his murdered friend, and then discovering the stolen cash. Roche describes Eddie's face as 'radiant' (81), even as he comprehends Raymie's treachery.

Then, presumably a few months later, the camera follows Power and Kathleen into a movie theatre. She is heavily pregnant. As they stroll arm in arm in the lobby past a group of teenage boys, laughter erupts behind them – and although the audience sees that Power is not the source of this amusement, he clearly thinks that the boys are laughing at him. He may be worried about insinuations that he is not the father of Kathleen's child, and of course Power himself must be wondering about the actual fact of paternity. In any case, he will always have to deal with the inevitable scorn befalling an old man with a young wife. 'In the old myth,' Roche says in his introduction (vi), 'Fionn MacCumhall actually wins back his Grania, and Diarmuid is killed by a wild boar that is chased his way. And when the victorious Fionn rides into town with his young bride everybody laughs at his love-foolishness.'

In the theatre Power's humiliation mounts when Eddie, looking prosperous, pops on the screen delivering a fast-paced spiel for his new store:

> What you want, I got. And if you can get it cheaper anywhere else then I want to know about it. Trojan Eddie's the name, bargan-zinies the game! A Walkman? I got it. A razor? I got it. A guitar? I got it. A flask? I got it. A keyboard? Had one last week. Too late. So listen, don't be done out of it, get down here now! Trojan Eddie's of William Street. Now!

Power's irritation subsides as other images fill the screen – a quiet ad for an Indian restaurant – but suddenly Eddie's face reappears, this time in a bigger close-up: 'What are yeh doin' sitting there?' he demands. 'I said *now!*' The final frames of *Trojan Eddie* show Power's face in the half-light, defeated.

This concluding moment – in which Eddie seems to taunt Power directly, even personally – represents an ambiguous turning of the tables. Mary Burke has suggested that Eddie's ability to ultimately detach himself from the pull of the Travelling community and re-enter legitimate society only serves to reinforce the idea of the 'uncivilized' Traveller.[8] But though Eddie emerges from the story as the victor, the audience understands that he too is flawed: his new empire is the product of a crime, and he has absorbed some of the questionable values held by Power. Eddie has gained the upper hand through dishonesty as well as luck. Power has become subservient through his own misguided ideas of love and happiness. Billy Roche's tale has come full circle.

---

[8] *Tinkers: Synge and the Cultural History of the Irish Traveller* (Oxford: Oxford University Press): 245.

# 17 | 'Anything But Stand Still': Billy Roche's *On Such As We* *

Patrick Lonergan

Like many of Billy Roche's plays, *On Such As We* dramatizes a clash between two Irelands, one traditional and the other modern (or perhaps modernizing). That conflict is presented in terms of a dispute between the play's protagonist Oweney, the owner of a Wexford barbershop, and a local businessman called P.J., who never appears onstage. Their antagonism is caused mainly by the decision of P.J.'s wife, Maeve, to begin a relationship with Oweney; the play concerns her uncertainty about whether to remain with a husband she no longer loves, or instead to join Oweney for a more fulfilling yet less secure life. The presentation of that dilemma allows audiences to understand the conflict at the heart of the play between an authentic Irish past and a gaudy, materialistic future. Given that it received its premiere in 2001 – at the peak of the Celtic Tiger era – *On Such As We* can therefore be seen as both pertinent and prophetic.

The play can also be seen as a response to the problem of acceleration in contemporary culture, an issue that was receiving a great deal of attention in both popular and academic literature at the time of the play's premiere. Those discussions were occasioned by a growing awareness that, in contemporary business, nothing lasts forever. Vinyl was replaced by compact discs, which are in turn being replaced by digital downloads; videotapes disappeared with the advent of the soon-to-be obsolete DVD; and perhaps, for reasons of environmental protection as well as fashion, the book may eventually be replaced by an electronic equivalent. 'To avoid frustration', notes Zygmunt Bauman, 'one would do better to refrain from developing habits and attachments or entering into lasting commitments. The objects of desire are better enjoyed on the spot and then disposed of; markets see to it that they are made in such a way that both the gratification and the obsoleteness occur in an instant.[1] The increased commodification of culture, that is, results in a situation where the gap between consumption and desire has been reduced to almost nothing.

*On Such As We* appeared at a time when many critics and scholars were attempting to come to terms with the transformation of culture occasioned by the combined impact of the mass media, digital culture, and globalization on our ability to receive and process information. In 2000, for example, James Gleik drew attention to the 'acceleration of just about everything' in global culture, noting that many aspects of human life, from commerce to employment to culture, had accelerated considerably. [2] That acceleration has resulted in a situation in which people now 'multitask' cognitively, Gleik suggests: that is, they have become used to performing a number of simple tasks simultaneously rather than, as would have been the case in the past, devoting their attention to one specific complicated activity. Eleven years earlier, David Harvey had related multitasking to the impact of capitalism, which, he stated, has been 'characterized by continuous efforts to shorten turnover times, thereby speeding up social processes while reducing the time-horizons of meaningful decision-making.'[3]

Both writers' insights seem accurate if somewhat generalized. The public have shown an enthusiasm for devices that are designed to save them time or that allow them to perform multiple tasks simultaneously: microwave ovens, remote controls, and speed-dialling telephones are common examples of that phenomenon. Gleik in 2000 described how a manufacturer of portable CD players was offering users the option to play back their CDs with the gaps between songs removed, saving the user perhaps forty seconds when

---

[1] Zygmunt Bauman, The *Individualized Society* (Cambridge: Polity Press, 2001): 156.

[2] James Gleik, *Faster: The Acceleration of Just About Everything* (London: Abacus, 2000): 162.

[3] David Harvey, *The Condition of Postmodernity* (Oxford: Blackwell, 1989): 229.

listening to a sixty-minute album. What is significant about this example, of course, is that it illustrates how the time we use to engage with culture has become more compressed. But it is also notable that Gleik's example has itself become outdated in a very short period of time, since digital music players such as the Apple iPod have largely supplanted portable CD players since the turn of the century.

For the present purposes, the most important form of acceleration occurred when capital's focus moved from production to culture. Responding to Frederic Jameson, Harvey notes (61) that the production of culture 'has become integrated into commodity production generally.' He continues:

> The mobilization of fashion in mass (as opposed to elite) markets provided a means to accelerate the pace of consumption not only in clothing, ornament and decoration but also across a wide swathe of life-styles and recreational activities (leisure and sporting habits, pop music styles, video and children's games, and the like). A second trend was a shift away from the consumption of goods and into the consumption of services – not only personal, business, educational, and health services, but also into entertainments, spectacles, happenings, and distractions. (285)

This alteration in the pacing of mass-mediated entertainment was not imposed by an elite on an unsuspecting and helpless public, states Harvey. Rather, as Gleik suggests, it was a reaction by those controlling the mass media to the exercise of viewers' decision-making – principally by means of the remote control. Gleik quotes Robert Levine, who cites studies showing that television no longer has viewers, but 'grazers': people who change channel up to twenty-two times in one minute, who 'approach the airwaves as a vast smorgasbord, all of which must be sampled, no matter how meagre the helpings.' [4] As a result of such 'grazing', audiences form superficial views of the programming, which reduces their satisfaction levels and their attention span. Networks have responded by ensuring that the audiences will not be given any reason to hit the remote control button. Gleik mentions how a 'new forward-looking unit within the NBC' has been taking 'an electronic scalpel to the barely perceptible instants when a show fades to black

---

[4] Gleik: 183. See Robert Levene, *A Geography of Time: The Temporal Misadventures of a Social Psychologist* (New York: Basic Books, 1997).

and then re-materializes as a commercial. Over the course of a night, this can save the network as much as fifteen precious seconds, maybe even twenty.' However, writes Gleik, saving time is not the main point of this exercise. 'The point', he argues, 'is that the viewer, at every instant, is in a hurry' (175).

Similarly, the growth of fast-cutting and double or triple cutting in cinema and television has meant that the speed with which people process images has increased. The Irish theatre producer Michael Colgan offers a useful example of the consequences of this transformation:

> I recently went to see *L.A. Confidential* with my sixteen-year-old daughter and my mother. It starts with cross-cutting, cameras flashing, simultaneous sounds, half-sentences, over-lapping dialogue, American slang, characters talking in unison, everything topping everything. I was giving it my best just to hold on to it, not helped by my mother who was giving it her complete best but was hopelessly lost and my daughter said 'What's wrong?' I said, 'Nana doesn't understand it' and Sophie said 'Doesn't understand what?' She had time to talk to us and she understood every single thing that was going on. The speed, the density was perfect for her. Her world is an entirely different world from ours. It's not a failure of the imagination to say it would be easier for my mother to sit through three and a half hours of *King Lear* than it would be for my daughter. My daughter would be bored by that.[5]

So, as Gleik and Harvey note, many people now perform their tasks in work differently, but the point here is that they too are watching theatre and other forms of culture differently. Colgan's example of a movie from 1997 illustrates that different generations have become used to receiving culture differently. His mother's reception of culture involves concentrating on one specific point for a protracted period. His daughter performs a number of cognitive tasks simultaneously: she is multitasking, in other words. Colgan's perceptual processes combine both extremes. He admires his mother's concentration and his daughter's versatility, but relates entirely to neither.

---

5 'Michael Colgan in Conversation with Jeananne Crowley', in *Theatre Talk: Voices of Irish Theatre Practitioners*, eds Lilian Chambers, Ger FitzGibbon and Eamonn Jordan (Dublin: Carysfort Press, 2001): 80-81.

Colgan's anecdote – together with the works of Bauman, Harvey, and Gleik – can be used to illustrate the way in which audiences' responses to theatre are changing, both in Ireland and internationally.[6] It is almost certainly the case that the organization of time within theatre is being altered. The traditional three or five act structure of plays has generally been replaced by a loosely structured series of short scenes (often between twelve and fifteen per play) that tend not to last longer than fifteen minutes each. The risk of an audience losing concentration is minimized with action taking place quickly enough to be perceived, but too quickly to be analysed, and by the frequently gratuitous use of shocking images such as explicit on-stage sex or intensely cruel violence.[7] Audiences have generally responded positively to the ways in which some new dramas attempt to provoke spontaneous emotional reactions from them rather than considered intellectual responses – since this is what they have become used to in almost every other visual medium, from cinema to television news reports.

If we now receive culture at a faster speed, it is also significant that the world has itself become a faster place. As Arjun Appadurai notes, 'few persons in the world today do not have a friend, relative or co-worker who is not on the road to somewhere else or already coming back home, bearing stories and possibilities.' [8] Irish dramatists are clearly no exception in this regard, as is evident from the success of such playwrights as Martin McDonagh and Conor McPherson in New York, of Enda Walsh in Germany, and of Frank McGuinness in London.

Rather like globalization itself, mobility is evident in ways that are difficult to measure. Freedom from restraint of one's mobility is

---

[6] This discussion appears in more detail in my book *Theatre and Globalization* (Basingstoke: Palgrave Macmillan, 2009), where I explore the impact of these processes on the development of the Irish monologue.

[7] The critic Aleks Sierz refers to the emergence of this development in Britain as an example of 'In-yer-face Theatre', but in fact these characteristics have become common in many other media – especially television and cinema. They are also common in drama outside of Britain. I discuss this issue in more detail in a chapter on Martin McDonagh in *Theatre and Globalization*. See Sierz, *In-Yer-Face Theatre* (London: Faber, 2001).

[8] Arjun Appadurai, *Modernity at Large: Cultural Dimensions of Globalization* (London and Minneapolis: University of Minneapolis Press, 1996): 7.

indispensable to the success of organizations and individuals in the globalized world; inhibition of mobility is increasingly being seen as an indicator of disadvantage. Zygmunt Bauman, who writes about these issues in great detail, suggests that, in our times, 'Mobility climbs to the rank of the uppermost among the coveted values – and the freedom to move, perpetually a scarce and unequally distributed commodity, fast becomes the main stratifying factor of our late-modern or postmodern times.'[9] As Bauman points out, one of the most interesting analyses of the current importance of freedom of movement is Richard Sennett's *The Corrosion of Character* (1999). Sennett illustrates the importance of mobility in our society by means of a perceptive comparison of Bill Gates – the most successful businessperson of the globalization era – with John D. Rockefeller. 'Gates seems to be free of the obsession to hold on to things', Sennett notes: 'His products are furious in coming forth and as rapid in disappearing, whereas Rockefeller wanted to own oil rigs, buildings or machinery for the long term. Lack of long-term attachment seems to mark Gates's attitude towards work.'[10] Rockefeller's power was signified by possessions occupying physical space, but Gates's power is signified by his freedom from temporal attachment – by the fact that his success is built on the short lifespan of everything he produces. Gates therefore becomes a significant example of a value that has come to dominate all of our lives: the temporary nature of our relationships with everything that we produce or consume. Sennett interestingly dubs Gates and those who share his values as examples of 'Davos Man', named after the Swiss resort at which, each year, the World Economic Forum meets.

In some sense P.J. in *On Such As We* can be understood as an Irish example of Sennett's 'Davos man.' He is no Bill Gates, but he seems to be similarly desperate to remain free of temporal or physical attachment. He has taken control of many of the small businesses in Wexford, replacing their individualized shop fronts and products with material described by Oweney as 'Neon, plastic, hollow crap.'[11] P.J.'s interest is in the impermanent and the temporary. As Maeve explains (33):

---

[9] *Globalization: The Human Consequences* (Cambridge: Polity Press, 1998): 2.

[10] Richard Sennett, *The Corrosion of Character* (New York: Norton, 1999): 61.

[11] Billy Roche, *On Such As We* (London: Nick Hern Books, 2001): 94.

He never stays put. When he's here, he wants to be there. When he's there he wants to be somewhere else. And he wants to knock everything down – the house where he was born in case somebody sees it, the old hotel for spite, the whole neighbourhood if necessary. Anything but stand still.

This description contrasts with Oweney, who is 'old-fashioned and proud of it.' Whereas P.J.'s actions are a denial of his past, Oweney is committed to a linear sense of history, as represented by his barbershop: 'My da had this place before me and his da before him and I'll be straight about it – I'm hopin' my young lad'll take over after me' (32). This rootedness to one location is emphasized throughout the play, as for example when the audience is told that Oweney does not have a car (27).

As is appropriate for a play set in a barbershop, the dominant image in the text is of the mirror – with P.J. and Oweney functioning dramatically as reflections of each other. P.J. generates obedience from people by hiring thugs to commit acts of violence on his behalf, but Oweney inspires loyalty by means of kindness and generosity. Oweney's sensitivity is evident when he tells Maeve that he will walk with her through a wood, but P.J. tears down an orchard at the back of his house in order to build a pool-room. Whereas P.J. does not want to have children, Oweney is on the other hand an apparently affectionate father to his own three children, as well as being a self-professed 'mother' (6) to Leonard, one of the young men to whom he leases accommodation. When one of P.J.'s hired thugs is sent to prison for an assault which P.J. had ordered him to commit, he receives no support; in contrast, Oweney shows great concern for his young tenant Leonard when he is summonsed to court for the theft of Christmas trees.

There might appear to be a rather simplistic morality at work here, with the overwhelmingly negative characteristics of P.J. contrasting favourably with the essential decency of Oweney. It could be easy for an audience to think that since P.J. is overwhelmingly bad, so too is the modernity that he represents – and that, similarly, the traditional values shown by Oweney are good simply because he himself seems a decent man. The fact that at the end of the play Oweney has taken P.J. 'down a peg or two' (94), and that Oweney is still in business while P.J. has left town, might lead us to believe that Roche's hero has been successful and that, by extension, we are to understand that traditionalism has triumphed over gaudy modernity. However, many aspects of the play combine to show that Roche is attempting instead to avoid creating such an impression.

Firstly, Oweney is not as admirable a person as we might assume, and Roche leaves many aspects of his character interestingly unresolved. Oweney is estranged from his wife, who forced him to leave their home. Furthermore, Oweney tells us that his 'oldest girl Sharon is still not talkin' to me. She turns away or crosses the street whenever she sees me comin' now' (32). When asked by Maeve to explain this, Oweney can only say that his wife asked him to leave because of his 'ramblin' and gamblin' and stayin' out late at night' (32) – an evasive explanation that no member of the audience can be satisfied with – though Maeve does not pry further, interestingly. The cause of this separation is not explained. Instead, Roche hints at possible causes. Oweney certainly gambles, as we find out late in the play's second act, when he tells us that he is 'after winnin' a nice handy little two hundred smackers for meself anyway. ... Twenty pound win double on Sergeant Major and Planxty Jones' (72). In other words, he bets against long odds. So this is one possible cause of his estrangement from his wife (as well as his lack of a car). It is therefore apparent that the audience is intended to regard Oweney as being in certain respects flawed.

Furthermore, the play concludes unsatisfactorily for many of the main characters. Maeve tells Oweney as consolation for her unwillingness to pursue a relationship with him that 'the two of us will live forever' in memory (90), because Oweney showed her a reflection of herself that was 'beautiful.' This vision is instantly subverted, however: Maeve then tells Oweney that she has decided to stay with her husband because she must make a success of her marriage: 'at the end of the day Oweney it's a *reflection* on me if I don't' (91, emphasis added).

Similarly, the other couple in the play – Sally and Leonard – end the action very happily and romantically. Yet a great deal of what we see of Sally is contradicted by what the other characters say about her. There is a hint that she has had some form of relationship, albeit probably a brief one, with Eddie, one of the play's least likeable characters. The play's last action is of Leonard crossing himself before getting into bed – an image that contrasts with a statement that Ritchie makes about how Sally 'caused quite a stir up there [at the convent where she lives] from time to time ... Sister Veronica had to put her on the pill and everything I believe' (19). Ritchie himself seems a very likeable old man, yet we are told that he treated his wife badly, and that she at one stage ran away to Swansea in order to be free from him. From these and many other examples, it seems that Roche is trying to direct our attention to an undercurrent in his description of an apparently idyllic setting. This is a play in which most of the characters appear to be very likeable – but much of what is reported about them shows that they are not just performing to the audience, but to each other as well.

Another significant example of this tension between appearance and reality is the play's presentation of popular culture. Although Oweney and some of the other characters are trying to resist the forces of modernization, he – and everyone else in the play – is highly literate in popular culture, albeit in its older manifestations. While Oweney is able to recount to Maeve the story of the 'Swan Lady' from Wexford (29) and Sally thinks that Matt's portrait of Leonard makes him look like 'Labhraic Loinseach' (61), the majority of references in the play are to popular culture. The play is filled with a variety of popular songs, all either American or English, most of them originating in the 1950s and 1960s. We also have references to American television programmes such as *Mister Ed* (about a talking horse) or to international events such as the sinking of the Titanic, or such global personalities as Che Guevara.

Furthermore, the play is clearly based on the Western genre of cinema, which, as Luke Gibbons has shown, has played an important role in the production of Irish culture. [12] In a public interview at the Peacock Theatre in 2001, the play's director Wilson Milam said that although Roche had never confirmed that he had intended to structure the play like a Western, Milam's own view was that the play certainly resembled one – *Shane* (1953) in particular, he thought. The play certainly uses many aspects of that genre: there is the presentation of Wexford as a small, self-contained unit being threatened by external forces, and there is also the showdown on the main street at the conclusion of the play. Furthermore, *On Such as We* is filled with references to the Western genre, as for example when Leonard recounts a scene at the courthouse on Christmas Eve (68): 'It was like the Wild West up there at one stage. Hank was up for breakin' your man's nose, there was another lad up for hittin' a

---

[12] Luke Gibbons, *Transformations in Irish Culture* (Cork: Cork University Press, 1997).

fella in the forehead with a hatchet and Malachy Morris was charged with knockin' off a horse and cart.'

All of Roche's plays are nostalgic – 'old fashioned and proud of it', like Oweney – but in *On Such As We*, that nostalgia is consistently destabilized. The sentimental portrayal of Oweney, Roche's use of old-fashioned music, and his use of the Western plot structure are all intended to celebrate the recent past. On the surface, Roche's play appears to be a critique of the attack by modernity on tradition. Yet it is also a celebration of certain forms of mass mediated popular culture.

Interestingly, however, if Roche's use of these forms is in fact a celebration of late modernity, the directorial style employed by Milam was in many ways a celebration of mobility, being like P.J. 'afraid to stand still.' Although written in two acts, the play combines a number of run-together scenes that take place over the course of two weeks. In its 2001 Peacock production, the action occurred, often simultaneously, in three performance spaces – so that when a character left one room, his or her instantaneous appearance into another room signalled a chronological shift of hours, days – even weeks. In the course of a play lasting less than two hours, the audience was therefore asked to keep up with sudden chronological shifts forward in time on almost thirty occasions – making the pace of the play remarkably fast, and ensuring that audiences' attention would never be allowed to waver. The audience, that is, was being asked to multitask cognitively—we were, like P.J., constantly in a state of being hurried – and the directorial approach was clearly an attempt to bring to the theatre the techniques of fast-cutting that had become more popular in cinema. In some ways, then, the directorial approach seemed to celebrate speed, mobility, acceleration – and thus to contradict (or at least contrast with) the themes of the play.

The marketing of the play could also be regarded as a celebration of mobility. Although the play can be seen as many things – new work from one of Ireland's leading playwrights, a 'Christmas' play, a love story – the Abbey simply used a portrait of Brendan Gleeson (shown below) to market the play. In the late 1980s and early 1990s, Gleeson occupied an important role in the Irish theatre, with his brilliant performance as Fluther Good in the Abbey's 1991 production of *The Plough and the Stars* as a highlight of a career that also involved playwrighting: Passion Machine produced his work in 1987 (*The Birdtable*) and 1994 (*The Last Potato*). But the

Abbey's use of Gleeson's portrait was due mainly to the fact that he had acquired a high profile abroad as an actor, notably with his performances in such internationally successful movies *The General* (Boorman, 1998) and *AI – Artificial Intelligence* (Spielberg, 2001). The Abbey's portrait of Gleeson provides no indication of the play's theme or plot; no value may be ascribed to Gleeson's character. All we are told is that Gleeson – whose face we know from his cinema performances – has returned to Ireland to perform in a play. And that knowledge is deemed sufficient to attract an audience.

## The Abbey Theatre's Marketing of *On Such As We*

The apparent triumph of traditionalism in the play is thus complicated in many ways. Roche undermines it by hinting at darker sides of his characters' lives, and with his use of popular culture. The manner in which the play was produced – with its overlapping scenes and its use of celebrity to market the play – also contrasts interestingly with Roche's apparent celebration of traditional values. And most importantly, there is the plot: Roche shows that, despite Oweney's admirable qualities, his lack of mobility means that he cannot be successful in the globalizing world, as is made evident at the play's conclusion, when Maeve returns to P.J. This shows that *On Such As We* must be regarded as a lament for a dying culture, rather than as a celebration of an embattled one.

As such, Roche illustrates the importance of mobility. P.J.'s success is represented through his power to move freely and without impediment; for all of his good qualities, Oweney's lack of mobility is represented as disadvantageous to him. So, as an act of social critique, the play's views on mobility are clear. Yet the play itself is an example of the significance of the need for cultural forms to be transferable across national boundaries: with its use of the Western genre and the fact that its linguistic register is from a globalized popular culture, the play's Wexford setting will not prevent anyone from understanding it. Roche's characterization and the play's music indicate regret for the passing of certain values; but the production's pace and innovative use of chronology show that those values have not just passed, but are gone forever. Thematically and structurally, Roche's play implies that the ability to move freely and quickly is a sign of success in the globalized world, but, characteristically, he invites audiences to contemplate – and ultimately to regret – that this is so.

* This essay is an edited version of a paper that appeared in *Ihla Do Desterro*, number 58 (2010).

## 18 | Stasis, rootlessness and violence in *Lay Me Down Softly*

Úna Kealy

A play on a page is only half alive. It needs actors, lighting, set, music, and crucially an audience to enable it to become what the playwright has imagined. Consequently, when a playwright directs his own text, that production is important and revealing in the life of the play. Such a production took place in October 2010 in Wexford town when Mosshouse Production Company, founded by Billy Roche, staged *Lay Me Down Softly* in association with the Wexford Arts Centre. Mosshouse is without Arts Council funding, meaning that resources were quite limited. And because Roche wanted this version of the play to tour, the challenge was a typical one facing any small scale theatre company: create a production on a shoestring that can pack into a small van and work in a variety of spaces with minimal equipment. While scarce funds and the technical demands of touring can mean compromises for some writers, directors, and designers, in this case necessity inspired a wonderfully simple solution for a play which recounts the events, set over three days, in a travelling roadshow.

Bui Bolg, the designers and builders for the production, used their expertise in creating props and puppets for street theatre to suggest the lurid and portable world of the play. Before the drama began to unfold in the Wexford Arts Centre, the audience entered a world of light and shadows via a stairway masked with candy striped canvas and naked bulbs, creating the impression of the 'Academy Boxing Arena' within the play's setting, Delaney's Travelling Road Show. A boxing ring – smaller than a real one – served as the stage centrepiece, while a small ticket kiosk, a turnstile, a large equipment box and a punching bag completed the set. Paul Keogan's lighting design used a few focused beams to enhance the road show atmosphere, creating separate areas in a tight performance space on a floor-level apron stage. Off-stage areas were bounded by velvet curtains that suggested a more prosperous past. Seated on three sides of the performance space, the audience created a backdrop of faces that completed the design and added to the claustrophobic world of the play. It was an approach that exposed the gaudy dilapidation of life on the road, amplifying the sense of transience that dominates the play and truly immersing the audience within the production.

**Figure 7:** Gary Lydon as Theo and Michael O'Hagan as Peadar in the 2010 Mosshouse production of *Lay Me Down Softly* at the Wexford Arts Centre, directed by Billy Roche. (Photograph by John Michael Murphy)

The boxing arena is all that the audience sees of the road show, and it constitutes a world of its own. The characters appearing on stage are those who work in the boxing booth: Theo Delaney, the show's owner-manager and a former amateur boxer; Peadar, an 'over the hill ex-boxer', cut man, and fixer; Dean, the principal fighter, brawny and full of bluster; Junior, fit and lean but injured and now working as a repair man; and Lily, who sells raffle tickets and sleeps with Theo to ease the loneliness of an empty life. Emer, Theo's estranged teenage daughter, who has run away from home, arrives into this world, and her presence becomes a catalyst for change.

As is usual in any Roche play, numerous characters inhabit the off-stage world and their reported actions add substance to the on-stage milieu, subtly intensifying the drama. Reported events from the past, especially those involving Joy, Emer's mother, poignantly reveal how opportunities for happiness have been squandered. In the present action of the play, comic relief comes from some unseen confrontations, such as Little Ernie's trouble with a local man nicknamed 'Wild Bill Hickock' who wins all the prizes on the rifle range. Other off-stage conflicts, such as Theo's beating of Rusty, a thieving employee, increase the tension on stage. This tension finds a natural focus in the boxing ring, where locals can contend against real prize fighters or vent their frustrations upon one another. The play opens as Dean boasts to Peadar and Theo of his previous night's victory when he beat a much older opponent. His bravado is short-lived, however, as Junior breaks the news that the defeated man's nephew – Joey Dempsey, a former professional boxer – has returned to avenge his uncle. In the ensuing action Dean predictably loses his fight against Dempsey, who insists on returning to box again. This time Junior agrees to fight him. The result is a draw and a big payday for Theo. But the money is barely counted when Emer and Junior, aided by Peadar, take it and run away together, leaving Peadar to face Theo's wrath.

*Lay Me Down Softly* creates a world of grubby glamour. Roche sets the play 'somewhere in Ireland' in the 1960s, which might hint at nostalgia – but the physical proximity of the performers and audience in the Mosshouse/Wexford Arts Centre production quickly exposed this life and its trappings as a threadbare and violent realm where beauty is found only in fragments that are cheap and shabby when fixed together, like the jigsaws that occupy Theo in his spare time. The setting marks a departure from Roche's previous plays, which are all set in small Irish towns.[1] The decision to create a location that is neither urban nor rural but somewhere in-between reflects a shift in Roche's themes: whereas earlier plays, including those in *The Wexford Trilogy*, showed characters confined by narrow streets and a correspondingly narrow mind-set, *Lay Me Down Softly* explores the contortion of personality and potentiality in the absence of family and familiar ground. The impermanent

---

[1] Although Roche's plays have become synonymous with Wexford town, in fact only *Amphibians*, *Poor Beast in the Rain* and *Belfry* are actually said to be set there, while *A Handful of Stars*, *On Such as We* and *The Cavalcaders* are set more anonymously in small towns 'somewhere in Ireland.'

marginal world of the play provides an apt environment to explore the effects of living outside a particular place that can be called 'home' – a point emphasized by Peadar when he repeats the words of Emer's mother, Joy:

> I asked her did she want to go back home again or anything, but she didn't. She said she didn't really know what that word meant any more – home![2]

Conveying this sense of impermanence, the stage directions state that a marquee is set on 'a rough wooden floor with tufts of grass growing up through it' (2), creating an on-stage image of a world hastily put together, and one that can just as easily disappear. At the opening of Act Two, Junior identifies the play's location as in the midlands 'Just outside Bridgewater somewhere' (45), and also mentions Stoneyville and Huntley. Yet these villages differ from each other only in that the bottles of milk produced there, otherwise so uniform, are imprinted with the names of the local dairies, suggesting that little differentiates the landscape that the characters traverse. The text includes references to the bigger west Waterford towns of Cappoquin and Dungarvan, but these places are vaguely 'elsewhere', thus emphasizing the ambiguity of the setting rather than providing points of orientation. In the same way, by giving features of the immediate locality generic names such as 'the shrine' and 'the milk train', the text suggests a kind of no-man's-land, a place existing on the outskirts of anonymous towns and villages that is not necessarily even Irish. It could be any peripheral waste land anywhere. Although it departs from a familiar and known geographical location, the visual stage picture described by the set directions calls for an attention to detail that recalls the old-fashioned public spaces (betting shop, shoe-repair shop, barber shop) of Roche's previous plays. Within the imagined activity and relative openness of a fairground field, the enclosed space and focused light of the boxing ring and the shadows surrounding it create a contained and atmospheric setting. Somewhat like the pool hall in *A Handful of Stars*, the Academy Boxing Arena in *Lay Me Down Softly* comes to life as daylight fades, revealing a turbulent world within a tightly defined arena – as indicated by the stage directions (2):

> *A ring is erected in a marquee tent and there is a raised dais of sorts at the back wall with benches for the bystanders. ... A small table and chairs are positioned close to the ring. ... There*

---

[2] Billy Roche, *Lay Me Down Softly* (London: Nick Hern Books, 2008): 62. All quotations from the text are taken from this edition.

*are a few steps leading up to a covered-in wooden kiosk with a*
*turnstile for punters ... A heavy punchbag dangles down.*

This stage picture alters little in the course of the play, and almost all changes are effected through lighting.The minimally invasive stage management keeps the dramatic focus on the characters themselves, allowing the rhythm and momentum of the unfolding drama to be sustained – a vital element in a play that must steadily heighten tension to create the suspense required in the final scene.

Though ostensibly a play concerned with physical battles, *Lay Me Down Softly* is ultimately about psychological pain. Roche harnesses the energy and intrinsic theatricality of boxing to explore an emotional violence that fractures relationships rather than jaw bones. Characters hurt each other through jealousy, bitterness, and rejection until, by the close of the play, Theo and Lily's relationship is cracked, Dean's ego is crushed, and Peadar and Theo's friendship reaches a point of irredeemable disintegration. Appropriately, the physical violence within the play – most notably in the fights between Dean and Dempsey, and Junior and Dempsey – takes place between scenes, thus maintaining focus on emotional rather than physical cruelty. At the conclusion, as the lights fade to black, Peadar sits waiting and ready to absorb the predictable and bitter violence of Theo's fury, which becomes more bloody and brutal in the imagination than would be possible if it were played out on stage. The final stasis recalls the ending of *A Handful of Stars* in which, as the lights come down, Jimmy Brady squats by a jukebox, alone, waiting for his inevitable arrest – which may involve a beating as well. In *Lay Me Down Softly* the audience must piece together crucial elements of the story for themselves to appreciate the subtext and emotional depth of the drama. Just as the spectators' physical presence completed the stage picture in the Wexford Arts Centre, the text requires that the audience interpret the significance of information, such as Peadar's liaison with Joy, Emer's mother, after Theo had abandoned her – which hints that Peadar, not Theo, is Emer's father. An accumulating dramatic tension is crucial to the play in production. That force arises from the interplay of characters, and Roche invests each of them with a contrasting energy. *Lay Me Down Softly* opens with characters focused and engaged in a specific physical activity, thus freeing the text from the burden of exposition and allowing the characters' physicality to establish an immediate rhythm for the drama. The stage directions are once again explicit in their detail (2):

*Lights rise on the boxing booth. It is Wednesday morning*
*and DEAN, in a lather of sweat, is skipping close to the*

*punchbag. PEADAR is working inside the ring, dismantling the ropes and testing their durability and looking underneath the ring for replacements etc. THEO is busy inside the wooden kiosk.*

Dean, throwing jabs while boasting of his previous night's success, provides a kind of punctuation for the minor but menacing confrontations, frustrations and threats that underlie the men's conversation. The dialogue, interspersed with monosyllabic questions and mutterings, suggests characters who are trapped in a world and a vocabulary that stunts their ability to express themselves and thereby resolve their particular frustrations. Those frustrations then explode in bouts of verbal violence – for example, when Theo, jealous that Lily might be courting the attention of one of the fairground hands, berates Peadar over a broken turnstile (7):

**THEO.** (*in a fury*). Are you goin' to take a look at that aul' turnstile our there for me or are you not, yes or no? – like I asked yeh.
**PEADAR.** What?
**THEO.** Instead of fuckin' around with that thing for him there. The ropes were alright the way they were. Lave them be, be fucked. You'll be puttin' powder on the floor next.
**PEADAR.** Junior, come on, you're better at this lark than me.
**JUNIOR.** What lark?
**PEADAR.** The turnstile is stickin' apparently.
**JUNIOR.** Yeah?
**THEO.** The whole thing dismantled, be Jaysus. For what? Bullshit!
**PEADAR.** Here we go again.
**JUNIOR.** What?
**THEO.** Never mind mutterin' there at all.
**PEADAR.** Yeh what?
**THEO.** I said less of your aul' guff there.

In the Mosshouse/Wexford Arts production Gary Lydon's Theo simmered with a barely controlled rage, which contrasted effectively with the stoical demeanour of Michael O'Hagan's Peadar. Lesley McGuire as Lily, with her shining black hair and cat-like sensuality, further heightened the tension on stage.[3] Calling attention to the pungent smells of sweat, dust, leather and rope, and making references to Theo's possessive jealousy, Lily adds an intoxicating

---

[3] Other cast members in the Mosshouse/Wexford Arts Centre production included Dermot Murphy as Dean, Anthony Morris as Junior, and Pagan McGrath as Emer.

element of sexual frustration to this testosterone-fuelled world. In the ensuing events and conversations, in which tempers are short and language is terse, it is apparent that Theo's control over his shabby empire is weakening and he must resort to threats and violence to maintain his authority. The ebb and flow of tension, expressed physically as well as through dialogue, capture a process of transition: the power dynamic between age and youth is shifting, and the alpha males are no longer so powerful. Theo wears glasses and does the books while Peadar's role is to care, repair, and maintain. It is the younger characters, Emer and Junior, who emerge as the dynamic force in the story and manage to escape the debilitating emotional violence of the road show.

Whether to maintain a status quo or to escape is a perennial conflict played out in each generation, and all the physical paraphernalia associated with boxing creates a symbolic arena in which this eternal power struggle is made manifest.

In addition to its generational struggles, *Lay Me Down Softly* dramatizes existential conflicts in term of space: between the problems of being settled in one place and the opposite but equal difficulties of being cast adrift in the world with no place of sanctuary. In its constant relocation, Delaney's Travelling Road Show offers freedoms from small-town life where change is rare and a rigid moral code demands the permanency of relationships, regardless of the unhappiness they may cause. This unhappiness is crystallized in the character of Lily, whose life in her home village of Knocknanoo was weighed down by the twin forces of a Rayburn and her husband. In their life together, Lily says, her husband preferred enduring unhappiness to the unknown eventualities of change (47): 'I mean he knew well enough I wasn't happy livin' there but it never even occurred to him to do anything about it. ... He didn't want to lose what he had, I suppose. What he had! A brown coat and a book of fuckin' dockets! Ha!'

Lily had security in Knocknanoo where things were predictable and permanent, as symbolized by the image omnipresent in the village: a woman in her coat and hat on her way to town, frozen forever in an impossible act of escape. The road show offers freedom from this unchanging and unstimulating life, but the alternative is another extreme where Lily must endure a life of constant relocation and instability, and where possessions and people are continually damaged. The opening line of *Lay Me Down Softly*, in which Theo asks Peadar to fix a broken turnstile, immediately suggests the abrasive quality of life on the road. The wear and tear of physical objects symbolizes a corresponding emotional deterioration that is played out in Lily and Theo's relationship, which is defined by sniping sarcasm. Whatever tenderness there once may have been between them has long since worn away. By the end of the play, Lily is ready to transfer her affections to Junior, simply because the harsh nature of such an itinerant life is Darwinian: as Lily instinctively knows, only those who can adapt quickly, allying themselves with those who are strongest, will survive. Thus while life on the road might offer freedom from the confines of small town life, this freedom comes at the price of foregoing sensitivity and tenderness. Roche's female characters seem to suffer this loss most keenly.

Lily will survive such a loss of tenderness because, in her own words, she is a 'a big strappin' heifer' of a woman (22). She knows that to be otherwise is to risk being left behind, as Joy was. Described by Theo as 'like glass' or 'porcelain' (24), Joy was too fragile to survive in a world that demands emotional and physical resilience. Joy might be regarded as a reincarnation of Nuala in *The Cavalcaders*: a character who also writes poetry, is emotionally vulnerable, and looks to men to fill an emotional need. Nuala's invitation to Terry to join her for a night when she suggests they will not simply have sex but read poetry and talk by the fire comes to fruition in *Lay Me Down Softly* when Peadar and Joy have a stolen night together in the Sea Breeze Hotel. Peadar describes the time he spent with Joy (63):

> Somewhere along the line I nipped out and got some kindling and coal and, although we weren't supposed to, I lit a fire in the grate and she read me one of her poems.
>
> > 'Wash me and comb me
> > And lay me down softly
> > Lay me down softly
> > At the end of the day ...'

The fire, the poetry and that sense of sanctuary directly echo Nuala's invitation to Terry:

> **NUALA.** Listen, I'm wantin' yeh to come over and see my little room sometime....Will yeh?
> **TERRY.** OK.

**NUALA.** I'll read you some of my poetry by candlelight. And I'll light a big fire and we'll lie down on the mat together.[4]

Terry ultimately rejects Nuala – and in her misguided search for tenderness, she gets pregnant by another and equally uncaring man and tragically commits suicide by drowning. Joy also yearns for tenderness and intimacy in a callous world, and she finds it – but only fleetingly. This moment of tenderness is literally life-giving in that Joy avoids Nuala's tragedy, returns to her brother's house and a life made possible despite (or perhaps because of) her pregnancy.

Like Nuala, Joy is abandoned by the men in her life, and this theme of abandonment recurs throughout the play: Theo was abandoned by his father, and in his turn abandoned Joy, who was then also abandoned by Peadar, while Lily left her husband and life in Knocknanoo but now spends her time in fear of being left by the side of the road herself. Through this preoccupation with abandonment, and other references to Joy's brother as a bull and her house as a labyrinth, *Lay Me Down Softly* becomes a drama of archetypes: Theo and Peadar recall the restless mythic adventurers Theseus and Pirithous, who attain power and possessions through violence and abduct women only to abandon them when a new challenge becomes more interesting. *Lay Me Down Softly* uses myth to interrogate the pain and passion of the human condition, transcending any particular people, place, or period.

The production of *Lay Me Down Softly* in the Wexford Arts Centre managed this feat of transcendence through precise direction and evocative design, thus illuminating universal and perennial problems of love, loss and longing. The lurid colours of the set, the dirty cuffs of the costumes, and the shabby velvet curtains evoked a dingy and demanding life that promised freedom from the mundane but in reality delivered only an alternative set of difficulties. The proximity of the audience to the performers encouraged those present to participate in a drama that, like so many of Billy Roche's works, explores a world of shadows and dark hurts. The minimal set and simple lighting design complemented a text that avoids the showy theatricality of physical violence in favour of a deeper, more painful emotional violence, expressed in the restrained and often monosyllabic poetry of everyday life. In the world of this production, as in our own world, things are temporary and easily damaged:

---

[4] Billy Roche, *The Cavalcaders and Amphibians: Two Plays* (London: Nick Hern Books, 2001: 84.

turnstiles stick, tents leak, and broken people do their best to survive. The Wexford production created and sustained an emotional intensity which transformed the glare of the lights, the smell of sweat, the smack of a punch, and the moan of a train into potent sensory signifiers of frustration, hope and freedom.

## 19 | Billy Roche's Secular Priests

Maureen Cech

Noting the absence of a 'governing myth' in Billy Roche's writing, Colm Tóibín contends that 'Catholicism means nothing in his work.'[1] It is true that the frequent sexual affairs among Roche's characters are usually unaccompanied by religious guilt, and that these characters seem free to explore their own aspirations and existential longings without carrying a burden of institutional morality. But in Roche's Wexford the role of religion is complicated – and the complications are richly dramatic. In *The Cavalcaders*, for example, the music of 'Uncle Eamon's Mass' (written by Roche himself) becomes a touchstone for the protagonist, Terry, challenging his conscience even as it conveys forgiveness. In *Belfry* Donal confronts the man who cuckolded him – Artie, the church sacristan – by innocently asking for a copy of his own baptismal certificate, and then tearing it into shreds and scattering it like confetti over Artie's head. 'That's what you think of me, isn't it?' Donal demands. 'I really don't exist as far as you're concerned. Sure I'm not a Christian at all am I?'[2]

Such complications may be most pronounced in Roche's portrayal of two priests: Father Pat in *Belfry* and Father Corish in *Tales from Rainwater Pond*. As minor characters, the priests remain on the periphery of the stories, just as Catholicism as an

---

[1] Colm Tóibín, 'The Talk of the Town', in *Dudes, Druids and Beauty Queens: The Changing Face of Irish Theatre*, ed. Dermot Bolger: 23. The essay is reprinted in this anthology.

[2] Billy Roche, *The Wexford Trilogy* (London: Nick Hern Books, 2000): 159. Subsequent citations from *Belfry* will be given parenthetically in the text.

institution is itself decentralized, but Roche avoids familiar caricatures of the Irish Catholic priest as domineering, abusive, or clueless. His priest characters are conceived in a much different spirit than other recent depictions of Irish clergy – such as Marina Carr's doddering Father Willow (*By the Bog of Cats*), whose senility makes him unable and unwilling to involve himself in the Kilbrides' family strife; or Martin McDonagh's pathetic sacrificial lamb Father Welsh (*The Lonesome West*), whose eccentric interpretation of Catholic doctrine allows him to wager his immortal soul on the flimsy bond between two spiteful brothers; or Channel 4's humorously improper trio of priests in *Father Ted*, whose comic irreverence is pure parody. Roche may not look up to priests the way he once did as an altar boy in Wexford, but neither does he look down on them, or use them as easy stereotypes. Instead, he treats his priests with the same candor and impartiality that he extends to all his characters. The results provide lessons in aesthetic fairness and social insight, even as the two priests offer an intriguing study in contrasts.

Father Pat's most striking feature is his youth. Actor Gary Lydon portrayed Pat in the debut of *Belfry* at the Bush Theatre in November 1991, only three years after playing the teen rebel Jimmy Brady in Roche's *A Handful of Stars*. In an interview with Conor McPherson, Roche points out that Father Pat is estranged because of his youth in a profession in which there are few young men to whom he can relate. McPherson agrees: this recently ordained priest is part of 'a dying breed. You don't get the young bucks going into the priesthood. So he really is a very isolated character.'[3] Pat (often referred to in the play without the honorific 'Father', and with no reference to his last name) is expected to hear the sins of others with a maturity and eloquence beyond his years. The loneliness weighs heavily on him, and he sometimes copes by turning to alcohol. Pat's drinking problem is no secret: Donal, one of his parishioners, inquires whether Pat is 'off the gargle now' (132). Early in the play, Pat admits to the sacristan Artie that he doubts his ability to serve as a spiritual guide for others. He describes having faltered in performing the last rites for an old man (146):

---

[3] 'Billy Roche in Conversation with Conor McPherson', in *Theatre Talk: Voices of Irish Theatre Practitioners*, ed. Lilian Chambers, Ger FitzGibbon and Eamonn Jordan (Dublin: Carysfort Press, 2001): 427. Excerpts from the interview are reprinted in this anthology.

He lost two children when he was a young man he was tellin'
me. He lost his wife, he lost his job, he lost his health and in the
end he lost his faith. And who could blame the man. And I'm
supposed to minister to him. I'm supposed to tell him what he
doesn't know, what he hasn't figured out already himself. I
don't know ... (*He shakes his head and sighs.*)

To the dying parishioner, Pat's vocation makes him a
representative of God, but Pat himself is overwhelmed with doubt
about his spiritual and moral authority. He feels that he has not
lived and suffered enough to provide spiritual advice to others.

In the midst of these doubts and mounting duties in the parish,
Pat misses the opportunity to guide Dominic, the mildly retarded
altar boy who is most in need of the priest's attention. Instead of
counselling Dominic, Pat reprimands him, and the role of advisor
for the troubled boy is taken on by Artie. The responsibility of
running the parish himself may have become too great for Pat, who
seems more concerned about the consequences he might face as a
result of Dominic's shenanigans than the circumstances
surrounding the boy's acting out. Dominic's most recent prank, in
which he played 'The House of the Rising Sun' on the church bells,
in fact prefigures Pat's own cry for help when (at the beginning of
Act Two) he rings the church bells 'as a sort of S.O.S.' In an attempt
to mollify Pat, Artie insists no one heard the song, perhaps
symbolizing the adults' general neglect of Dominic and
foreshadowing his tragic death. Pacing and smoking anxiously, Pat
says: 'I mean to say if the bishop hears about this he'll be down on
me. He won't be down on you or Father Matthews, Artie. It's me
he'll be after.' The usually mild-mannered Pat appears unwilling to
extend forgiveness to Dominic (155):

> **DOMINIC.** I'm sorry Father.
> **PAT.** Oh you're sorry now are yeh? You're sorry! That's
> supposed to make everything alright is it? You're sorry. If I
> remember correctly you were sorry too when yeh climbed out
> onto the roof of the chapel last year and when yeh changed the
> hands of the clock. You were sorry when you got caught goin'
> up into the pulpit. You're sorry!

Pat makes Artie promise not only to keep Dominic out of the
belfry, but even to keep him out of Pat's sight, and threatens further
punishment. Here Pat's age, inexperience, and ultimately his
immaturity become most apparent in a display of self-concern and a
refusal to forgive a penitent. Dramatically, this anxious, unsure
character is foiled against the large, constant presence of the Church
(the setting of the play a constant reminder), which includes those

in charge of him – Father Matthews and the unnamed bishop, who are never seen but whose presences are felt – and his colleagues in the manse whom he says he cannot face (166). Like many of Roche's characters, Pat feels lost and trapped, overshadowed by the image of a confident self he feels he can never become.

Act Two begins with the sound of the church bell ringing, but not for religious services. Pat, in the midst of a breakdown, is making a cry for help – which Artie answers, coming to Pat's aid much as he did in the days when Pat was an altar boy in trouble. Now Pat confesses to Artie that he has returned to drinking. In having the priest confess to the sacristan, Roche reverses the normal hierarchy, undercutting the priest's political and spiritual authority while also dramatizing him as a completely human character. Christopher Murray points to Roche's role reversal as a means by which the audience is 'asked to see Father Pat as trapped in the same way as most characters of the play.'[4] The scene of Pat's confession is the belfry, a site whose spiritual aura has already been diminished by Artie's affair with Angela, Donal's wife.

In this encounter Pat unburdens himself in what Benedict Nightingale, reviewing the original production at the Bush Theatre, called 'an angry, self-accusing tirade, packed with insecurity, helplessness, longing and pain.'[5] Pat focuses on his clerical collar as a symbol – not of a vocation, but of alienation from others (165): 'I've lashin's of acquaintances yeah. No friends though. Thanks to this garb here. I mean to say Artie nobody talks natural when I'm around in this get-up. What am I talkin' about, I don't talk normal meself when I'm around.' Pat feels that he is wasting his best years by missing out on experiences that an average young man takes for granted: friends, sexual relationships, and, ultimately, a family of his own:

> I mean it's a queer auld lonely life boy. Yeh know you're walking down a street and yeh see this lovely woman gettin' out of a car or somethin' or a little family goin' by on the other side of the road or yeh hear a crowd of young people laughin' and singin' inside some public house. I'm tellin' yeh Artie my heart

---

[4] Christopher Murray, 'Billy Roche's Wexford Trilogy: Setting, Place, Critique', in *Theatre Stuff: Critical Essays on Contemporary Irish Theatre*, ed. Eamonn Jordan (Dublin: Carysfort Press, 2000): 218. A revised version of the essay is reprinted in this anthology.

[5] Benedict Nightingale, 'Elegy in a Country Church,' *London Times*, 22 November 1991.

sinks sometimes when I think of all the things I'll never see and do and hear.

Pat's sense of loss is conveyed most poignantly in his memory of a woman he once befriended (165):

> When I was a young student in the seminary I was sent out to Rome one summer. I met this girl out there – knocked around with her for the duration of my stay. Ah yeh should have seen her Artie. She was like poetry in motion I'm not coddin' yeh … The pair of us sittin' in the shade of an auld fountain or skippin' up a side street away from the summer rain. The sound of her dress swishin' against her legs when she walked. And her laugh. Ah Jaysus Artie, you should have seen her laugh boy. Poetry in motion I swear.

If Pat's reminiscence of his time in Rome epitomizes what he believes he surrendered, his following comments – about what drew him to the priesthood – suggest how he once romanticized a clerical life: he wistfully asks Artie if he remembers 'when I was an altar boy here? I fell in love with the place didn't I? The smell of it! The whole atmosphere of it' (166). Pat's confession ends in tears that seem cathartic, as he agrees with Artie: 'Sure people are very good alright aren't they when yeh give them half a chance. People can be very kind.'

By the end of *Belfry* Pat's very doubts and conflicts have made him a more empathetic character. As he comes to terms with his own flaws, he is better able to identify with the difficulties of others. In the play's final scene, as Angela leaves the sacristy, Pat notices Artie's lovelorn gaze and 'suddenly understands' the love that Artie holds for her (186). Well acquainted with unfulfilled desires and hopeless wishes, Pat cannot be judgemental about Artie's love for a married woman, although it is doubtful that he knows about their affair. In a way, Pat's experience with the Church is like Artie's with Angela, and at the conclusion both men must make their way in a world that has been de-romanticized.

Pat's religious belief is never in question. Roche emphasizes, in his conversation with McPherson, that 'For Father Pat, the Mass is not just symbolism. God is coming down onto that altar.' In the midst of Pat's desperate confession, he hastens to assure Artie that he has not lost his faith: 'I mean I still believe and all the rest of it. I always believe – but sometimes I don't know what it's all about yeh know' (165). What Pat has lost is his sense of vocation. And in that imaginative gap between faith and vocation there is ample space for the portrayal of a fully three-dimensional character. 'When I started to write Father Pat', Roche tells McPherson,

I was as riddled with prejudice as any young man would be in this country. He was going to be a typical priest and he just refused to be. I learned so much from that.

An even less typical priest appears in Roche's collection of short stories, *Tales from Rainwater Pond* (2006). Father Corish presents a striking contrast to the insecure Father Pat: he has clearly conquered his conflicts with the priesthood – if he ever had them in the first place.

Corish is decidedly older than Pat. A blustery, sometimes rowdy former hurler, he wears his past like a badge of honour and seems unapologetic about his choices and behaviour. For both priests, the clerical collar symbolizes the demands of their vocation – but whereas Pat feels alienated and even choked by the collar, Corish often removes it to transform himself as he challenges a man to a fistfight or asks a woman to dance. Corish ventures into the romantic/sexual relationships whose absence Pat laments, and his antics establish him as something of a comic figure, as opposed to Pat's semi-tragic character. His athletic boasting and his tendency to get into fights suggest that he has a sturdy build, or at least the remnants of one. If 'Some Silent Place' were to be cast as a movie, Brendan Gleeson would be a natural choice to play Father Corish.

This priest is first introduced, albeit briefly, in the story 'Table Manners' as he is attending a poetry reading with a female companion, Nancy Byrne. First described as being in a hurry to join the audience, slightly messy after a meal, Corish seems a tad bumbling. The reading moves him beyond words:

> 'I'm speechless', Father Corish said ... 'I mean ... I'm ...' and he threw his plump hands into the air to indicate that words failed him. And Nancy Byrne just nodded in mute agreement by his side.[6]

Later he is spotted possibly holding hands with Nancy during the evening performance, a passing observation alerting the reader that this small-town priest may be leading a complicated life (204).

Roche's initial introduction of Father Corish, several stories before 'Some Silent Place', in which he plays a major role, demonstrates the interconnectedness of the tales and the place of

---

[6] *Tales from Rainwater Pond* (Kilkenny: Pillar Press, 2006): 190. Subsequent citations from this collection will be given parenthetically in the text.

this priest in the repertory of the town. Characters become familiar faces (we know their stories) and locations become old haunts (we have been there before), together weaving the fabric of the community. Roche builds the reader's sense of Wexford through relationships and associations, reiterations and different points of view of the town's stories. He invites the reader to become one of the townspeople through an intimate and colloquial narrative voice that shares asides throughout each story. In 'Some Silent Place' the reader is told that the 'ruddy complexioned priest' is generally not called 'Father', but is 'affectionately (and sometimes not so affectionately) known as Corish by all and sundry' (245). The townspeople's familiarity with him is acknowledged through the exclusive use of his last name – his first name is never divulged, just as Pat's last name is never used – and Corish is quickly sketched as a character who elicits feelings of fondness and closeness. As the chaplain of the county hurling team, he serves in a mentoring capacity for its young men, particularly for the resident bad-boy Mick Hyland, over whom he has been given specific responsibility. Corish, Mick and the team's youngest player, Kevin Troy, form what is referred to as the 'Blessed Trinity', travelling to and from games together (253).

Corish comes with a reputation that precedes him, and much of what is learned emerges through stories and hearsay. As is typical of Roche's work – particularly *Tales from Rainwater Pond*, in which all of the stories are connected in some way to the titular pond – 'Some Silent Place' relies heavily on characters' reputations and the currency of gossip. Corish is referred to as the wayward, smoking, drinking, swearing priest known for taking off his collar when it suits him, to join a fistfight or charm a woman (255). After he is forcibly dragged 'red faced and cursing' from a bar by Mick, whom he was defending from the needling of a few fellow drinkers, the remaining men discuss the rumours surrounding Corish's current placement in a country parish. He is famous for his temper – and after a rather vicious brawl with a hurler, Corish is said by one bar patron to have been 'hauled up in front of the bishop and everything' and transferred to 'the arse hole of nowhere' (265).

Corish's conduct with women furthers his cloudy reputation. The suggestion made about him and Nancy Byrne in 'Table Manners' is developed in 'Some Silent Place': Nancy sometimes joins the Blessed Trinity on the way to games, during which she waits for Corish at a nearby hotel. He sneaks away to meet her while the team has its post-game meal and returns smelling of alcohol and, according to Mick, 'the reek of hoochie coochie' (254). When Mick is informed that Nancy will not be joining them for the game due to an illness, he asks if she is not 'what-do-you-call-it or anything?' Rather than reacting to Mick's joke that Nancy is pregnant, Corish merely ignores him. In fact, he seems more ruffled by Mick's insinuation that he is inebriated after Mass from drinking sacramental wine (264). After Corish makes a show of dancing with a woman at a bar (having removed his collar), Mick playfully threatens to tell Nancy, as though the two are in a committed relationship. Corish seems to enjoy this ribbing. Not only does he bring up his dance partner 'out of the blue', essentially boasting, but he also displays just 'the hint of a cheeky grin', as though he were just one of the boys. Confirming Corish's unorthodox behaviour, Mick asks Kevin, 'You'd never think he was a priest, would you?' (262).

Wayward indeed, Corish seems more the hurler of his youth than a priest. As the team's chaplain, he occasionally tries to offer moral guidance, but his reprimands usually trail off with a helpless 'I don't know ...' (248, 252). The story's central conflict arises from Mick's strategic seduction of Anne Green, wife of Donie Green, the team's coach. When the affair is made public, Corish attempts to counsel Mick, who responds by accusing the priest of hypocrisy and calling attention to his broken vow of chastity. Again, Corish does not deny this aspect of his relationship with Nancy; in fact he acknowledges it in order to regain control of the conversation (281):

> 'Leave me and her out of this now,' Father Corish was telling him. 'This is not about me. This is about ...'
> 'It's alright for you to knock her off is that what you're tellin' me?'
> 'No. I'm sayin' this is not about me. And it's not about Nancy either – who by the way is not very well so I'll thank you not to bring her name into it.'

The argument becomes circular and, seeing this, the priest threatens to remove his collar and 'sort this thing man to man if that's the only language you understand.' Surprisingly inarticulate for one whose vocation relies on the spoken word, Corish tends to turn to his fists when language fails. Saddened by Mick's stubbornness or by his own helplessness, or perhaps both, Corish bows his head as he watches Mick take off with Anne. He stands as if in prayer, with 'his hands hooked to his hips like a set of clumsy, outmoded wings' (283). The very life experiences that lend Corish credibility have undermined his clerical authority for Mick, a fellow black sheep.

Like the chastened Pat, Corish does not pass judgement. His relationship with Nancy Byrne appears all too similar to Mick and Anne's; rumours and reports place both couples in similar situations, seen out together in restaurants and holding hands across the table. Yet while Corish's relationship with Nancy is obviously contrary to his vows, it is treated with sympathy: Nancy is suffering from an unnamed illness (likely cancer), and Corish takes up caring for her.

These loving duties consume much of his time and attention – while Mick, without Corish in his corner, has little sway with the coaches and is removed from the hurling team. What little is directly narrated about Corish and Nancy's relationship seems genuinely caring: their clasping of hands in sorrow is juxtaposed to Mick's strategic seduction of Anne, and to Anne's sudden departure from her home and family to move in with Mick .

Corish is characterized as such an unconventional priest that seeing him actually performing in a ceremonial role is rather a shock for Kevin Troy. While waiting for the priest during a funeral, Kevin reflects on the oddity of seeing him conduct a religious service (262-263):

> This was the first time Kevin had seen Father Corish in all his finery and it was strange to discover him immersed in the mystery of it all, to hear him saying 'The Prayers of the Faithful,' or to experience him genuflecting and holding the consecrated Holy Host aloft; and later on, as he accompanied the coffin down the main aisle and out to the windy cemetery at the back of the churchyard, to see him swing the thurible, the incense wafting in sanctifying plumes all around him.

As with Father Pat, Corish's commitment to his faith is not questioned – it is not even discussed. And the form of prose fiction makes it easier for Roche to place the priest in his sacred setting, with a full description of Catholic ritual. Nevertheless, the scene concludes by demystifying the image of reverence, almost as if one were viewing an actor backstage: Kevin watches the sacristan assisting Corish as he disrobes, 'the florid faced priest puffing on a cigarette, shifting it from one hand to the other as the sacristan struggled to get the embroidered chasuble and long white alb over his big red head' (264).

Corish also serves a more secular role as he introduces Kevin to the mythic world of hurling in master hurl maker Tadgh O'Toole's workshop, and Roche describes in great detail the hushed sanctity of this shrine. With Corish's 'blessing', Kevin is allowed to look around the shop: a repository of hurling legends, and heroes honoured as icons, where repairing a hurl is a meditative ritual (260). To Kevin the relics in Tadgh's workshop seem as holy as the sacramentals that Corish used at the funeral service.

Tending to his flock and caring for others emerges as an obvious priority for Corish, despite his raucous reputation and unconventional ways. Indeed, he does take on the traditional priestly role as a spiritual guide and plays a pivotal role in the reconciliation between Anne and her husband Donie. Anne comes to realize that making a home with the careless Mick Hyland is not what she had imagined their affair would be. She asks Corish to take her home, and he enlists Kevin as the driver. It is during Corish's late-night retrieval of Anne that another opportunity for judgement occurs, and again he avoids it. As Kevin drives them toward Donie's house, Corish sits with Anne in the backseat, comforting her and essentially hearing Confession (285-286):

> 'What's he goin' to say when he sees me?' Anne wept.
>
> 'You let me worry about that,' Father Corish told her. 'That's not your problem now ... I'll take care of all that ... He's a bigger man than that ... I mean to say we're not talkin' about ... Don't cry now.'
>
> Anne whimpered something through her tears. Kevin couldn't make out what it was.
>
> 'No one thinks that at all,' Father Corish assured her in a hushed tone of voice. 'I mean, Jesus Christ tonight Anne, you know us all longer than that ... I mean. You made a mistake. Everyone makes mistakes. No one's above it. Nobody's what-do-you-call-it ... perfect or anything.'

The scene continues with Corish – here called 'Father' more than at any other point in the story – listening to Anne's sins, so to speak, but more importantly, insisting that she will not be judged by others and that he will act as her intercessor with Donie. Kevin watches them in the rearview mirror as he drives, able to overhear only bits and pieces of the secularized sacrament taking place behind him. Roche keeps Anne's confession private from both Kevin and from the reader. Although Corish has failed as a moral guide for Mick, his life experience lends credibility to his reassurance of Anne and mediation with Donie. The words Kevin hears lack any reference to prayer, to atonement, or even to consequences; Corish simply comforts Anne as an understanding friend.

Donie's reunion with Anne hinges upon Corish's presence and intervention. Corish negotiates with Donie on his own, but is seen by Kevin and Anne as first explaining, then appealing, and finally pleading. After Donie's initial reluctance, Corish returns to the car, assuring Anne that she is 'all right' and returns her to her husband (287-288). Whatever Corish says to Donie is unknown, just as whatever Anne says to Corish remains a secret. In summing up the episode, Corish turns to Kevin and simply remarks, 'And that's that' (288) – perhaps a comment on the mystery of confession, forgiveness, and the priest's role.

Unlike *Belfry*, 'Some Silent Place' does have a judgemental character, but it is not the priest. It is actually the young Kevin Troy who ends up most disappointed by the actions of those around him. Kevin's youthful naïveté and pure feelings for Anne lead him to judge her more harshly than Corish or even her husband, Donie. Kevin is forced to face his own sense of disappointment after confronting his own romanticized notions of women, love, and relationships. Once Anne has fallen from the pedestal on which he has placed her, Kevin feels cold toward her, even when she reaches to him for comfort when Corish is pleading with Donie on her behalf (286-87). Upon seeing Anne reunited with Donie and both then acting as though the affair had never occurred, Kevin wonders if the entire incident had been 'some sort of mysterious ritual enacted solely for his benefit' (293). Roche likens this painful and significant episode in Kevin's growth to an initiation ceremony, similar to his introduction to the world of seriously competitive hurling. The groin injury that Kevin sustains during an important game is a literal and metaphorical initiation into the complexities of adulthood.

In presenting one priest who questions his vocation and another who often seems to ignore it, Billy Roche is neither denigrating nor elevating traditional clerical behaviour or Church politics. Colm Tóibín observes that Roche tells an Irish story other than that of national heroism; in a similar way, through his priest characters, Roche tells a spiritual story other than that of rigid religiosity. His priests are sympathetic, human figures who express genuine emotion and hold integral places in the community. They are neither heroes nor fools.

Father Corish successfully fulfills many of his priestly duties, just in a secularized manner, unshackled by traditional precepts. Father Pat provides a poignant parallel to Artie's own crises of love and identity. These priest characters seem very similar to the rest of Roche's Wexford cast – complete with inescapable pasts, anxieties, and disappointments. Fully aware of their own humanity, they are not trying to be bigger than they are – although Corish's exaggerations of his own reputation as both a hurler and a ladies' man are used to comedic effect, endearing him to the reader as well as to his own companions.

Tóibín is correct to say that Roche does not use Catholicism as a governing myth: in this version of Wexford, the inhabitants do not judge themselves by traditional religious standards. But neither are they so judged by the priest figures who clearly understand them. Roche's atypical priests are deconstructing the authoritarian reputation of the Catholic clergy, and in many respects amending this reputation for an Irish society that is increasingly secular.

Throughout his body of work, Roche has been concerned with reputation and identity in a small town, and the individual's struggle against an inherited past. For many of Roche's characters that inheritance is a family shadow, such as the stigma of illegitimacy or the reputation of a drunken father; for priests that inheritance is the past practice of an authoritarian Church. Paula Murphy notes that while Roche challenges 'small-town life and its tribal laws', he crafts characters 'accurately, without sentimentalizing and without patronizing.'[7] Rocked by scandal in recent decades, Catholic communities worldwide have become distrustful of the clergy. And although *Belfry* premiered prior to the abuse scandals, Murphy says that Roche's 'refreshing' portrayal of Father Pat, and of the relation between Church and laity, suggests 'the spirit with which the current problems within Irish Catholicism might be addressed.' Fathers Pat and Corish, who explore their own modern anxieties beyond the boundaries of convention and the strictures of dogma, might sometimes seem not to be priests at all. But they might also contribute to a paradigm change in the characterization of priest figures in modern Irish literature.

---

[7] Paula Murphy, 'The Hermeneutics of Heredity: Billy Roche's *Wexford Trilogy*', *Irish Studies Review*, 14/3 (August 2006): 365.

## 20 | A Strange Sort of Allure: Transformations of Wexford in *Tales From Rainwater Pond*

Hilary Sophrin

'I absolutely love Joyce's *Dubliners*', Billy Roche has said. 'It's a beautiful piece of work and, like Chekhov, it's so understated.'[1] Roche's own short story collection, *Tales from Rainwater Pond* (2006), is similarly understated in its portrayal of a community through the characters' secret thoughts, paralyzing flaws, and epiphanic moments. The book presents a series of interwoven narratives, with major characters in some stories reappearing as minor characters in others, just as the denizens of Joyce's Dublin constitute a wandering repertory company. Although Roche's setting is a town, his native Wexford, rather than a city, his characters seem convinced, as much as any Dubliner, that the world revolves around them. In another interview, included in this anthology, the author tells Conor McPherson that 'the quintessential Wexford man has no idea that he belongs to a small town. He thinks that he comes from a big cosmopolitan place.'

A significant difference lies in each writer's shaping of fictional space. One aims for exact topography, rendering an urban landscape so precisely that it remains recognizable even when most labyrinthine. The other asserts his aesthetic freedom by remapping a town's streets, buildings, and surrounding environment. According to Roche, 'Joyce once said that if Dublin disappeared, the city could be reconstructed from his pages. My work is different. It's

---

[1] Jimmy Lacey, 'Stories in the Key of Life: Jimmy Lacey Interviews Billy Roche', *The Irish Book Review*, II, 3 (Spring 2007): 33.

firmly grounded in Wexford, but it's not a transcription of the town. It's a transformation.'[2]

Two of Roche's transformative strategies, *relocation* and *magnification*, were already evident in his early novel *Tumbling Down* (1986). The autobiographical narrative chronicles a year of Wexford life as observed by an earnest young man who tends bar in his father's pub, The Rock. The original pub, The Shamrock Bar, which Roche's father leased and managed during Billy's formative years, was located next to The Small Hotel on Anne Street, toward the edge of town. Roche moved the fictional pub, The Rock, and the hotel with it, to Circular Quay at the heart of Wexford, which offers a stunning view of the harbour and the sea beyond. This new placement establishes The Rock as a kind of portal to the outside world, especially for the novel's impressionable protagonist. The pub's physical setting now matches its emotional setting as the nerve centre of community life.

Roche also magnifies several Wexford sites. He situates much of his novel's action around a market area known as the Bull Ring which, in the real Wexford, is a small square – fronted by a statue of 'The Pikeman', an iconic representation of the rebels of 1798, and bounded at the back by narrow alley of market stalls. Across the street a plaque pays tribute to Jem Roche, Ireland's heavyweight boxing champion in the early 1900s. In *Tumbling Down* Billy Roche, Jem's grandson, enlarges the Bull Ring into an arena for romantic encounters, comedic chases, and 'the music of the streets' in the voices of hawkers and tradesmen.

---

[2] Quoted in *Undergraduate Research in English Studies*, ed. Laurie Grobman and Joyce Kinkead (Urbana, IL: National Council of Teachers of English, 2010): 124.

**The Bull Ring (with stalls in back)**

**The Ballast Bank**

Another example of magnification is the transformation of the Ballast Bank in Wexford Harbour into 'Useless Island.' Created in 1931 opposite Paul Quay, the Ballast Bank provided a site for loading and unloading the sand and gravel essential to stabilize ships without cargo. Now empty, except for the remains of an old brick building, the bank stretches for only about 150 metres. But Roche's fictional island is big enough so that characters can explore it, hide on it, and even daydream about building a casino there. *Tumbling Down* also lends an air of mystery to this barren spot: an island of stone and clay 'that looked like it must have sprung from the sea centuries ago ... Even the fisherman stayed well clear of it and the absence of life lent that place a ghostly, enchanted air.'[3] In Roche's *Amphibians* (1992), spending a night alone on Useless Island is dramatized as an adolescent rite of passage. Wild boars are said to roam the island's expanses.

*Tales from Rainwater Pond* employs yet another strategy for transforming the Wexford landscape: the *conflation* of two sites into a single setting that becomes a unifying presence in the book. Rainwater Pond is a composite of two real places just outside Wexford, Otter Pond and Blue Pond. These small pools are located about one mile from the Quay, down railroad tracks that run parallel to the sea. On the shore side rests Otter Pond: a shallow, circular pool ideal for group outings. On the other side of the tracks, hidden behind brambles and bushes, is Blue Pond, Otter Pond's deep and dark twin.

**Otter Pond**                    **Blue Pond**

Roche's amalgamation, Rainwater Pond, possesses both the openness of the seaside and the mystery of a secluded vale. It is a site for innocent recreation by middle-class townspeople, but also a menacing place frequented by 'hard cases ... fairly tribal about their

---

[3] *Tumbling Down*, revised edition (Wexford, Tassel Publications, 2008): 1.

territory.'[4] To emphasize the water's depth, Roche adapts a common Wexford saying about Blue Pond, attributing it to the lonely narrator of 'One Is Not a Number' (70): 'Rainwater Pond was a dark and treacherous place, bottomless they say. You could throw a stone or a coin in there and watch it fall, go home and have your tea and go to the pictures and come home and go to bed and sleep and dream and wake up and go to work or to school or whatever and it would still be falling when you came home for your dinner.' Two of Roche's tales feature characters who drown in the pond – 'down deep, down among the eels and the tiny fishes and all the other old rusty things that dwelt down there' (42)

In fact, Rainwater Pond is a microcosm of the town's life. Its waters collect memories as well as artefacts, embodying the past and present of all the characters: lives shaped by loneliness, love, betrayal, and death. The pond is a place for lovers' trysts, sexual spying, athletic training, group outings, isolated meditation, and even a contemplated murder. It is Wexford's mirror, perhaps its collective unconscious. Like Egdon Heath in Thomas Hardy's *The Return of the Native*, Rainwater Pond becomes a dominant inanimate presence, and a character in its own right.

Of the twelve stories in Roche's collection, eight are told through third-person narration, and the overall tone of that omniscience is nostalgic, pensive, and occasionally ominous as in 'Verdant' and 'Mystic.' Most often, the tales revolve around a particular memory, which in a small town can become one song on a continuous loop. The first story in the collection, 'Haberdashery', infuses a memory scene with character and mood by incorporating a romantic lament from the mid-1960s. Roche originally conceived 'Haberdashery' as a play, with the same working title.[5] Now, as the opening tale, it conveys a distinctive first-person voice. The narrator, Leo Cullen, recalls riding to a teenage outing at Rainwater Pond with Evelyn, the girl of his dreams, sitting on the crossbar of his bicycle (5):

> We sang *The Sun Ain't Gonna Shine Anymore*, and, needless to say, I was in heaven – Evelyn leaning into me and looking up at me, her husky voice singing and her strong little hand touching mine from time to time as we bumped from sleeper to sleeper.

---

[4] 'The Day Off' in *Tales from Rainwater Pond* (Kilkenny: Pillar Press, 2006): 142. Subsequent citations from the tales are given parenthetically in the text.

[5] Roche explains the evolution of 'Haberdashery' in the conversation with Conor McPherson that is excerpted in this collection.

'When you're in love,' she said, 'you die a little every day.' Only
a little? I couldn't help thinking as her face shone before me in
the broken, mounted mirror.

Leo's thirty years of yearning for Evelyn remain unspoken, except
to the reader, and yet she clearly understands his feelings – both
before and after her marriage to Andy Carrington, owner of the local
haberdashery. For much of the story Leo reverts to the past, to that
day at the pond when Andy won Evelyn's heart and took her away
from his brother, Peter. As Evelyn stood at the edge of Rainwater
Pond, she whimsically tossed her birthday present, a beautiful locket
given to her by the three boys, into the water. All the picnickers tried
diving in after it, except for Peter: 'I think he paid the price for it too.
She sulked all the way home ... I often picture it lying down there at
the bottom of Rainwater – glistening, rusting, dying ... And that was
it. Peter had lost her' (6).

In the present action of the story Leo, now a middle-aged baker,
spends as much time as possible at the haberdashery just to bask in
Evelyn's presence, and he is even more preoccupied than Andy by
her illness, which is terminal. As Peter drives Evelyn to the hospital
for treatment, Leo remains alone outside the store: 'I stood there in
the drizzling rain and watched the car disappear around the bend. I
knew I'd never see her again' (12).

Leo masks his pain with banter and a preoccupation with his
drumming (he plays in a local band called The Toreadors), and the
percussion of his practice sessions conveys the power of his hidden
emotions, especially at the very end of the story. In a subsequent
tale, 'A Lucky Escape', Leo appears as a minor character, a joker on
the bandstand, while the narration focuses on the Toreadors' lead
singer, Tommy Day: another man hopelessly in love with an
unattainable woman. In this story the narration begins with the
reminiscence of an all-knowing witness, a lifelong resident of the
town (44): 'Tommy Day? Yeah, I know Tommy Day. Tommy Day the
singer, you mean? Yeah!'

He used to sing with a dance band called the Toreadors once
upon a time ... A nifty sort of fellow. You'd often see him coming out
of a side street or nipping up a back street or slipping in and out of
betting shops and all the rest of it. That's more or less how he lived
his life really. Plenty of talent. No ambition. No plan. Some people
are like that. Until they wake up one morning and realize it's all
over.

How does the unnamed narrator know so much about Tommy Day? It may be simply that both men have spent their whole lives in a small community where everyone's business is common knowledge. But as the story progresses, the narrator parses Tommy's deepest feelings about Clare Kearney, a local girl he noticed from the bandstand one night: 'From the moment he saw her and heard her name spoken out loud I'm afraid it was all over for him. And I'm sorry to have to report that from that day on Tommy's life was just another sad, sad song that he'd never get to sing' (46). Ultimately the reader is forced to wonder if the narrator – who was apparently asked at the beginning of the story if he happened to know Tommy Day – might, coincidentally, be Tommy Day himself.

Tommy's budding romance with Clare is cut short when Marty Maher, a Lothario, comes home from England. After Marty wins Clare's heart, the narrator describes Tommy brooding at Rainwater Pond (51):

> A train trundled by and a passenger looked out and wondered about the gang of wayward boys who basked beside this strange looking lagoon. The stranger seemed to wonder too about Tommy's lonely frown and he appeared to understand. Perhaps that's the answer, Tommy thought as the man's face evaporated. Get on a train and go away.

Tommy's thought, like the train, simply flashes past. As in Joyce's *Dubliners*, some characters may consider leaving home, or at least revealing their deepest emotions, but in the end they hold back and fail to act.

A fuller epiphany comes a moment later when Tommy and his friends encounter a group of garrulous older men ambling around the pond with blackthorn sticks and dogs. Tommy wonders if this is all that's in store for himself and his mates in forty years time – 'Men without women!' A moment later he sees Clare walking to the pond with Marty Maher, and here the narrative voice seems to simulate Tommy talking to himself (52): 'He must learn to despise her otherwise the pain will be too hard to endure. He must relinquish all hope. The nape of her neck though!' In this passage, and throughout *Tales from Rainwater Pond*, Roche's brief and poignant language, often in Wexford dialect, conveys feelings that another writer might amplify into a long paragraph.

When Marty Maher abandons the pregnant Clare, the town assumes (and her mother hopes) that Tommy will propose. Clare has expressed a wish to leave town, and maybe Ireland itself, so that she could 'be myself for a change', but Tommy remains content to live a hometown life without grand aspirations. He briefly considers leaving with Clare, but he is not serious – and as it turns out, neither is she, because Marty Maher eventually returns to town and marries her. The narrator says that Clare had two more children and then became widowed, but that Tommy kept his distance. As the years go by, he begins to fulfill the destiny foreshadowed by those old men at Rainwater Pond (59): 'Most weekdays he rambles the roads now with Shamey Shiggins and Apache Byrne: walking sticks, dogs, the lot, talking about everything under the sun – this, that and the other. They marvel at the people dying all around them.' The story ends ironically, as Tommy avoids an encounter with Clare, who is now a grandmother (60):

> She called out to him from the other side of the road. She seemed genuinely pleased to see him too. He was tempted to go on over and talk to her, but he didn't in the end, he just walked on by. Better not start all of that up again, eh? A lucky escape really when you think of it.
> *Yes It's All Only Make Believe.*[6]

The power of the pond is even more evident in 'Maggie Angre', another story of loss. The title character, described as 'awkward and ugly', sits at the water's edge each day, forcing herself to relive the memory of her brother's drowning. Maggie blesses herself as she prepares to plunge into the 'black and bottomless' pool. The elegiac poetry of Roche's writing is evident here more than in any other story, and his mournful and poetic phrases illuminate this quiet moment: 'And even still his voice echoed here, echoed through the trees, was blown on out to sea only to return year in and year out to this desolate and magnetic place' (32).

Maggie believes her daily presence at the Pond is her redemption. She knew from a young age that she was not normal, though her brother Steven always made her feel special. She describes herself in the reflection in a shop window as 'rough looking' and masculine with a 'pock-marked face.' The town and her father ignored her, but her brother was an ideal protector: 'Steven

---

[6] The last line is the title of Conway Twitty's hit song of 1958, which is part of Tommy Day's repertoire. The allusion exemplifies Roche's use of musical refrains in the tales to add bite (in this case as a choric commentary on Tommy's relationship with Clare) even while evoking an era that seems more innocent.

would stand up for her if he ever heard tell of anyone saying anything against her or anything. He'd put on his coat and go down after them' (37).

Steven was handsome, brave, and well liked in the town. Yet one fateful day, as the boys and Maggie began their swim at Rainwater Pond, he inexplicably drowned. Now contemplating the murky water, Maggie is overcome by guilt for being unable to save Steven, as he might have saved her. Ironically, his death motivated her to become a strong swimmer – the only reason she is admired at all in the town. (In 'Haberdashery', when Maggie Angre is unable to retrieve Evelyn's necklace from the pond, everyone realizes that it must be lost forever.)

Maggie re-enacts her brother's drowning moment by moment when she swims, retracing the strokes Steven made: 'Here's where he splashed, here's where he kicked, here's where he called out her name' (39). Then the point of view shifts as Maggie addresses Steven directly for three full pages, culminating in a poignant realization (42):

> My poor Da was dying alive about you though, Steven, you know. He was never the same at all after you were gone. He just couldn't get over it. I mean he never put much pass on me one way or another but after you were gone I sort of disappeared too. In a way, I supposed you could say, Steven, I perished too.

The past and present are intertwined most vividly in this story, often blurring the protagonist's concept of time. In the beginning, as Maggie recalls the fateful day, she is uncertain about the weather: 'It was a fine afternoon. There was a blue sky. Or was it raining? No, it was … It was all kinds of weather on the day he drowned and it was no particular time of day, it was all day and every day and all day long there were sun showers' (33). Later, as she relives the drowning once again, the pond seems to become a spiritual black hole: when Maggie climbs back on the bank, 'there was nothing, nothing but the ghost of the echo of her name somewhere, nothing but grey sky and the grey water and the greyness of the two dirty swans below.' Only a moment later, the ever-changing pond reflects a moment of catharsis as Maggie sits calmly, gazing 'down into the tranquil waters where two white swans swam' (43).

Although 'Maggie Angre' features the pond more prominently than any other story, all the tales revolve around this image of life's mysteries. Roche has described his central setting as nothing less than a Jungian symbol:

Rainwater Pond in this collection, and water in general throughout my work, represents the unconscious, I suppose: the past, the future, the womb, the tomb, the sexual other world. My characters are constantly looking at their future selves or searching for the person they used to be or could be or whatever. They fall in, they drown, they swim toward salvation, and they watch it from a passing train.[7]

At the pond many of the characters weave in and out of one another's stories. In Maggie's reminiscence about Steven, for example, a girl appears 'out of nowhere – a beautiful apparition in the clearing of a cluster of crab apple trees. She was accompanied by a crippled boy who lurked in the long grass like he was her guardian angel' (36). Later, in 'One Is Not a Number', the boy – Matty – becomes the narrator of his own tale, which deals with his perverse fixation on the wild and lovely Imelda. The clubfooted Matty stands alone in the pond and dreams about an alternate life. He imagines that the water has healing powers, and he loves the way that it refracts the image of his distorted limbs, creating an illusion of wholeness. Matty's submerged body is transformed (70): 'And he was the other me, the real me, the one marooned inside me, the invisible one who stood beside me or behind me in times of trouble, the one Imelda (or anyone else here either for that matter) didn't even know yet. My other self so to speak!'

Matty never achieves a fraction of this alternative self. He sullenly stalks Imelda her whole life, even when she begins an affair with a newcomer to town. Ishmael (as Matty calls him after seeing a copy of *Moby Dick* lying on the table) rents one of the cottages surrounding Rainwater Pond. In many of the tales the pond is a completely isolated place, surrounded by brambles and small trees. But here, as in 'Table Manners', the pond lies near a quiet grouping of small cottages, and thus becomes the focus of a dynamic love triangle: Imelda, Ishmael, and Imelda's husband, Ely, who is also unfaithful.

Matty describes the restless Imelda as a 'palm tree growing in the wrong country.' But the characters in this story, like those in 'A Lucky Escape', merely daydream about transcending their routine lives: they remain bound inextricably to the town. The only one who leaves is Ishmael, who never belonged to begin with. Years later Imelda, like Maggie Angre's brother, drowns in Rainwater Pond, enigmatic to the last. Earlier Matty had characterized Imelda as

---

[7] Jimmy Lacey: 33-34.

essentially mysterious (95): 'I mean you never know what she's thinking. You watch her sometime. Try and figure her out. You won't be able. And she changes all the time too, you know. She wears jeans and she's one thing. Put her in a dress and she's another. You know?' Like the pond, Imelda is shadowy and unfathomable.

'One Is Not a Number' includes a cameo appearance by Tommy Day, performing with his band at a dancehall – in a scene where Matty, now drunk, once again becomes an outcast. *Tales from Rainwater Pond* is full of such intriguing cross-references. Another occurs when a priest, Father Corish, accompanied by a woman named Nancy Byrne, attends a poetry reading in the story 'Table Manners' – and then in 'Some Silent Place', the final story in the collection, the priest becomes a central character and his long-term relationship with Nancy is illuminated.

Somehow Father Corish is able to reconcile his private and public lives when he celebrates the mystery of the Mass, and when he provides compassionate counselling at a crucial point in the story. Corish, the chaplain of the county hurling team, is proud of his own athletic past, whether real or imagined, and tries relentlessly to push the team's surly veteran star, Mick Hyland, into playing shape. An innocent young hurler, Kevin Troy, is deeply impressed by the gruelling training regimen at Rainwater Pond (278-279):

> In the winter months he'd use it as a training ground, running round and round the shadowy lagoon with a sturdy schoolbag full of rocks and heavy stones strapped to his back, Father Corish urging and goading him on. Kevin couldn't believe it when he first witnessed his rigorous routine. Round and round he'd go with a hurl in his hand, catching the balls that Father Corish would peg to him every so often and driving them across to the far side of the pond ... then up the steep mound of marly earth that stood like a mountain close by, and down the other side to catch another ball and send it sailing skywards.

For Kevin and the reader, the effect is epic, almost as if Cuchulain were hurling across country, bounding over fields in a few steps. Roche enhances the tale's mythic quality when the priest and Mick take Kevin to Tadgh O'Toole's workshop, a veritable shrine of hurling; and again when hurling action is dramatized through the majestic prose of 'the Scribe', the most old-fashioned of sports writers. The story is mythologized even more by Rainwater Pond, which is now a solitary and secret spot. As a training ground, the

pond is Mick's 'very own purgatory of pain' (279). It is also the site
of Mick's trysts with Anne Green, the coach's wife, and the pain in
this story is psychological and moral as well as physical. At the end
of 'Some Silent Place', the main characters – all 'spiritually altered
somehow' (296) – talk about the next hurling season, and think
about such unresolved problems as Nancy Byrne's failing health and
Anne Green's patched-up marriage. *Tales from Rainwater Pond*
concludes with hints of transformation, if not redemption.

Since publishing his collection in 2006, Roche has performed
several of the stories on stage. His shows have been closer in spirit
to the stage recitations of Charles Dickens than to the enacted
monologues of Conor McPherson, because the authorial voice seems
to convey either omniscient understanding ('Maggie Angre') or
simple emotional identification ('Haberdashery'). But after his
successful presentations at The Irish Repertory Theatre in New
York, as part of the '1st Irish Festival' in 2009, Roche immediately
turned to adapting 'One is Not a Number' for performances by
another actor, Gary Lydon, in Cork and Dun Laoghaire. Lydon
brought a bitter ferocity to Matty's first-person narration, and with
that added distance the story more clearly assumed the shape of a
monologue play.[8]

In adapting these stories theatrically, Roche has relied more on
poetic prose than on set design to dramatize a sense of the pond. In
the New York production of 'Maggie Angre', for example, small
props and dark lighting helped to suggest the ever-present
'subconsciousness' of the pond: the audience saw Billy Roche
standing next to an empty crate, a rusty bicycle, an old shopping cart
filled with trash, and a dirty brick wall (evoking the 'old stone
quarry' where Steven had stood before he drowned). During the
interval following Roche's performance, The Walker Brothers'
version of 'The Sun Ain't Gonna Shine Anymore' was played,
foreshadowing a scene in the second monologue, 'Haberdashery',
when Leo remembers riding his bike towards Rainwater Pond with
Evelyn on the crossbar.

Roche had first performed 'Haberdashery' in 2006 at the very
store in Wexford, now called Kellys of Cornmarket, that he had

---

[8] See the review of *One Is Not a Number* by Rachel Andrews, *Irish
Theatre Magazine*, October 31, 2009. These performances were
directed by Johnny Hanrahan. Roche provided original music,
somewhat eerie, for moments in the story when Matty hums or
sings.

envisioned when writing the story. The audience walked down the street from the Wexford Arts Centre, and stood inside below the large staircase leading to the main floor. The setting was especially apt because of the first lines of the story: 'I was standing below in the shop when she appeared on the stairs like a beautiful apparition, her lovely face slipping from shadow to sunlight as she stepped from step to step' (1). The Wexford audience was literally standing in the same place as the narrator.

**The former haberdashery**    **Inside Kellys of Cornmarket**

Another Rainwater Pond story, 'Table Manners', inspired the film *The Eclipse*, which was co-scripted by Roche and Conor McPherson, and then directed by McPherson in 2009. In April 2010 it was honoured with an award for Best Screenplay by the Irish Film and Television Academy. In Roche's original story Michael Farr, a teacher assisting at a literary festival in Wexford, serves as the chauffeur for a visiting poet, Kitty Shaw, who is staying the week at a cottage next to Rainwater Pond. Kitty writes about the darker sides of love, and Michael is transfixed by her voice and words: 'Poems about sinners and lovelorn creatures for the most part, poor things who were guilty of all sorts of unforgivable things: murder and abortion and betrayal and unkindness of every kind' (189). Kitty's poetry expresses the deeper consciousness of the town, which also

includes Michael's desires. It voices sentiments normally held
beneath the surface of Rainwater Pond – as in 'Maggie Angre', when
the title character dives into the murky water: 'And while she was
down there, Maggie confided in herself again, and the things she
told herself were not for human ears: sins and other odd ephemeral
things that cannot be caught or put into words' (42).

The film makes several key changes. Michael is no longer
married but widowed, and thus the audience can more easily relate
to his infatuation with the visiting writer. That writer is now Lena
Morelle, a British fantasy novelist who is drawn to ghost stories. And
Michael is in the midst of a real ghost story: he is literally haunted
by the presence of his wife, and he has horrifying encounters with
the spirit of his father-in-law even before that troubled man
commits suicide. The film also moves the setting from Wexford to
Cork – and yet the Cobh landscape approximates the quiet, almost
subliminal effect of Rainwater Pond. In Cobh, McPherson says, 'the
period buildings with their scale and elegance add so much to the
feel of the story where past and present, the dead and the living,
need to be palpably within reach of each other.'[9]

One scene that is similar in the short story and film involves a
visit to an old abbey where Kitty/Lena and Michael spend a rainy
afternoon looking at cracked graves, hundreds of years old. In the
short story Roche uses the setting of Wexford's Saint Selskar Abbey
and describes the woman as a beautiful Gothic statue, idealized in
Michael's infatuated eyes: 'He caught sight of her now, standing at
an old gravestone, her gaze fastened on some scribbled inscription.
She had all the poise of a fallen angel: slightly sinful, her skin
translucent, her hair aflame and her body full and feline' (196). The
film captures this muted romantic tone through images and music
rather than words, but its roots in the short story remain vital.

---

[9] McPherson, 'Director's Statement', on-line at Magnolia Pictures:
    http://www.magpictures.com/presskit.aspx?id=2bb7e122-e994-
    448c-b207-d4808a6059a6

**Saint Selskar Abbey**

In fact, the substitution of Cobh for Wexford is analogous to Roche's own transformation of his hometown. 'I don't really write about a place', he has said. 'I write about people and I use the sense of place to enhance the story. In that sense I'm not realistic. I change names and locations and move buildings around, whatever it takes to enhance the story.'[10] Roche's Wexford is based on the grit and salt air of a real town, with a familiar pattern of streets and shops, and hills 'tumbling down' to the harbour. But in his writing the town and environs are prototypes – like architectural models, not always to scale – that can be rearranged for different effects. And Roche plays with time as well as space: his Wexford incorporates the town's past not as a setting for historical events, but as a repository of personal stories, especially buried secrets. It is a surprisingly pre-modern world, generally free of new technology, where ordinary lives can assume mythic shape.

In the short stories, those shapes are reflected by the surface of Rainwater Pond, while the water's depths seem to hold everything: conscious motives, unconscious drives, and all that keeps the characters bound by circumstance. Roche dramatizes the pond's

---

[10] Jimmy Lacey: 32.

mesmerizing effect in a darkly funny scene in 'Haberdashery' when Leo dives down to retrieve the necklace that Evelyn had capriciously thrown into the dark pool. Although his efforts are in vain, as are everyone's, Leo plunges into the pond with eyes wide open (6):

> Jesus it was deep. And murky. But it had a strange sort of allure too though, you know. All the queer things trapped in the weeds – dead dogs and prams and rusty wheels and tyres and the buckled skeleton of an old bicycle and what-have-you. And that sort of what-do-you-call-it ... under water sound. Sort of hypnotic or something.

# Billy Roche: A Bibliography

(In order of date of publication – and, for plays, the dates and sites of first performances)

## Novel

*Tumbling Down* (Dublin: Wolfhound Press, 1986). Revised edition (Wexford: Tassel Publications, 2008).

## Plays

*The Wexford Trilogy: A Handful of Stars, Poor Beast in the Rain, Belfry* (London: Nick Hern Books, 1992).
*A Handful of Stars* was originally performed at the Bush Theatre in London on February 15, 1988.
*Poor Beast in the Rain* was originally performed at the Bush on November 18, 1989.
*Belfry* was originally performed at the Bush on November 13, 1991.
*Amphibians* (London: Warner Chappell Plays, 1992). The play was originally performed in London at the Barbican Centre on September 3, 1992.
*The Cavalcaders* (London: Nick Hern Books in association with the Royal Court Theatre, 1994). The play was originally performed in Dublin at the Peacock Theatre on July 14, 1993. [These two dramas were subsequently published together as *The Cavalcaders and Amphibians: Two Plays* (London. Nick Hern Books. 2001). The slightly revised version of *Amphibians* reprinted in this edition was first performed at the Wexford Y.W.C.A. on June 1, 1998.]
*On Such As We* (London: Nick Hern Books, The Abbey Theatre Playscript Series, 2001). The play was originally performed in Dublin at the Peacock Theatre on December 7, 2001.
*Lay Me Down Softly* (London: Nick Hern Books, 2008). The play was originally performed in Dublin at the Peacock Theatre on November 14, 2008.

## Screenplays

*Trojan Eddie: A Screenplay* (London: Methuen, 1997). The film was
   released in Ireland and the UK in 1996.
*The Eclipse* (2009), coauthored with Conor McPherson as an
   adaptation of Roche's short story 'Table Manners'. The film was
   released in Ireland and the UK in 2010.

## Short Stories

'Maggie Angre', *in New Writing from Ireland: A Soho Square
   Anthology*, ed. Colm Tóibín (Winchester, MA: Faber and Faber,
   1994).
'Northern Lights' in *Ascent*, XXVIII, 3 (Spring 2004).
'Sussex Gardens': commissioned by BBC Radio 3 and read by the author
   on The Verb: April 9, 2005.
'Haberdashery': read by the author on BBC Radio 4 (Write to Perform)
   on October 8, 2006.
*Tales from Rainwater Pond* (Kilkenny: Pillar Press, 2006). The
   collection includes: 'Haberdashery'; 'Northern Lights'; 'Maggie
   Angre' (revised); 'A Lucky Escape'; 'One Is Not a Number'; 'On a
   Blackthorn Limb'; 'The Day Off'; 'Mystic'; 'Table Manners'; 'Sussex
   Gardens'; 'Verdant'; 'Some Silent Place'.
'The Dog and Bone': companion piece to 'Sussex Gardens' read on BBC
   Radio 3 (The Verb) by Simone Kirby on July 15, 2011. Forthcoming
   in *Lampeter Review*.

## Essays

Afterword to *The Wexford Trilogy* (London: Nick Hern Books, 1992):
   187-189.
Foreword to *African Shadows: North East Africa*, 1989-94:
   Photographs by Pádraig Grant (Taghmon, Wexford: House of Munn,
   1994).
'Billy Roche in conversation about memories of Wexford cinemas', in
   *Here's Looking at You, Kid! Ireland Goes to the Pictures*, ed.
   Stephanie McBride and Roddy Flynn (Dublin: Wolfhound Press,
   1996): 116-118.
'My Summer Job: Blood, Sweat and Tears', *Irish Times*, August 8, 1996.
'Tom Murphy and the Continuous Past' (2007), *Princeton University
   Library Chronicle*, LXVII , 1 and 2 (Autumn 2006-Winter 2007):
   620-631.
Untitled reminiscence in *'Close-Up Magic': 40 Years at the Bush
   Theatre*, ed. Neil Burkey (London: Third Millennium Publishing,
   2011): 76-79.

## Interviews

Battersby, Eileen, 'The Boy from Wexford', *The Irish Times*, March 2, 1995.

---, 'Dreamer without the Angst', *The Irish Times*, April 7, 2007.

Kerrane, Kevin, 'The Poetry of the Street: An Interview with Billy Roche', *Irish Studies Review*, 14/3 (August 2006): 369-378.

Lacey, Jimmy, 'Stories in the Key of Life', *The Irish Book Review*, II, 3 (Spring 2007): 31-34.

McKeon, Belinda, 'Gambling with Their Hopes and Dreams', *The Irish Times*, August 16, 2005.

McPherson, Conor, 'Billy Roche in Conversation with Conor McPherson', in *Theatre Talk: Voices of Irish Theatre Practitioners*, eds Lilian Chambers, Ger FitzGibbon, and Eamonn Jordan (Dublin: Carysfort Press, 2001): 409-423.

O'Mahoney, John, 'Tales of a Small Town', *Sunday Times* (London), February 6, 2000.

Spencer, Charles, 'A Walk with Billy Roche', *The Daily Telegraph* (London), October 30, 1992.

Wallace, Arminta, 'A Year to Remember', *The Irish Times*, November 19, 2008.

Woolgar, Claudia, 'Tumbling Down to London: Claudia Woolgar Talks to Billy Roche about His Plays', *Theatre Ireland*, 29 (Autumn 1992): 6-9.

## A Selected Bibliography of Criticism

Carr, Mary, 'The Plays of Billy Roche', *Journal of the Irish Theatre Forum*, 1.1 (Summer 1997), on-line at <http://www.ucd.ie/irthfrm>.

Clarity, James F., 'Failure in Pop Music Breeds Success on Stage', *The New York Times*, August 16, 1993.

Donohoe, Aileen, 'The Pull of the Past', *Fortnight*, No. 358 (February 1997): 31-32.

Dromgoole, Dominic, 'Billy Roche' in *The Full Room* (London: Methuen, 2002): 242-245.

Lawley, Paul, 'Billy Roche', *Contemporary Dramatists*, fifth edition, ed. K. A. Berney (London, St. James Press, 1993): 565-567.

Lonergan, Patrick, 'From Mass Media to New Media in Contemporary Irish Drama: Billy Roche's *On Such As We* and Paul Meade's *Skin Deep, Ilha de Desterro*, 58 (2010: 309-332).

Murphy, Paula, 'The Hermeneutics of Heredity', *Irish Studies Review*, 14/3 (August 2006), 359-368.

---, 'Passages Through a Two-Way Mirror: Billy Roche's *The Cavalcaders* and *Amphibians*', in *Passages: Movements and Moments in Text and Theory*, ed. Maeve Tynan, Maria Beville, and Marita Ryan (Newcastle upon Tyne: Cambridge Scholars Publishing: 2009): 120-27.

Murray, Christopher, 'Billy Roche's *Wexford Trilogy*: Setting, Place, Critique', in *Theatre Stuff: Critical Essays on Contemporary Irish Theatre*, ed. Eamonn Jordan (Dublin: Carysfort Press, 2000): 209-223.

Schnierer, Peter Paul, 'Billy Roche', in *The Methuen Drama Guide to Contemporary Irish Playwrights*, ed. Martin Middeke and Peter Paul Schnierer (London,Methuen, 2010): 423-438.

Tóibín, Colm, 'The Talk of the Town', in *Dudes, Druids and Beauty Queens: The Changing Face of Irish Theatre*, ed. Dermot Bolger (Dublin: New Island, 2001): 18-29.

Walsh, Martin W., 'Ominous Festivals, Ambivalent Nostalgia: Brian Friel's *Dancing at Lughnasa* and Billy Roche's *Amphibians*', *New Hibernia Review* 14:1 (2010): 127-41.

Wilcher, Robert, 'Billy Roche', *Dictionary of Literary Biography*, second series: Volume 233: *British and Irish Dramatists Since World War II*, ed. John Bull (Detroit: Gale Group, 2001): 240-244.

# Contributors

**Patrick Burke** lectured in English, Drama and Theatre for 36 years at St. Patrick's College, Dublin City University, where he served as first director of the MA in Theatre Studies. He has published widely on the work of Brian Friel, Tom Murphy, J.M. Synge and T.C. Murray, and has frequently presented papers at international literary conferences. He is also an experienced actor and director with the Dublin Shakespeare Society.

**Maureen Cech** is an assistant librarian in Special Collections at the University of Delaware. She holds a Master of Arts degree in Library Science from the University of Maryland, College Park, as well as a Master's degree in English from the University of Delaware. Her professional interests include literary manuscripts and teaching with primary sources.

**Katherine Clarke** is an Irish journalist and editor based in New York. She holds a Master's degree in arts journalism from Columbia University and has written for the *Wall Street Journal, WSJ Magazine,* the *New York Observer* and the Yale School of Drama's *Theater* magazine.

**Dominic Dromgoole** is currently the artistic director of Shakespeare's Globe Theatre in London. He began his career at the Bush Theatre as an assistant director, and then (1990-96) as artistic director. In that time the Bush premiered 65 new plays – including early work by Billy Roche, Conor McPherson, and Sebastian Barry. He has directed major productions in England, the U.S. and Romania, and is the author of *The Full Room: An A-Z of Contemporary Playwriting* and *Will and Me: How Shakespeare Took Over My Life.*

**Úna Kealy** is a lecturer in the Department of Creative and Performing Arts in Waterford Institute of Technology and is a critic for *Irish Theatre Magazine*. She completed a Doctorate in the University of Ulster, Coleraine on the work of George Fitzmaurice while working as Company Manager for Big Telly Theatre Company. As a theatre producer she has worked extensively with theatre companies and venues in Northern Ireland, and as a playwright has written and produced two plays for young children.

**Kevin Kerrane** is a professor of English at the University of Delaware, where his work ranges from the history of journalism, including documentary film, to Irish literature and drama. He is the co-editor (with Ben Yagoda) of *The Art of Fact: A Historical Anthology of Literary Journalism*, and the author of *Dollar Sign on the Muscle: The World of Baseball Scouting*. His essays have appeared in *Irish Review*, *New Hibernia Review*, *Sports Illustrated*, and on-line at *salon.com*.

**Larry Kirwan**, born in Wexford, is an Irish-American writer and musician, most noted as the lead singer for the Irish rock band, Black 47, based in New York City. He has written and produced eleven plays and musicals, including several dealing with Irish history and politics; five of these are collected in his book *Mad Angels*. He has also written a memoir (*Green Suede Shoes: An Irish-American Odyssey*) and a novel (*Rockin' the Bronx*). He is presently working on a musical, *Transport*, with the Australian author Thomas Kenneally.

**Patrick Lonergan** is Course Director for drama and theatre studies (both undergraduate and graduate) at NUI Galway, and the academic director of the Synge Summer School. He is the author of *Theatre and Globalization: Irish Drama and the Celtic Tiger Era*, which was awarded the 2009 Theatre Book Prize by the Society for Theatre Research (UK). He has edited seven books dealing with Irish literature and drama – including *Synge and His Influences: Centenary Essays from the Synge Summer School* – and has lectured in many countries on literary and theatrical topics. His most recent book (2012) is *The Theatre and Films of Martin McDonagh*.

**Alexander McKee** is currently an Assistant Professor in the Department of English at the University of Delaware. His article on 'Samuel Beckett's Critique of Irish Ireland' appeared in *New Hibernia Review* in Spring 2010. He has also published work on

British filmmaker Peter Greenaway and South African poetry of the apartheid era.

**Belinda McKeon** has written on the arts for *The Irish Times* for over ten years, and has published essays and fiction in such journals as *The Guardian, Paris Review, and Dublin Review.* Her novel, *Solace*, was named a Kirkus Outstanding Debut of 2011, was honoured as the Bord Gáis Energy Irish Book of the Year 2011 at the Irish Book Awards, and won the *Sunday Independent* Best Newcomer award. She curated Ireland's largest poetry festival, DLR Poetry Now, from 2008 to 2011, and has also curated a number of literary events in the U.S. Her plays have been staged in both Dublin and New York, and she is currently under commission to the Abbey Theatre.

**Conor McPherson** began writing plays as a student at University College Dublin, and was the founder of Fly By Night Theatre Company in Dublin. In 1998, in London, he received the Critics' Circle Award as most promising playwright, and *The Weir* won the Laurence Olivier BBC Award as best new play. In addition to later successes as a dramatist, he has directed for the stage – most notably a 2005 revival of Billy Roche's *Poor Beast in the Rain* at the Gate Theatre in Dublin – and for the screen, including two of his own film scripts and a third co-authored with Billy Roche: *The Eclipse*, which was named Best Film at the 2010 Irish Film and Television Awards. McPherson and Roche also shared honours for Best Screenplay.

**Christopher Murray** is Emeritus Professor of Drama and Theatre History, in the School of English, Drama and Film, University College Dublin. A former editor of Irish University Review and chair of the International Association for the Study of Irish Literatures, (IASIL), he is author of *Twentieth-Century Irish Drama: Mirror Up to Nation* (1997) and *Sean O'Casey: Writer at Work: A Biography* (2004). He has edited *Brian Friel: Essays, Diaries, Interview 1964-1999, Samuel Beckett: 100 Years: The Centenary Essays, Selected Plays of George Shiels*, and *Alive in Time: The Enduring Drama of Tom Murphy*. He is currently writing a book on Friel for the Methuen Drama Companion Series.

**Benedict Nightingale** retired as the chief theatre critic of *The Times* of London in 2010, after reviewing plays for 47 years – including stints at *The Guardian* and the *New Statesman*, and for one theatre season (1983-84) as a Sunday theatre columnist for *The*

*New York Times*. His diary of that season was published as *Fifth Row Center: A Critic's Year On and Off Broadway*. In 1986 he was appointed Professor of English with special reference to Drama at the University of Michigan, Ann Arbor, and in 1990 he began his distinguished work for *The Times*. He is currently working on a book about his greatest experiences in theatre.

**Hilary Sophrin** teaches English at Padua Academy in Wilmington, Delaware. While earning a Master's degree in Irish Studies at New York University (with a thesis on the work of Billy Roche), she worked at the Irish Repertory Theatre as a production assistant for Roche's show based on *Tales From Rainwater Pond*.

**Colm Tóibín** has won many awards as a journalist, novelist, dramatist, and essayist, and his work has been translated into thirty languages. A native of Enniscorthy, County Wexford, he studied at University College Dublin, lived in Spain for three years, and then wrote and edited for several journals in Ireland before launching an independent literary career. His most recent works include a short story collection, *The Empty Family*; a play, *Testament*, directed by Garry Hynes for the 2011 Dublin Theatre Festival; a memoir, *A Guest at the Feast*; and two books of essays, *All a Novelist Needs: Colm Tóibín on Henry James* and *New Ways to Kill Your Mother*. He is currently a distinguished professor of humanities at Columbia University.

**Martin W. Walsh** holds a PhD from Cambridge University and currently heads the Drama program at the Residential College of the University of Michigan. He is widely published in early drama and early popular culture and festivity, and has worked as an actor, director, dramaturge, and translator in drama from the medieval period to Brecht, Beckett, and such contemporary Irish playwrights as Marina Carr and Martin McDonagh. He is completing a large-scale study of the popular cultural aspects surrounding the feast and figure of Martin of Tours.

# Index

**Carysfort Press** was formed in the summer of 1998. It receives annual funding from the Arts Council.

The directors believe that drama is playing an ever-increasing role in today's society and that enjoyment of the theatre, both professional and amateur, currently plays a central part in Irish culture.

The Press aims to produce high quality publications which, though written and/or edited by academics, will be made accessible to a general readership. The organisation would also like to provide a forum for critical thinking in the Arts in Ireland, again keeping the needs and interests of the general public in view.

The company publishes contemporary Irish writing for and about the theatre.

Editorial and publishing inquiries to:
Carysfort Press Ltd.,
58 Woodfield,
Scholarstown Road,
Rathfarnham,
Dublin 16,
Republic of Ireland.

T (353 1) 493 7383
F (353 1) 406 9815
E: info@carysfortpress.com
www.carysfortpress.com

**HOW TO ORDER**

*TRADE ORDERS DIRECTLY TO:*
Irish Book Distribution
Unit 12, North Park, North Road,
Finglas, Dublin 11.

T: (353 1) 8239580
F: (353 1) 8239599
E: mary@argosybooks.ie
www.argosybooks.ie

*INDIVIDUAL ORDERS DIRECTLY TO:*
eprint Ltd.
35 Coolmine Industrial Estate,
Blanchardstown, Dublin 15.
T: (353 1) 827 8860
F: (353 1) 827 8804 Order online @
E: books@eprint.ie
www.eprint.ie

*FOR SALES IN NORTH AMERICA AND CANADA:*
Dufour Editions Inc.,
124 Byers Road,
PO Box 7,
Chester Springs,
PA 19425,
USA

T: 1-610-458-5005
F: 1-610-458-7103

**The Theatre of Conor McPherson: 'Right beside the Beyond'**

Edited by Lilian Chambers and Eamonn Jordan

Multiple productions and the international successes of plays like *The Weir* have led to Conor McPherson being regarded by many as one of the finest writers of his generation. McPherson has also been hugely prolific as a theatre director, as a screenwriter and film director, garnering many awards in these different roles. In this collection of essays, commentators from around the world address the substantial range of McPherson's output to date in theatre and film, a body of work written primarily during and in the aftermath of Ireland's Celtic Tiger period. These critics approach the work in challenging and dynamic ways, considering the crucial issues of morality, the rupturing of the real, storytelling, and the significance of space, violence and gender. Explicit considerations are given to comedy and humour, and to theatrical form, especially that of the monologue and to the ways that the otherworldly, the unconscious and supernatural are accommodated dramaturgically, with frequent emphasis placed on the specific aspects of performance in both theatre and film.

ISBN: 978 1 904505 61 7   €20

## The Story of Barabbas, The Company

Carmen Szabo

Acclaimed by audiences and critics alike for their highly innovative, adventurous and entertaining theatre, Barabbas The Company have created playful, intelligent and dynamic productions for over 17 years. Breaking the mould of Irish theatrical tradition and moving away from a text dominated theatre, Barabbas The Company's productions have established an instantly recognizable performance style influenced by the theatre of clown, circus, mime, puppetry, object manipulation and commedia dell'arte. This is the story of a unique company within the framework of Irish theatre, discussing the influences that shape their performances and establish their position within the history and development of contemporary Irish theatre. This book addresses the overwhelming necessity to reconsider Irish theatre history and to explore, in a language accessible to a wide range of readers, the issues of physicality and movement based theatre in Ireland.

ISBN: 978-1-904505-59-4   €25

## Irish Drama: Local and Global Perspectives

Edited by Nicholas Grene and Patrick Lonergan

Since the late 1970s there has been a marked internationalization of Irish drama, with individual plays, playwrights, and theatrical companies establishing newly global reputations. This book reflects upon these developments, drawing together leading scholars and playwrights to consider the consequences that arise when Irish theatre travels abroad.

Contributors: Chris Morash, Martine Pelletier, José Lanters, Richard Cave, James Moran, Werner Huber, Rhona Trench, Christopher Murray, Ursula Rani Sarma, Jesse Weaver, Enda Walsh, Elizabeth Kuti

ISBN: 978-1-904505-63-1   €20

## What Shakespeare Stole From Rome

Brian Arkins

What Shakespeare Stole From Rome analyses the multiple ways Shakespeare used material from Roman history and Latin poetry in his plays and poems. From the history of the Roman Republic to the tragedies of Seneca; from the Comedies of Platus to Ovid's poetry; this enlightening book examines the important influence of Rome and Greece on Shakespeare's work.

ISBN: 978-1-904505-58-7   €20

## Polite Forms

Harry White

*Polite Forms* is a sequence of poems that meditates on family life. These poems remember and reimagine scenes from childhood and adolescence through the formal composure of the sonnet, so that the uniformity of this framing device promotes a tension as between a neatly arranged album of photographs and the chaos and flow of experience itself. Throughout the collection there is a constant preoccupation with the difference between actual remembrance and the illumination or meaning which poetry can afford. Some of the poems 'rewind the tapes of childhood' across two or three generations, and all of them are akin to pictures at an exhibition which survey individual impressions of childhood and parenthood in a thematically continuous series of portraits drawn from life.

Harry White was born in Dublin in 1958. He is Professor of Music at University College Dublin and widely known for his work in musicology and cultural history. His publications include "Music and the Irish Literary Imagination" (Oxford, 2008), which was awarded the Michael J. Durkan prize of the American Conference for Irish Studies in 2009. "Polite Forms" is his first collection of poems

ISBN: 978-1-904505-55-6   €10

## Ibsen and Chekhov on the Irish Stage

Edited by Ros Dixon and Irina Ruppo Malone

*Ibsen and Chekhov on the Irish Stage* presents articles on the theories of translation and adaptation, new insights on the work of Brian Friel, Frank McGuinness, Thomas Kilroy, and Tom Murphy, historical analyses of theatrical productions during the Irish Revival, interviews with contemporary theatre directors, and a round-table discussion with the playwrights, Michael West and Thomas Kilroy.

*Ibsen and Chekhov on the Irish Stage* challenges the notion that a country's dramatic tradition develops in cultural isolation. It uncovers connections between past productions of plays by Ibsen and Chekhov and contemporary literary adaptations of their works by Irish playwrights, demonstrating the significance of international influence for the formation of national canon.

Conceived in the spirit of a round-table discussion, *Ibsen and Chekhov on the Irish Stage* is a collective study of the intricacies of trans-cultural migration of dramatic works and a re-examination of Irish theatre history from 1890 to the present day.

ISBN: 978-1-904505-57-0   €20

## Tom Swift Selected Plays

With an introduction by Peter Crawley.

The inaugural production of Performance Corporation in 2002 matched Voltaire's withering assault against the doctrine of optimism with a playful aesthetic and endlessly inventive stagecraft.

Each play in this collection was originally staged by the Performance Corporation and though Swift has explored different avenues ever since, such playfulness is a constant. The writing is precise, but leaves room for the discoveries of rehearsals, the flesh of the theatre. All plays are blueprints for performance, but several of these scripts – many of which are site-specific and all of them slyly topical – are documents for something unrepeatable.

ISBN: 978-1-904505-56-3    €20

## Synge and His Influences: Centenary Essays from the Synge Summer School

Edited by Patrick Lonergan

The year 2009 was the centenary of the death of John Millington Synge, one of the world's great dramatists. To mark the occasion, this book gathers essays by leading scholars of Irish drama, aiming to explore the writers and movements that shaped Synge, and to consider his enduring legacies. Essays discuss Synge's work in its Irish, European and world contexts – showing his engagement not just with the Irish literary revival but with European politics and culture too. The book also explores Synge's influence on later writers: Irish dramatists such as Brian Friel, Tom Murphy and Marina Carr, as well as international writers like Mustapha Matura and Erisa Kironde. It also considers Synge's place in Ireland today, revealing how *The Playboy of the Western World* has helped to shape Ireland's responses to globalisation and multiculturalism, in celebrated productions by the Abbey Theatre, Druid Theatre, and Pan Pan Theatre Company.

Contributors include Ann Saddlemyer, Ben Levitas, Mary Burke, Paige Reynolds, Eilís Ní Dhuibhne, Mark Phelan, Shaun Richards, Ondřej Pilný, Richard Pine, Alexandra Poulain, Emilie Pine, Melissa Sihra, Sara Keating, Bisi Adigun, Adrian Frazier and Anthony Roche.

ISBN: 978-1-904505-50-1    €20.00

## Constellations - The Life and Music of John Buckley

Benjamin Dwyer

Benjamin Dwyer provides a long overdue assessment of one of Ireland's most prolific composers of the last decades. He looks at John Buckley's music in the context of his biography and Irish cultural life. This is no hagiography but a critical assessment of Buckley's work, his roots and aesthetics. While looking closely at several of Buckley's compositions, the book is written in a comprehensible style that makes it easily accessible to anybody interested in Irish musical and cultural history.     *Wolfgang Marx*

As well as providing a very readable and comprehensive study of the life and music of John Buckley, Constellations also offers an up-to-date and informative catalogue of compositions, a complete discography, translations of set texts and the full libretto of his chamber opera, making this book an essential guide for both students and professional scholars alike.

ISBN: 978-1-904505-52-5    €20.00

## 'Because We Are Poor': Irish Theatre in the 1990s

Victor Merriman

"Victor Merriman's work on Irish theatre is in the vanguard of a whole new paradigm in Irish theatre scholarship, one that is not content to contemplate monuments of past or present achievement, but for which the theatre is a lens that makes visible the hidden malaises in Irish society. That he has been able to do so by focusing on a period when so much else in Irish culture conspired to hide those problems is only testimony to the considerable power of his critical scrutiny." Chris Morash, NUI Maynooth.

ISBN: 978-1-904505-51-8    €20.00

## 'Buffoonery and Easy Sentiment':
## Popular Irish Plays in the Decade Prior to the Opening of The Abbey Theatre

Christopher Fitz-Simon

In this fascinating reappraisal of the non-literary drama of the late 19th - early 20th century, Christopher Fitz-Simon discloses a unique world of plays, players and producers in metropolitan theatres in Ireland and other countries where Ireland was viewed as a source of extraordinary topics at once contemporary and comfortably remote: revolution, eviction, famine, agrarian agitation, political assassination.

The form was the fashionable one of melodrama, yet Irish melodrama was of a particular kind replete with hidden messages, and the language was far more allusive, colourful and entertaining than that of its English equivalent.

ISBN: 978-1-9045505-49-5    €20.00

## The Fourth Seamus Heaney Lectures, 'Mirror up to Nature':

Ed. Patrick Burke

What, in particular, is the contemporary usefulness for the building of societies of one of our oldest and culturally valued ideals, that of drama? The Fourth Seamus Heaney Lectures, 'Mirror up to Nature': Drama and Theatre in the Modern World, given at St Patrick's College, Drumcondra, between October 2006 and April 2007, addressed these and related questions. Patrick Mason spoke on the essence of theatre, Thomas Kilroy on Ireland's contribution to the art of theatre, Cecily O'Neill and Jonothan Neelands on the rich potential of drama in the classroom. Brenna Katz Clarke examined the relationship between drama and film, and John Buckley spoke on opera and its history and gave an illuminating account of his own *Words Upon The Window-Pane*.

ISBN 978-1-9045505-48-8   €12

## The Theatre of Tom Mac Intyre:  'Strays from the ether'

Eds. Bernadette Sweeney and Marie Kelly

This long overdue anthology captures the soul of Mac Intyre's dramatic canon – its ethereal qualities, its extraordinary diversity, its emphasis on the poetic and on performance – in an extensive range of visual, journalistic and scholarly contributions from writers, theatre practitioners.

ISBN 978-1-904505-46-4  €25

## Irish Appropriation Of Greek Tragedy

Brian Arkins

This book presents an analysis of more than 30 plays written by Irish dramatists and poets that are based on the tragedies of Sophocles, Euripides and Aeschylus. These plays proceed from the time of Yeats and Synge through MacNeice and the Longfords on to many of today's leading writers.

ISBN 978-1-904505-47-1  €20

## Alive in Time: The Enduring Drama of Tom Murphy

Ed. Christopher Murray

Almost 50 years after he first hit the headlines as Ireland's most challenging playwright, the 'angry young man' of those times Tom Murphy still commands his place at the pinnacle of Irish theatre. Here 17 new essays by prominent critics and academics, with an introduction by Christopher Murray, survey Murphy's dramatic oeuvre in a concerted attempt to define his greatness and enduring appeal, making this book a significant study of a unique genius.

ISBN 978-1-904505-45-7  €25

## Performing Violence in Contemporary Ireland

Ed. Lisa Fitzpatrick

This interdisciplinary collection of fifteen new essays by scholars of theatre, Irish studies, music, design and politics explores aspects of the performance of violence in contemporary Ireland. With chapters on the work of playwrights Martin McDonagh, Martin Lynch, Conor McPherson and Gary Mitchell, on Republican commemorations and the 90th anniversary ceremonies for the Battle of the Somme and the Easter Rising, this book aims to contribute to the ongoing international debate on the performance of violence in contemporary societies.

ISBN 978-1-904505-44-0 (2009)  €20

## Ireland's Economic Crisis - Time to Act. Essays from over 40 leading Irish thinkers at the MacGill Summer School 2009

Eds. Joe Mulholland and Finbarr Bradley

Ireland's economic crisis requires a radical transformation in policymaking. In this volume, political, industrial, academic, trade union and business leaders and commentators tell the story of the Irish economy and its rise and fall. Contributions at Glenties range from policy, vision and context to practical suggestions on how the country can emerge from its crisis.

ISBN 978-1-904505-43-3 (2009)  €20

## Deviant Acts: Essays on Queer Performance

Ed. David Cregan

This book contains an exciting collection of essays focusing on a variety of alternative performances happening in contemporary Ireland. While it highlights the particular representations of gay and lesbian identity it also brings to light how diversity has always been a part of Irish culture and is, in fact, shaping what it means to be Irish today.

ISBN 978-1-904505-42-6 (2009)  €20

## Seán Keating in Context: Responses to Culture and Politics in Post-Civil War Ireland

Compiled, edited and introduced by Éimear O'Connor

Irish artist Seán Keating has been judged by his critics as the personification of old-fashioned traditionalist values. This book presents a different view. The story reveals Keating's early determination to attain government support for the visual arts. It also illustrates his socialist leanings, his disappointment with capitalism, and his attitude to cultural snobbery, to art critics, and to the Academy. Given the national and global circumstances nowadays, Keating's critical and wry observations are prophetic – and highly amusing.

ISBN 978-1-904505-41-9  €25

### Dialogue of the Ancients of Ireland: A new translation of Acallam na Senorach

Translated with introduction and notes by Maurice Harmon

One of Ireland's greatest collections of stories and poems, The Dialogue of the Ancients of Ireland is a new translation by Maurice Harmon of the 12th century *Acallam na Senorach*. Retold in a refreshing modern idiom, the *Dialogue* is an extraordinary account of journeys to the four provinces by St. Patrick and the pagan Cailte, one of the surviving Fian. Within the frame story are over 200 other stories reflecting many genres – wonder tales, sea journeys, romances, stories of revenge, tales of monsters and magic. The poems are equally varied – lyrics, nature poems, eulogies, prophecies, laments, genealogical poems. After the *Tain Bo Cuailnge*, the *Acallam* is the largest surviving prose work in Old and Middle Irish.

ISBN: 978-1-904505-39-6 (2009)   €20

### Literary and Cultural Relations between Ireland and Hungary and Central and Eastern Europe

Ed. Maria Kurdi

This lively, informative and incisive collection of essays sheds fascinating new light on the literary interrelations between Ireland, Hungary, Poland, Romania and the Czech Republic. It charts a hitherto under-explored history of the reception of modern Irish culture in Central and Eastern Europe and also investigates how key authors have been translated, performed and adapted. The revealing explorations undertaken in this volume of a wide array of Irish dramatic and literary texts, ranging from *Gulliver's Travels* to *Translations* and *The Pillowman*, tease out the subtly altered nuances that they acquire in a Central European context.

ISBN: 978-1-904505-40-2 (2009)   €20

### Plays and Controversies: Abbey Theatre Diaries 2000-2005

Ben Barnes

In diaries covering the period of his artistic directorship of the Abbey, Ben Barnes offers a frank, honest, and probing account of a much commented upon and controversial period in the history of the national theatre. These diaries also provide fascinating personal insights into the day-to- day pressures, joys, and frustrations of running one of Ireland's most iconic institutions.

ISBN: 978-1-904505-38-9 (2008)   €20

## Interactions: Dublin Theatre Festival 1957-2007. Irish Theatrical Diaspora Series: 3

Eds. Nicholas Grene and Patrick Lonergan with Lilian Chambers

For over 50 years the Dublin Theatre Festival has been one of Ireland's most important cultural events, bringing countless new Irish plays to the world stage, while introducing Irish audiences to the most important international theatre companies and artists. Interactions explores and celebrates the achievements of the renowned Festival since 1957 and includes specially commissioned memoirs from past organizers, offering a unique perspective on the controversies and successes that have marked the event's history. An especially valuable feature of the volume, also, is a complete listing of the shows that have appeared at the Festival from 1957 to 2008.

ISBN: 978-1-904505-36-5  €20

## The Informer: A play by Tom Murphy based on the novel by Liam O'Flaherty

The Informer, Tom Murphy's stage adaptation of Liam O'Flaherty's novel, was produced in the 1981 Dublin Theatre Festival, directed by the playwright himself, with Liam Neeson in the leading role. The central subject of the play is the quest of a character at the point of emotional and moral breakdown for some source of meaning or identity. In the case of Gypo Nolan, the informer of the title, this involves a nightmarish progress through a Dublin underworld in which he changes from a Judas figure to a scapegoat surrogate for Jesus, taking upon himself the sins of the world. A cinematic style, with flash-back and intercut scenes, is used rather than a conventional theatrical structure to catch the fevered and phantasmagoric progression of Gypo's mind. The language, characteristically for Murphy, mixes graphically colloquial Dublin slang with the haunted intricacies of the central character groping for the meaning of his own actions. The dynamic rhythm of the action builds towards an inevitable but theatrically satisfying tragic catastrophe. ' [The Informer] is, in many ways closer to being an original Murphy play than it is to O'Flaherty...' Fintan O'Toole.

ISBN: 978-1-904505-37-2 (2008)  €10

## Shifting Scenes: Irish theatre-going 1955-1985

Eds. Nicholas Grene and Chris Morash

Transcript of conversations with John Devitt, academic and reviewer, about his lifelong passion for the theatre. A fascinating and entertaining insight into Dublin theatre over the course of thirty years provided by Devitt's vivid reminiscences and astute observations.

ISBN: 978-1-904505-33-4 (2008)  €10

## Irish Literature: Feminist Perspectives

Eds. Patricia Coughlan and Tina O'Toole

The collection discusses texts from the early 18th century to the present. A central theme of the book is the need to renegotiate the relations of feminism with nationalism and to transact the potential contest of these two important narratives, each possessing powerful emancipatory force. Irish Literature: Feminist Perspectives contributes incisively to contemporary debates about Irish culture, gender and ideology.

ISBN: 978-1-904505-35-8 (2008)   €20

## Silenced Voices: Hungarian Plays from Transylvania

Selected and translated by Csilla Bertha and Donald E. Morse

The five plays are wonderfully theatrical, moving fluidly from absurdism to tragedy, and from satire to the darkly comic. Donald Morse and Csilla Bertha's translations capture these qualities perfectly, giving voice to the 'forgotten playwrights of Central Europe'. They also deeply enrich our understanding of the relationship between art, ethics, and politics in Europe.

ISBN: 978-1-904505-34-1 (2008)   €20

## A Hazardous Melody of Being:
## Seóirse Bodley's Song Cycles on the poems of Micheal O'Siadhail

Ed. Lorraine Byrne Bodley

This apograph is the first publication of Bodley's O'Siadhail song cycles and is the first book to explore the composer's lyrical modernity from a number of perspectives. Lorraine Byrne Bodley's insightful introduction describes in detail the development and essence of Bodley's musical thinking, the European influences he absorbed which linger in these cycles, and the importance of his work as a composer of the Irish art song.

ISBN: 978-1-904505-31-0 (2008)   €25

## Irish Theatre in England: Irish Theatrical Diaspora Series: 2

Eds. Richard Cave and Ben Levitas

Irish theatre in England has frequently illustrated the complex relations between two distinct cultures. How English reviewers and audiences interpret Irish plays is often decidedly different from how the plays were read in performance in Ireland. How certain Irish performers have chosen to be understood in Dublin is not necessarily how audiences in London have perceived their constructed stage personae. Though a collection by diverse authors, the twelve essays in this volume investigate these issues from a variety of perspectives that together chart the trajectory of Irish performance in England from the mid-nineteenth century till today.

ISBN: 978-1-904505-26-6 (2007)   €20

## Goethe and Anna Amalia: A Forbidden Love?

Ettore Ghibellino, Trans. Dan Farrelly

In this study Ghibellino sets out to show that the platonic relationship between Goethe and Charlotte von Stein – lady-in-waiting to Anna Amalia, the Dowager Duchess of Weimar – was used as part of a cover-up for Goethe's intense and prolonged love relationship with the Duchess Anna Amalia herself. The book attempts to uncover a hitherto closely-kept state secret. Readers convinced by the evidence supporting Ghibellino's hypothesis will see in it one of the very great love stories in European history – to rank with that of Dante and Beatrice, and Petrarch and Laura.

ISBN: 978-1-904505-24-2  €20

## Ireland on Stage: Beckett and After

Eds. Hiroko Mikami, Minako Okamuro, Naoko Yagi

The collection focuses primarily on Irish playwrights and their work, both in text and on the stage during the latter half of the twentieth century. The central figure is Samuel Beckett, but the contributors freely draw on Beckett and his work provides a springboard to discuss contemporary playwrights such as Brian Friel, Frank McGuinness, Marina Carr and Conor McPherson amongst others. Contributors include: Anthony Roche, Hiroko Mikami, Naoko Yagi, Cathy Leeney, Joseph Long, Noreem Doody, Minako Okamuro, Christopher Murray, Futoshi Sakauchi and Declan Kiberd

ISBN: 978-1-904505-23-5 (2007)  €20

## 'Echoes Down the Corridor': Irish Theatre - Past, Present and Future

Eds. Patrick Lonergan and Riana O'Dwyer

This collection of fourteen new essays explores Irish theatre from exciting new perspectives. How has Irish theatre been received internationally - and, as the country becomes more multicultural, how will international theatre influence the development of drama in Ireland? These and many other important questions.

ISBN: 978-1-904505-25-9 (2007)  €20

## Musics of Belonging: The Poetry of Micheal O'Siadhail

Eds. Marc Caball & David F. Ford

An overall account is given of O'Siadhail's life, his work and the reception of his poetry so far. There are close readings of some poems, analyses of his artistry in matching diverse content with both classical and innovative forms, and studies of recurrent themes such as love, death, language, music, and the shifts of modern life.

ISBN: 978-1-904505-22-8 (2007)  €25 (Paperback)
ISBN: 978-1-904505-21-1 (2007)  €50 (Casebound)

## Modern Death: The End of Civilization

Carl-Henning Wijkmark. Trans: Dan Farrelly

Modern Death is written in the form of a symposium, in which a government agency brings together a group of experts to discuss a strategy for dealing with an ageing population.

The speakers take up the thread of the ongoing debates about care for the aged and about euthanasia. In dark satirical mode the author shows what grim developments are possible. The theme of a 'final solution' is mentioned, though the connection with Hitler is explicitly denied. The most inhuman crimes against human dignity are discussed in the symposium as if they were a necessary condition of future progress.

The fiercely ironical treatment of the material tears off the thin veil that disguises the specious arguments and insidious expressions of concern for the well-being of the younger generation. Though the text was written nearly thirty years ago, the play has a terrifyingly modern relevance.

ISBN: 978 1 904505 28 0 (2007)  €8

## Brian Friel's Dramatic Artistry: 'The Work has Value'

Eds. Donald E. Morse, Csilla Bertha and Maria Kurdi

Brian Friel's Dramatic Artistry presents a refreshingly broad range of voices: new work from some of the leading English-speaking authorities on Friel, and fascinating essays from scholars in Germany, Italy, Portugal, and Hungary. This book will deepen our knowledge and enjoyment of Friel's work.

ISBN: 978-1-904505-17-4 (2006)  €25

## The Theatre of Martin McDonagh: 'A World of Savage Stories'

Eds. Lilian Chambers and Eamonn Jordan

The book is a vital response to the many challenges set by McDonagh for those involved in the production and reception of his work. Critics and commentators from around the world offer a diverse range of often provocative approaches. What is not surprising is the focus and commitment of the engagement, given the controversial and stimulating nature of the work.

ISBN: 978-1-904505-19-8 (2006)  €30

## Edna O'Brien: New Critical Perspectives

Eds. Kathryn Laing, Sinead Mooney and Maureen O'Connor

The essays collected here illustrate some of the range, complexity, and interest of Edna O'Brien as a fiction writer and dramatist. They will contribute to a broader appreciation of her work and to an evolution of new critical approaches, as well as igniting more interest in the many unexplored areas of her considerable oeuvre.

ISBN: 978-1-904505-20-4 (2006)  €20

## Irish Theatre on Tour

Eds. Nicholas Grene and Chris Morash

'Touring has been at the strategic heart of Druid's artistic policy since the early eighties. Everyone has the right to see professional theatre in their own communities. Irish theatre on tour is a crucial part of Irish theatre as a whole'. Garry Hynes

ISBN 978-1-904505-13-6 (2005)  €20

## Poems 2000-2005 by Hugh Maxton

Poems 2000-2005 is a transitional collection written while the author – also known to be W.J. Mc Cormack, literary historian – was in the process of moving back from London to settle in rural Ireland.

ISBN 978-1-904505-12-9 (2005)  €10

## Synge: A Celebration

Ed. Colm Tóibín

A collection of essays by some of Ireland's most creative writers on the work of John Millington Synge, featuring Sebastian Barry, Marina Carr, Anthony Cronin, Roddy Doyle, Anne Enright, Hugo Hamilton, Joseph O'Connor, Mary O'Malley, Fintan O'Toole, Colm Toibin, Vincent Woods.

ISBN 978-1-904505-14-3 (2005)  €15

## East of Eden: New Romanian Plays

Ed. Andrei Marinescu

Four of the most promising Romanian playwrights, young and very young, are in this collection, each one with a specific way of seeing the Romanian reality, each one with a style of communicating an articulated artistic vision of the society we are living in. Ion Caramitru, General Director Romanian National Theatre Bucharest.
ISBN 978-1-904505-15-0 (2005)  €10

## George Fitzmaurice: 'Wild in His Own Way', Biography of an Irish Playwright

Fiona Brennan

'Fiona Brennan's introduction to his considerable output allows us a much greater appreciation and understanding of Fitzmaurice, the one remaining under-celebrated genius of twentieth-century Irish drama'. Conall Morrison

ISBN 978-1-904505-16-7 (2005)  €20

## Out of History: Essays on the Writings of Sebastian Barry

Ed. Christina Hunt Mahony

The essays address Barry's engagement with the contemporary cultural debate in Ireland and also with issues that inform postcolonial critical theory. The range and selection of contributors has ensured a high level of critical expression and an insightful assessment of Barry and his works.

ISBN: 978-1-904505-18-1 (2005) €20

## Three Congregational Masses

Seoirse Bodley

'From the simpler congregational settings in the Mass of Peace and the Mass of Joy to the richer textures of the Mass of Glory, they are immediately attractive and accessible, and with a distinctively Irish melodic quality.' Barra Boydell

ISBN: 978-1-904505-11-2 (2005) €15

## Georg Büchner's Woyzeck,

A new translation by Dan Farrelly

The most up-to-date German scholarship of Thomas Michael Mayer and Burghard Dedner has finally made it possible to establish an authentic sequence of scenes. The wide-spread view that this play is a prime example of loose, open theatre is no longer sustainable. Directors and teachers are challenged to "read it again".

ISBN: 978-1-904505-02-0 (2004) €10

## Playboys of the Western World: Production Histories

Ed. Adrian Frazier

'The book is remarkably well-focused: half is a series of production histories of Playboy performances through the twentieth century in the UK, Northern Ireland, the USA, and Ireland. The remainder focuses on one contemporary performance, that of Druid Theatre, as directed by Garry Hynes. The various contemporary social issues that are addressed in relation to Synge's play and this performance of it give the volume an additional interest: it shows how the arts matter.' Kevin Barry

ISBN: 978-1-904505-06-8 (2004) €20

## The Power of Laughter: Comedy and Contemporary Irish Theatre

Ed. Eric Weitz

The collection draws on a wide range of perspectives and voices including critics, playwrights, directors and performers. The result is a series of fascinating and provocative debates about the myriad functions of comedy in contemporary Irish theatre. Anna McMullan

As Stan Laurel said, 'it takes only an onion to cry. Peel it and weep. Comedy is harder'. 'These essays listen to the power of laughter. They hear the tough heart of Irish theatre – hard and wicked and funny'. Frank McGuinness

ISBN: 978-1-904505-05-1 (2004)   €20

## Sacred Play: Soul-Journeys in contemporary Irish Theatre

Anne F. O'Reilly

'Theatre as a space or container for sacred play allows audiences to glimpse mystery and to experience transformation. This book charts how Irish playwrights negotiate the labyrinth of the Irish soul and shows how their plays contribute to a poetics of Irish culture that enables a new imagining. Playwrights discussed are: McGuinness, Murphy, Friel, Le Marquand Hartigan, Burke Brogan, Harding, Meehan, Carr, Parker, Devlin, and Barry.'

ISBN: 978-1-904505-07-5 (2004)   €20

## The Irish Harp Book

Sheila Larchet Cuthbert

This is a facsimile of the edition originally published by Mercier Press in 1993. There is a new preface by Sheila Larchet Cuthbert, and the biographical material has been updated. It is a collection of studies and exercises for the use of teachers and pupils of the Irish harp.

ISBN: 978-1-904505-08-2 (2004)   €35

## The Drunkard

Tom Murphy

'The Drunkard is a wonderfully eloquent play. Murphy's ear is finely attuned to the glories and absurdities of melodramatic exclamation, and even while he is wringing out its ludicrous overstatement, he is also making it sing.' The Irish Times

ISBN: 978-1-90 05-09-9 (2004)   €10

## Goethe: Musical Poet, Musical Catalyst

Ed. Lorraine Byrne

'Goethe was interested in, and acutely aware of, the place of music in human experience generally - and of its particular role in modern culture. Moreover, his own literary work - especially the poetry and Faust - inspired some of the major composers of the European tradition to produce some of their finest works.' Martin Swales

ISBN: 978-1-9045-10-5 (2004) €25

## The Theatre of Marina Carr: "Before rules was made"

Eds. Anna McMullan & Cathy Leeney

As the first published collection of articles on the theatre of Marina Carr, this volume explores the world of Carr's theatrical imagination, the place of her plays in contemporary theatre in Ireland and abroad and the significance of her highly individual voice.

ISBN: 978-0-9534257-7-8 (2003) €20

## Critical Moments: Fintan O'Toole on Modern Irish Theatre

Eds. Julia Furay & Redmond O'Hanlon

This new book on the work of Fintan O'Toole, the internationally acclaimed theatre critic and cultural commentator, offers percussive analyses and assessments of the major plays and playwrights in the canon of modern Irish theatre. Fearless and provocative in his judgements, O'Toole is essential reading for anyone interested in criticism or in the current state of Irish theatre.

ISBN: 978-1-904505-03-7 (2003) €20

## Goethe and Schubert: Across the Divide

Eds. Lorraine Byrne & Dan Farrelly

Proceedings of the International Conference, 'Goethe and Schubert in Perspective and Performance', Trinity College Dublin, 2003. This volume includes essays by leading scholars – Barkhoff, Boyle, Byrne, Canisius, Dürr, Fischer, Hill, Kramer, Lamport, Lund, Meikle, Newbould, Norman McKay, White, Whitton, Wright, Youens – on Goethe's musicality and his relationship to Schubert; Schubert's contribution to sacred music and the Lied and his setting of Goethe's Singspiel, Claudine. A companion volume of this Singspiel (with piano reduction and English translation) is also available.

ISBN: 978-1-904505-04-4 (2003) €25

### Goethe's Singspiel, 'Claudine von Villa Bella'

Set by Franz Schubert

Goethe's Singspiel in three acts was set to music by Schubert in 1815. Only Act One of Schuberts's Claudine score is extant. The present volume makes Act One available for performance in English and German. It comprises both a piano reduction by Lorraine Byrne of the original Schubert orchestral score and a bilingual text translated for the modern stage by Dan Farrelly. This is a tale, wittily told, of lovers and vagabonds, romance, reconciliation, and resolution of family conflict.

ISBN: 978-0-9544290-0-3 (2002)  €14

### Theatre of Sound, Radio and the Dramatic Imagination

Dermot Rattigan

An innovative study of the challenges that radio drama poses to the creative imagination of the writer, the production team, and the listener.
"A remarkably fine study of radio drama – everywhere informed by the writer's professional experience of such drama in the making...A new theoretical and analytical approach – informative, illuminating and at all times readable." Richard Allen Cave

ISBN: 978- 0-9534-257-5-4 (2002)  €20

### Talking about Tom Murphy

Ed. Nicholas Grene

Talking About Tom Murphy is shaped around the six plays in the landmark Abbey Theatre Murphy Season of 2001, assembling some of the best-known commentators on his work: Fintan O'Toole, Chris Morash, Lionel Pilkington, Alexandra Poulain, Shaun Richards, Nicholas Grene and Declan Kiberd.

ISBN: 978-0-9534-257-9-2 (2002)  €12

### Hamlet: The Shakespearean Director

Mike Wilcock

"This study of the Shakespearean director as viewed through various interpretations of HAMLET is a welcome addition to our understanding of how essential it is for a director to have a clear vision of a great play. It is an important study from which all of us who love Shakespeare and who understand the importance of continuing contemporary exploration may gain new insights." From the Foreword, by Joe Dowling, Artistic Director, The Guthrie Theater, Minneapolis, MN

ISBN: 978-1-904505-00-6 (2002)  €20

## The Theatre of Frank Mc Guinness: Stages of Mutability

Ed. Helen Lojek

The first edited collection of essays about internationally renowned Irish playwright Frank McGuinness focuses on both performance and text. Interpreters come to diverse conclusions, creating a vigorous dialogue that enriches understanding and reflects a strong consensus about the value of McGuinness's complex work.

ISBN: 978-1904505-01-3. (2002)  €20

## Theatre Talk: Voices of Irish Theatre Practitioners

Eds Lilian Chambers, Ger Fitzgibbon and Eamonn Jordan

"This book is the right approach - asking practitioners what they feel." Sebastian Barry, Playwright "... an invaluable and informative collection of interviews with those who make and shape the landscape of Irish Theatre." Ben Barnes, Artistic Director of the Abbey Theatre

ISBN: 978-0-9534-257-6-1 (2001)  €20

## In Search of the South African Iphigenie

Erika von Wietersheim and Dan Farrelly

Discussions of Goethe's "Iphigenie auf Tauris" (Under the Curse) as relevant to women's issues in modern South Africa: women in family and public life; the force of women's spirituality; experience of personal relationships; attitudes to parents and ancestors; involvement with religion.

ISBN: 978-0-9534257-8-5 (2001)  €10

## 'The Starving' and 'October Song':

Two contemporary Irish plays by Andrew Hinds

The Starving, set during and after the siege of Derry in 1689, is a moving and engrossing drama of the emotional journey of two men.

October Song, a superbly written family drama set in real time in pre-ceasefire Derry.

ISBN: 978-0-9534-257-4-7 (2001)  €10

## Seen and Heard: Six new plays by Irish women

Ed. Cathy Leeney

A rich and funny, moving and theatrically exciting collection of plays by Mary Elizabeth Burke-Kennedy, Siofra Campbell, Emma Donoghue, Anne Le Marquand Hartigan, Michelle Read and Dolores Walshe.

ISBN: 978-0-9534-257-3-0 (2001)  €20

## Theatre Stuff: Critical essays on contemporary Irish theatre

Ed. Eamonn Jordan

Best selling essays on the successes and debates of contemporary Irish theatre at home and abroad. Contributors include: Thomas Kilroy, Declan Hughes, Anna McMullan, Declan Kiberd, Deirdre Mulrooney, Fintan O'Toole, Christopher Murray, Caoimhe McAvinchey and Terry Eagleton.

ISBN: 978-0-9534-2571-1-6 (2000)  €20

## Under the Curse. Goethe's "Iphigenie Auf Tauris", A New Version

Dan Farrelly

The Greek myth of Iphigenie grappling with the curse on the house of Atreus is brought vividly to life. This version is currently being used in Johannesburg to explore problems of ancestry, religion, and Black African women's spirituality.

ISBN: 978-09534-257-8-5 (2000)  €10

## Urfaust, A New Version of Goethe's early "Faust" in Brechtian Mode

Dan Farrelly

This version is based on Brecht's irreverent and daring re-interpretation of the German classic. "Urfaust is a kind of well-spring for German theatre... The love-story is the most daring and the most profound in German dramatic literature." Brecht

ISBN: 978-0-9534-257-0-9 (1998)  €10